Rumi: The Big Red Book

Rumi:
The Big Red Book

The Great Masterpiece Celebrating
Mystical Love and Friendship

Odes and Quatrains from *The Shams*

The Collected Translations of

Coleman Barks

Based on the work of John Moyne, Nevit Ergin,
A. J. Arberry, and Reynold Nicholson

HarperOne
An Imprint of HarperCollinsPublishers

HarperOne

Further acknowledgments and permissions for the illustrations contained in the book can be found on page 477–478 and constitute as a continuation of this copyright page.

HarperCollins Web site: http://www.harpercollins.com

HarperCollins®, 📖®, and HarperOne™ are trademarks of HarperCollins Publishers

FIRST EDITION

Interior design by Laura Lind Design

Calligraphy by Mohamed Zakariya

Library of Congress Cataloging-in-Publication Data is available upon request.

ISBN 978–0–06–190582–7

10 11 12 13 14   RRD(H)   10 9 8 7 6 5 4 3 2 1

This book is for all those who
love what Rumi and Shams love.

Contents

10. *AN-NUR*, LIGHT 123

11. *ASH-SHAKUR*, THE GRATEFUL 135

12. *AL-LATIF*, THE SUBTLE, THE INTRICATE 147

13. BAWA MUHAIYADDEEN 160

II. QUATRAINS (*Rubai*) 359

28. TAURUS: THE BULL 365

29. URSA MAJOR: THE GREAT BEAR, THE BIG DIPPER 369

30. CORONA BOREALIS: THE NORTHERN CROWN 373

35. VIRGO: THE VIRGIN 390

36. ORION: THE HUNTER 393

37. LEO: THE LION 397

38. THE MILKY WAY: OUR HOME ADDRESS SEEN FROM THE SIDE 401

39. BIJOU: THE BLACK HOLE 406

40. COLUMBA: NOAH'S DOVE 411

41. DRACO: THE DRAGON 415

42. CAPRICORN: THE SEA GOAT 419

43. HERCULES: THE HERO 423

44. PEGASUS: THE WINGED HORSE 427

45. LEPUS: THE HARE 432

50. CETUS: THE SEA MONSTER, OR KRAKEN 451

51. ANDROMEDA: THE CHAINED QUEEN 456

52. SCORPIO: THE SCORPION 462

Introduction

RUMI'S LIFE

Jelaluddin Rumi was born near the city of Balkh in what is now Afghanistan, then on the eastern edge of the Persian Empire, on September 30, 1207. He descended from a long line of Islamic jurists, theologians, and mystics. When Rumi was still a young man, his family left Balkh ahead of the invading armies of Genghis Khan, who was extending his empire westward, eventually all the way to the Adriatic. It is said that Rumi's father, Bahauddin, loaded ninety camels with just books for the journey. Theirs was a profoundly learned lineage.

Rumi and his family went to Damascus and on to Nishapur, where the poet and teacher Fariduddin Attar recognized the teenage boy as a great spirit. He is reported to have said, as he saw Bahauddin walking toward him with Rumi a little behind, "Here comes a sea, followed by an ocean." To honor this insight he gave Rumi a copy of his wonderful *Ilahinama* (*The Book of God*).

The family eventually settled in Konya, now in south-central Turkey, where Bahauddin resumed his role as head of the *medrese*, the dervish learning community. Rumi was still in his twenties several years later when his father died and he became head of the *medrese*. He gained a wide reputation as a devout scholar, and his school reportedly numbered over ten thousand students. Broadly speaking, the work of Rumi's community was to open the individual and the collective heart. Its members used music and poetry and movement. They sat in silence. They listened to discourses. Stories, jokes, meditation—everything was used. They fasted and they feasted. (The cook Ahim Baaz was a very important figure in Rumi's community. You can visit his tomb in Konya today.) The members of Rumi's community walked together. They worked in the garden and the orchard. They observed animal behavior very carefully; it was a kind of scripture they read for signs.

This was not a renunciate group. Everyone had a family and a line of useful work; they were masons, grocers, weavers, hatmakers, carpenters, tailors, and bookbinders. Everyone was deeply engaged. These were affirmative, ecstatic makers. Some call them Sufis. I like to say they were living the way of the heart.

A few years after Bahauddin's death in 1231, Burhan Mahaqqiq, a hermit meditator in the remote mountain region north and east of Konya, returned and found that his teacher, Rumi's father, had died. He decided to devote the rest of his life to training his teacher's son. For nine years he led Rumi on many, sometimes three consecutive, forty-day fasts (*chillas*). Rumi became a joyful adept in this mystical tradition.

Rumi's oldest son, Sultan Velad, saved 147 of his father's personal letters, so, amazingly, we have a somewhat accurate sense of what his daily life was like eight centuries ago. He was deeply involved in the details of community life. In one letter he begs a man to put off, for fifteen days, collecting the money he is owed by another man. In another he asks a wealthy nobleman to help a student out with a small loan. Someone's relatives had moved into the hut of a devout old woman, and he tries to solve the situation. Sudden lines of poetry are scattered throughout the practical business contained in the letters. His life was grounded in daily necessities and in the ecstatic simultaneously.

In the late fall of 1244, Rumi met Shams Tabriz, a fierce man-God, or God-man. Shams had wandered through the Near East in search of a soul friend on his level. Shams was sometimes lost in mystical awareness for three or four days. He took work as a mason to balance his visionary bewilderment with hard physical labor. When he was paid, he contrived to slip his wages into another worker's jacket before he left. He never stayed anywhere long. Whenever students began to gather around him, as they inevitably did, he excused himself for a drink of water, wrapped his black cloak around himself, and was gone. Because of this restless searching, he was known as *Parinda*, or the Flier or Bird. He prayed that God's hidden favorite be revealed to him, so that he could learn more about the mysteries of divine love. An inner voice came, *What will you give in return?*

"My head," said Shams.

The one you seek is Jelaluddin of Konya, son of Bahauddin of Balkh.

Shams arrived in Konya on November 29, 1244. He took lodging at the caravanserai of the sugar merchants, pretending to be a successful seller of sugar. But all he had in his room was a broken water pot, a ragged mat, and a headrest of unbaked clay. One day, as Shams sat at the gate, Rumi came by riding a donkey, surrounded by students. Shams rose and took the bridle.

"Money changer of the current coins of esoteric significance, knower of the names of the Lord, tell me. Who is greater, Muhammad or Bestami?"[1]

"Muhammad is incomparable among the saints and prophets."

"Then how is it he said, 'We have not known You as You should be known,' while Bestami cried out, 'How great is my glory!'"

Rumi fainted when he heard the depth of the question and fell to the ground. When he revived, he answered, "For Muhammad the mystery is always unfolding, while Bestami takes one gulp and is satisfied."

The two tottered off together. They spent weeks and months at a time together in the mystical conversation known as *sohbet*.

Another version of their meeting is: One day Rumi was teaching by a fountain in a small square in Konya. Books were open on the fountain's ledge. Shams walked quickly through the students and pushed the books into the water.

"Who are you and what are you doing?" Rumi asked.

"You must now live what you have been reading about."

Rumi turned to the books in the fountain, one of them his father's precious spiritual diary, the *Maarif*.

Shams said, "We can retrieve them. They will be as dry as they ever were." He lifted out the *Maarif* to show him. Dry.

"Leave them," said Rumi.

With that relinquishment of books and borrowed awareness, Rumi's real life began, and his real poetry too. "What I had thought of before as God," Rumi said, "I met today in a human being."

The meeting with Shams was the central event in Rumi's life. They were together in Konya for about three and a half years. Twice during that time the jealousy of Rumi's disciples drove Shams away, and twice Rumi sent his son Sultan Velad to bring him back. What happened next is the subject of extensive debate among scholars. Shams either left on his own, disappearing without a trace, as he had evidently threatened several times to do, or was killed by a group of the jealous disciples, including one of Rumi's sons, Ala al-Din. The latter is the version that has come down in the oral tradition among the Mevlevi dervishes, the order begun by Sultan Velad.

In this version Shams came to Sultan Velad in a dream after he had been killed and told him the circumstances of the murder. The son then kept that painful information from Rumi. He let him go out on long searches for Shams, to Damascus and elsewhere. The situation became a kind of reverse analogue for the Joseph story, in which Joseph's brothers pretend that the beloved one is dead, telling Jacob, the father, that he has been killed by a wolf. Here Rumi is *not* told that the beloved one has been killed by a group of his students, one of them his son. Both stories involve the central figure living for years under a misconception about the person dearest to them. The Joseph story, of course, resolves beautifully when Joseph, through his dream-interpreting skills, comes to be in charge of the granaries of Egypt and then later reunites with his family.

Rumi is reunited with Shams in the poetry, and in his inmost core. Perhaps a conventional religious community cannot contain the wild originality of a Shams Tabriz until it becomes embodied in someone like Rumi, who can be a bridge between wild gnostic experience and more traditional belief. This mysterious event comes on one of Rumi's journeys in search of Shams. Suddenly, walking a Damascus street, Rumi feels that he *is* their friendship, that he no longer needs to look for Shams. Whatever miracle they were together, he *is now* in himself. Call off the search.

Rumi translator and biographer Franklin Lewis has done formidable research, and he sees the story differently.[2] He feels that Shams was not murdered, that he left on his own, perhaps so that Rumi's soul growth could move to another level. It is true that Shams was a mystic who demanded *movement*, always more, of whatever came, always more blessings, more ecstatic praise. It must have been strenuous to have been around Shams, almost impossible for some. Shams once said that if you could lift up the Kaaba and take it out of the world, you would then see that what we all had been praying to, five times a day, was the divine glory *in each other*. That notion is difficult to place in a conventional theology. It must have been unacceptable to a segment of Rumi's community to have had their beloved teacher totally absorbed in the company of such a wild man. So Franklin Lewis thinks that Shams disappeared on his own and that his tomb is elsewhere, not in Konya, maybe out on the road toward Tabriz, in the town of Khuy. A minaret there is called by his name. Nothing is certain. Shams shall remain elusive.

I tend to believe that the jealous murder of Shams Tabriz actually happened. One thing is sure. With the disappearance of Shams, whether by violence or his own choice, Rumi's poetry went deeper. The core of longing became more radiant and vital, reflecting the depth of the communion that was the majestic friendship between Rumi and Shams.

Rumi had two wives. The first, Gowher Khatun, by whom he had two sons, Ala al-Din and Sultan Velad, died in 1242. Then he married Kira Khatun, by whom he had a son, Mozaffer, and a daughter, Malika. There is a wonderful hagiographic story about Kira Khatun. One day she peered through a slit in the door into the room where Rumi and Shams were sitting in *sohbet* (mystical conversation). She saw one of the walls open and six majestic beings enter. The strangers bowed and laid flowers at Rumi's feet, although it was the middle of winter. They remained until the time for dawn prayers, which they motioned for Shams to lead. He excused himself, and Rumi performed the duties. When prayers were over, the six left through the wall. Rumi came from the chamber and, seeing his wife in the hall, gave her the flowers, saying, "Some visitors brought these for you."

The next day she sent her servant to the perfumers' market with a few leaves and blossoms from the bouquet. The perfumers were baffled, unable to identify the flowers, until a spice trader from India recognized them as flowers that grew only in Ceylon (Sri Lanka). The servant went back with this astonishing news, and just as he was telling it, Rumi came in and told her to take good care of the flowers, because Indian saints had brought them from the paradise that human beings had lost. As long as Kira Khatun lived (she died nineteen years after Rumi), the flowers stayed fresh and fragrant, and just a single leaf applied to a diseased eye or other injured part brought instantaneous healing.

Rumi is known in the popular mind, of course, as the first whirling dervish. Shams seems to have taught him this form of physical and auditory meditation, *sema*. It was called deep listening, and it was said that whatever one was striving for would increase in *sema*. Rumi sometimes composed poetry while turning. He gives several reasons for putting music and poetry and movement together in his soul-growth work. In one of his *Discourses* he says:

> Responding to the prayers of the first Caliph, Abu Bakr, God made the Romans a major recipient of his mercy and Roman Anatolia the most beautiful of all landscapes. The people here, though, could not receive such grace. They had little taste for the inner life or the unseen world. For that reason I was attracted away from Khorasan (Persia), so that my children in this community could change the Roman copper to gold. They themselves would become the philosopher stones which cause this alchemy. But since Roman Anatolia was not ready for the gifts I had to give, I devised poetry, with music, to entrance the inhabitants toward spiritual truth. The people who live in this region are very blessed, lively and curious and fond of art, but as a sick child must be coaxed with sweetening to take medicine, they must be persuaded with poetry to acquire a longing for the soul.

Many stories have come down to us, through the hagiographic sources, about Rumi and children, about Rumi and beggars, the rejected of society, and especially about Rumi and animals. He was very in tune with the animal mind, much like an indigenous shaman. Every year Rumi went to a place near Konya where there were hot springs. Near a large lake music festivals were arranged, and Rumi gave discourses. One day the ducks that live on the lake were so vociferous that no one could hear the talk. Rumi yelled at them, "Either you give this discourse, or let me!" Complete silence. And during the remaining weeks he was there, no duck made a noise. When it came time for him to return to Konya, he went to the edge of the lake and gave the ducks permission to quack as much as they wanted, whereupon duck chatter resumed.

Here's another story I love. Some butchers purchased a heifer and were leading her to be slaughtered. Suddenly she broke free and ran. They shouted at her, but that just made her more crazed. No one could get near her. Rumi was walking the same road with his disciples some distance behind. When the heifer saw him, she trotted over and stood beside him very still as though communing with his spirit. He rubbed and patted her neck. When the butchers came to claim their property, he pleaded for her life. His students joined in the discussion. Rumi used the situation: "If a simple animal, being led to its death, can take such lovely refuge with me, how much more beautiful must it be when a human being puts heart and soul in the care of God?" The entire group, dervishes and butchers alike, found such joy in these words that they began to play music, and dancing and spontaneous poetry continued into the night.

One last animal story. Rumi was giving a longer than usual discourse in the square. People wandered away. The sun was going down. All that was left was a line of seven dogs sitting on their haunches listening attentively. "These are my true students," he said.

For the last twelve years of his life Rumi wrote, or dictated, one long luminous poem, the *Masnavi*, sixty-four thousand lines of poetry divided into six books. There is nothing quite like it in world literature. It surges like an ocean (his image) around many subjects. It is a self-interrupting, visionary work, with sometimes humorous, even bawdy, commentary on the health of the soul. Passages from the Qur'an are discussed, along with folktales, jokes, and remarks to people physically present as the poetry is being composed. Rumi dictated this sublime work of art to his scribe, Husam Chelebi, as they walked around Konya, through the nearby gardens of Meram, during teaching sessions, and in the streets and public places. Husam was a student of Shams, so this long poem can be considered an extension of Rumi's conversation, and union, with the friend. Perhaps the best image for the unified diversity of this wandering poem is the way that Rumi interacted with his community—sometimes tending to the growth of the group, sometimes addressing the needs of individuals. Readers of the *Masnavi* may enter it at any point.

Rumi died at sunset on December 17, 1273. His tomb in Konya is still visited by thousands each month. I once had a dream in which I was inside the tomb, and Rumi was arriving from outside. As he came in the door, he was so surrounded by enthusiastic friends that I could not see him. He had become all those who love him. He disappeared into them. One of the inscriptions on his tomb is: "Do not look for him here, but rather in the hearts of those who love him." It is said that representatives of all religions came to his funeral. When asked why, they each said that Rumi and his poetry had been a way of deepening their own faith. In this volume and in all my renderings of Rumi, I emphasize this universalist aspect. In bringing this great planetary poet over into the twenty-first century, it does not seem right to stress how we are divided into religions with mutually exclusive truths, but rather how we are moving along inside this Mystery like a family.[3]

The anniversary of his death is called his *urs*, or wedding night. He felt that union with the presence of the one he calls the beloved, or the friend, was as natural as breathing. Union with that companion transpires throughout and animates the universe. Above the door of his tomb on the inside is the double *hu* (see the calligraphy at the beginning of chapter 18, Shams Tabriz).

> *I belong to the beloved,*
> *have seen the two worlds as one,*
> *and that one call to and know,*
> *first, last, outer, inner,*
> *only that breath breathing human being.*

THE SOUL ESSENCE OF SHAMS TABRIZ

In my brief biography of Rumi, I have focused on his relationship with Shams Tabriz. Out of their deep, spiritually intimate friendship came this book. Rumi called his "big red book," the *Divani Shamsi Tabriz* (*The Works of Shams Tabriz*). It has come to be known as *The Shams* and is widely acknowledged as one of the great works of world literature. There are about three thousand poems in it, about six times as many as there are here.

The poems arose out of the friendship of Rumi and Shams. Their blended presence was the source and energy of the poetry in the *ghazals* (odes) and *rubai* (quatrains). Perhaps if we are ever to meet the elusive Shams, it will be in Rumi's book. Rumi often remarks in various ways that he does not know where his language comes from or who it belongs to. Shams in his *Discourses* (*Maqalat*) says this: Mevlana (Rumi) knows that the writer wrote in three scripts:

> *One that he could read and only he,*
> *one that he and others could read,*
> *and one that neither he nor anyone else could read.*
> *I am that third script.*

So Shams himself is, in the words of the poem, an *unknowable* part of the script. Rumi is more accessible.

Rumi is one of the great souls, and one of the great spiritual teachers. He shows us our glory. He wants us to be more alive, to wake up. *Mevlana* comes from the same root as "reveille"—a bugle call to lift us from our spiritual torpor. He wants us to see our beauty, in the mirror and in each other.

Rumi's message can be stated in many ways. It is the core of the core of every religion. It is the longing in a human being to live in unlimited freedom and joy, to move inside beauty, that most profound need of the human soul to flow with the namelessness that animates, luxuriates, burns, and transpires through form, enlivening *what is* as steam, mist, torrent, saliva, blood, ocean, cloud, coffee, wine, butterfly, tiger, hummingbird, energy, and delight.

I feel blessed to have spent much of the second half of my life working on the poetry of Rumi. I am seventy-three now (2010). I began when I was thirty-nine in 1976 at Robert Bly's Great Mother Conference in Ely, Minnesota. Robert brought a stack of A. J. Arberry's translation of Rumi's odes[4] and proposed one afternoon that we do a writing exercise. We were to try rephrasing Arberry's scholarly translations into lively American free verse in the lineage of Walt Whitman, William Carlos Williams, and Galway Kinnell. It was love at first sight for me, though I kept it mostly to myself.

Back in Athens, Georgia, teaching three classes in the English Department, I would go up, after a day of explicating poetry, to the Bluebird Cafe, then at the corner of Hull and Washington, sit there with hot tea, and try to disappear into my newfound devotion. What a relief it was to leave the explicating mind behind. These poems could not be explained. They had to be entered, inhabited. I did that pretty much every day for eight years, before Threshold Books published my first Rumi translations, *Open Secret*, in 1984.[5] The poetry remains an unfolding mystery. When I first began reading and rephrasing the Arberry translations in the fall of 1976, what I felt was a new freedom inside a wild presence. It was very soul-nourishing, a kind of practice for me.

I have a friend who works in prisons. She says the prisoners have a phrase they use among themselves for where they are: *in medium*. There is an old Sufi story about practices. A man is visited in prison by a friend who he hopes will help him escape by bringing a file or some tool for physically escaping, but all he brings is a prayer rug. He begins to do five-times prayer, and after a period he realizes that the place where his forehead touches the rug, the point called the *qibla*, is a diagram of the workings of the tumblers of the lock on his cell door. He escapes. I have been in the medium of this practice for thirty-four years.

Rumi often speaks of the bird who sits in the cage even though the cage door is open. He does not fly off. I sometimes feel like that bird. I was told by a teacher once that these translations are beautiful ("They have to be, for they are coming out of Rumi's love"), but that there is a danger in them for me, because they could become "ecstatic self-hypnosis." So it has sometimes been. My love for the beauty of the poetry has felt like enough, but it is not enough.

The poetry is meant to lead the listener into an experience, into a *presence* or *presences*. I have had a dream about this. I am being pointed into a cave by my friend the poet Galway Kinnell.[6] His strong right arm extends toward the side of a mountain indicating the large entrance to a cave. Over the opening are words in fire, *RASA SHAMSI*. *Rasa* means "essence" in Hindi. I walk up and into the cave, along a passageway bending to the right, and come to a deep cylindrical shaft opening down and up. On the walls of the shaft are sages in meditation on ledge niches as though for giant candles. It is fire-lit and profoundly quiet. Maybe this internal cave community is the *essence* of Shams Tabriz. He is not physically there. A great square wooden chair, his seat, is empty. It faces out over the abyss. I am directed to sit on the left of the empty seat. Someone else will sit on the right. The feel of the great hall and the magnificence of the meditators are images that stay with me. I would claim that the presence of Shams was in the excitement I felt when I was first trying to bring Arberry's scholarly translations over into the American free-verse tradition. It is a grandiose claim, and so be it.

I want to try and say something about my sense of what it is like inside a Rumi poem. Plotinus has a wonderful metaphor for the predicament of human consciousness: a net thrown into the sea. This is what we are with our longings, our works of art, our loves. We are the net. Soul is the ocean we are in, but we cannot hold on to it. We cannot *own* any part of what we swim within, the mystery we love so. Yet the longing we feel is there because of soul. To some degree we are what we are longing for. Some part of the ocean swims inside the fish. In Plotinus's view the visible universe—the entire cosmos, nature, ourselves, and all that we do—is a net thrown into the ocean of soul:

> The cosmos is like a net thrown into the sea, unable to make that in which it is its own. Already the sea is spread out, and the net spreads with it as far as it can, for no one of its parts can be anywhere else than where it is. But because it has no size, the Soul's nature is sufficiently ample to contain the whole cosmic body in one and the same grasp.
>
> —*Ennead IV,* Section 9[7]

There is great poignancy and beauty and longing in the situation, and to paraphrase Plotinus again, as we begin to recognize that beauty, we become more beautiful ourselves.

Say *The Shams* is floating in the Plotinian ocean, a deepening, widening place of soul. The poems are being spoken spontaneously, perhaps in response to soul-growth questions in Rumi's community. When we enter these poems, we enter a conversation in progress on the deepest human level. Soul is all around us, nourishing, illuminating, encouraging, as fine as light, but grounded in a specific friendship with a particular human being, a man named "The Sun," who grew up in Tabriz. Radiant soul intelligence.

C. S. Lewis says that in reading great literature, we transcend ourselves, and we are never more ourselves than when we do that. We feel a buoyancy, an alchemical quintessence, a shimmering aliveness that is both still and in motion. Rumi's originals have no titles in Persian, so the effect is even more watery. These are works in progress in a life in progress, oceanic living tissue, always reconfiguring itself. A music, in a dance around an enlightened being, or several enlightened friends, men and women. What a liveliness. You feel it coming through, even eight centuries later. The no-form joy of surrendered souls, playing. The poetry of *The Shams* is a connection to universal energy, the center itself. I feel that is true.

There is an interesting synchronicity between Rumi and Whitman. A year before he died, Whitman published a poem called "A Persian Lesson." In it, a "greybeard Sufi" is talking to students in a Persian rose garden. Whitman gives the Sufi his own voice:

"Finally my children, to envelope each word, each part of the rest,
Allah is all, all, all—is immanent in every life and object,
May-be at many and many-a-more removes—yet Allah, Allah, Allah is
  there.

"Has estray wander'd far? Is the reason-why strangely hidden?
Would you sound below the restless ocean of the entire world?
Would you know the dissatisfaction? The urge and spur of every life;
The something never still'd—never entirely gone? The invisible need of every
  seed?

"It is the central urge in every atom,
(Often unconscious, often evil, downfallen,)
To return to its divine source and origin, however distant,
Latent the same in subject and in object, without one exception."

Whitman, as the greybeard Sufi, and Rumi claim that there is a core impulse in all things to return to the source. Whitman and Rumi often speak with similar voices. It is appropriate to put Rumi into the Whitman free-verse lineage, which is the strongest strand of American poetry, and the most soul- and self-searching. But there are differences. Whitman, more often, is the beach-walking observer, whereas Rumi often proposes a risk. Danger is present:

Love comes with a knife . . .
You have been walking the ocean's edge,
holding up your robes to keep them dry.
You must dive naked under and deeper under,
a thousand times deeper. Love flows down.[8]

The *lover* in Rumi is the conductor who carries universal energy from the center to the periphery. The *you* in this poetry is that center. "Anything anyone says is your voice,"[9] says the one speaking this poetry. The pronouns are the greatest mystery. Someone knocks on a door. Someone answers. The two become each other, and four hundred thousand. This is true of Whitman too. His great identity poem, *Song of Myself*, begins with *I*:

I celebrate myself, and sing myself,
And what I assume you shall assume,

and ends with *you*:

Missing me one place search another,
I stop somewhere waiting for you.

This complex, lifelong process, the blending of soul essences, is the pervasive experiment of Rumi's poetry.

PART I
Odes (*Ghazals*)

Names for the Mystery

Rumi did not give his poems titles, nor are they divided in the standard editions, as here, into thematic categories. I have chosen to give the odes titles to make them more accessible to modern readers. The twenty-seven categories are meant to open new depths and dimensions in the poems. Eighteen are from the Sufi Ninety-Nine Beautiful Names of Allah, in Arabic.[1] All of those are preceded by a form of *Al*, the Arabic equivalent of "The." The calligraphy was done by Mohamed Zakariya in the *celi sülüs* script, specially commissioned for this volume. Two of the categories are teachers I have met during my life, Bawa Muhaiyaddeen and Osho. Shams Tabriz is also one of the names for Mystery, as is the great Indian saint Ramana Maharshi. The other categories, of my own devising, are: Dissolving the Concept of "God," Playing, Tenderness Toward Existence, Everything and Everyone Else, and the one that is implied in every list of the ninety-nine names, The Name That Cannot Be Spoken or Written.

1.

Al-Fattah, The Opener

I have come to love the sound of the names of God. *Al-Fattah* is my favorite. The homemade American mystic Joe Miller used to stand up and yell *Ya Fattah!* ("O Opener!") in an audience whenever he heard something he liked. There is an opening that is beyond thought. In Rumi's poetry it is often associated with spring. It is in the soul's life, that natural opening where we stay fresh and young. When we act out of mean-spiritedness, the closing up of the ego, we feel locked out of life. Rumi suggests that we "put the head under the feet." We must not be led by the mind, but by a spontaneity in the heart-center, the soul, which is always starting out, beginning again. It cannot be said with words. Music and song do better.

JARS OF SPRINGWATER   —

Jars of springwater are not enough anymore.
Take us down to the river.
The face of peace, the sun itself.

No more the slippery cloudlike moon.
Give us one clear morning after another,
and the one whose work remains unfinished,
who is our work as we diminish,
idle, though occupied, empty, and open.

GOD IN THE STEW

Is there a human mouth that does not give out soul sound?
Is there love, a drawing together of any kind,
that is not sacred?

Every natural dog sniffs God in the stew.

The lion's paw trembles like the rose petal.
He senses the ultimate spear coming.

In the shepherd's majesty wolves and lambs tease each other.
Look inside your mind. Do you hear the crowd gathering?
Help coming, every second.

Still you cover your eyes with mud.
Watch the horned owl. Wash your face.

Anyone who steps into an orchard
walks inside the orchard keeper.

Millions of love-tents bloom on the plain.
A star in your chest says, None of this is outside you.

Close your lips and let the maker of mouths talk,
the one who says *things*.

UNDRESSING

Learn the alchemy true human beings know:
the moment you accept what troubles you've been given,
the door will open.
Welcome difficulty as a familiar comrade.
Joke with torment brought by the friend.
Sorrows are the rags of old clothes and jackets

that serve to cover, then are taken off.
That undressing,
and the naked body underneath,
is the sweetness that comes after grief.

FLIGHTPATHS

Today I see Muhammad ascend.
The friend is everywhere, in every action.
Love, a lattice.
Body, a fire.
I say, Show me the way.

You say, Put your head under your feet.
That way you rise through the stars
and see a hundred other ways to be with me.

There are as many as there are
flightpaths of prayer at dawn.

MOUNTAINTOP TROUGH

We are here like profligates,
three camels with muzzles plunged in provender.

Other camels rage with their lips stuck out,
foaming, but they remain down below in the valley.

This windy mountaintop trough is ours.
It sustains and protects, and you do not arrive here
by just straining your neck to *look* at the mountain.

You must start out and continue on.
You have to leave the place
where everyone worries about rank and money,
where dogs bark and stay home.

Up here it is music and poetry and the divine wind.

Be the date tree that gave fruit to Mary,
the *Let-it-be* of her heart.

Say a small poem. Love the exchange.

An autumn willow has no fruit,
so how could it dance in the wind of *Do-not-fear?*
It rattles and talks with nothing to offer.

Give voice to a poem.
Let it end with praise for the sun,
and the friend within the sun.

OPEN WINDOW

How would it be if you appeared
in this open window?

It would be as though my hands and feet
were suddenly untied, and life was pouring back in.

I would say, I have not smiled
or laughed since you left.
Wine has had no effect.

And you would tease, *Such melancholy*.
It may be catching.

Then I would wrap my shroud around
and offer my neck to your blade.

Cure this headache permanently.
You are the soul light in my eyes.

Words drift out on the air.
Let the musicians play now.
The stringed instruments, the tambourine and drum,
since no reed flute is here today.

A NORTHERN WIND

Every second the question comes,
How long will you stay dregs?
Rise. Do not keep stirring the heavy sediment.
Let murkiness settle.

Some torches, even when they burn with spirit,
give off more smoke than light.

No matter how hard you stare into muddy water,
you will not see the moon or the sun.

A northern wind arrives that burnishes grief
and opens the sky.

The soul wants to walk out in that cleansing air
and not come back.

The soul is a stranger trying to find a home,
somewhere that is not a *where*.
Why keep grazing on *why*?

Good falcon soul,
you have flown around foraging long enough.

Swing back now toward the emperor's whistling.

ENTRANCE DOOR

How lover and beloved touch is familiar and courteous,
but there is a strange impulse in that
to create a form that will dissolve all other shapes.

Remember, the entrance door to the sanctuary
is *inside* you.

We watch a sunlight dust dance,
but nobody knows what music those particles hear.

Each of us has a secret companion musician to dance to.
Unique rhythmic play, a motion in the street
that we alone know and hear.

Shams is a king of kings like Mahmoud,
but there is not another pearl-crushing dervish Ayaz like me.

THE OPENER

Hangovers come with love,
yet love is the cure for hangovers.

A shrill pipe, and the battalion scatters.
Al-Fattah is here.

Bitter goes sweet in the mouth.
Lightning burns through cloud cover.

A water carrier's call
becomes thunder on the desert road.

We are told to deepen.
As the storm of Shams Tabriz moves across the sky,
ocean waves lift and scour the shore.

THE SOURCE OF JOY

No one knows what makes the soul wake up so happy.
Maybe a dawn breeze has blown the veil from the face of God.

A thousand new moons appear.
Roses open laughing.

Hearts become perfect rubies like those from Badakshan.
The body turns entirely spirit.

Leaves become branches in this wind.
Why is it now so easy to surrender,
even for those already surrendered?

There is no answer to any of this.
No one knows the source of joy.

A poet breathes into a reed flute,
and the tip of every hair makes music.

Shams sails down clods of dirt from the roof,
and we take jobs as doorkeepers for him.

THE SILENT ARTICULATION OF A FACE

Love comes with a knife, not some shy question,
and not with fears for its reputation.

I say these things disinterestedly.
Accept them in kind.

Love is a madman, working his wild schemes,
tearing off his clothes, running through the mountains,
drinking poison, and now quietly choosing annihilation.

A tiny spider tries to wrap an enormous wasp.
Think of the spiderweb
woven across the cave where Muhammad slept.

There are love stories,
and there is obliteration into love.

You have been walking the ocean's edge,
holding up your robes to keep them dry.

You must dive naked under and deeper under,
a thousand times deeper. Love flows down.

The ground submits to the sky and suffers what comes.
Tell me, is the earth worse for giving in like that?

Do not put blankets over the drum.
Open completely.

Let your spirit listen
to the green dome's passionate murmur.

Let the cords of your robe be untied.
Shiver in this new love beyond all above and below.
The sun rises, but which way does the night go?

I have no more words. Let the soul speak
with the silent articulation of a face.

CRY OUT YOUR GRIEF

Cry out all your grief, your disappointment.
Say them in Farsi, then Greek.

It does not matter whether you are from Rum or Arabia.
Praise the beauty and kindness praised
by every living being.

You hurt and have sharp desire,
yet your presence is a healing calm.

Sun, moon, bonfire, candle, which?
Someone says your flame is about to be dowsed,
but you are not smoke or fire.

You are infinitely more alive. Say how that is.
This fluttering love will not stay much longer in my chest.

Soon it will fly like a falcon to its master,
like an owl saying *Huuuu*.

THE HEART ACTS AS TRANSLATOR

I went inside my heart to see how it was.
Something there makes me hear the whole world weeping.

Then I went to every city and small town,
searching for someone who could speak wisdom,
but everyone was complaining about love.

That moaning gave me an idea.
Go back inside and find the answer.
But I found nothing.

The heart acts as a translator
between mystical experience and intelligence.

It has its own inhabitants
who do not talk with someone just wandering through.

And remember. Muhammad said of the place
in human beings that we call the heart,
This is what I value.

WE ARE TIRED OF SECRET JOY

With the sacredness you give and describe,
turn us upside down,
that other people may know you are here.

We are tired of secret joy,
bashfulness and being ashamed.

Reasons for holding back fly off like doves.
You speak your subtle truth to this ring of blank faces,
and someone suddenly finds something in a pile of ashes.

Why am I talking?
You know what is happening.
Simply say it.

Walk around to each of us and pour the wine,
and spoon out that eggplant fricassee concoction.

FASTING

There is a hidden sweetness in the stomach's emptiness.
We are lutes, no more, no less.
If the soundbox is stuffed full of anything, no music.
If the brain and belly are burning clean with fasting,
every moment a new song comes out of the fire.
The fog clears, and new energy
makes you run up the steps in front of you.
Be emptier, and cry like the reed instruments cry.
Emptier, write secret with the reed pen.
When you are full of food and drink,

Satan sits where your spirit should,
an ugly metal statue in place of the Kaaba.
When you fast, good habits gather like friends
who want to help. Fasting is Solomon's ring.
Do not give it to some illusion and lose your power,
but even if you have, if you have lost all will and control,
they come back when you fast, like soldiers appearing
out of the ground, pennants flying above them.
A table descends to your tents, Jesus' table.
Expect to see it when you fast, this table
spread with other food, better than the broth of cabbages.

IN THE ARC OF YOUR MALLET

Do not go anywhere without me.
Let nothing happen in the sky apart from me,
or on the ground, in this world or that world,
without my being in its happening.

Vision, see nothing I don't see.
Language, say nothing. The way the night
knows itself with the moon, be that with me.
Be the rose nearest to the thorn that I am.
I want to feel myself in you when you taste food,
in the arc of your mallet when you work.
When you visit friends,
when you go up on the roof by yourself at night.

There is nothing worse
than to walk out along the street without you.
I don't know where I'm going.
You are the road and the knower of roads,
more than maps, more than love.

THE TORRENT LEAVES

Rise up nimbly and go on your strange journey
to the ocean of meanings where you become one of those.
From one terrace to another through clay banks,
washing your wings with watery silt,
follow your friends. The pitcher breaks.
You are in the moving river, living water.
How long will you make clay pitchers
that have to be broken to enter you?

The torrent knows that it cannot stay on this mountain.
Leave, and do not look away from the sun as you go.
Through him you are sometimes crescent, sometimes full.

LOCKED OUT OF LIFE

Again it happens in my sleep.
A core of wakefulness opens.
But I have ways of ignoring that.

You say, How long will you beg from others,
when there are things born of you
that emperors want?

Why waste time in meanness?
Who else can say what you say to me?

If I could repeat it,
people passing by would be enlightened and go free.

You are an ocean in my chest,
where everyone changes places,
believer-unbeliever, cynic-lover, dervish-king.

Last night, you came to my sleep asking, *How are you?*

Locked out of life, waiting, weeping.

GRANITE AND GLASS

You are granite.
I am an empty wine glass.

You know what happens when we touch.
You laugh like the sun coming up laughs
at a star that disappears into it.

Love opens my chest,
and thought returns to its confines.

Patience and rational considerations leave.
Only passion stays, whimpering and feverish.

Some men fall down in the road like dregs thrown out.
Then totally reckless the next morning
they gallop out with new purposes.

Love is the reality,
and poetry is the drum that calls us to that.

Do not keep complaining about loneliness.
Let the fear-language of that theme
crack open and float away.

Let the priest come down from his tower,
and not go back up.

A GARDEN IS QUESTIONING THE DAWN

Good health to you, my teacher,
wherever you are, source of beauty and trust.

How are you with these troubles we bring?
They wonder about you in heaven, in hell,
in pure soul and broad daylight.

Do you hear this flattery we sing to an empty sky?
Longing that comes with a crown,
Moses talking to Pharaoh,
blind hands feeling their way,
what do these things mean?

A garden is questioning the dawn.
Khidr's secret springwater under a violent sky,
an ox standing here in the thick leather of his skin.

My soul sits in silence, and then asks again,
Where are *you* in all of *this*?

WHAT A FINE SONG

The first stork has come,
the soul-bird that brings us the clothing
of new leaves and roses that we call spring.

Joseph's face rises in every well.
Last year, fruit fell.
Now the buried seeds from those
are opening their eyes underground.

A dungeon door loosens in the grass.
Marys who are ready to, become pregnant.

Men who have been quietly studying
lift their faces toward majesty.

You belong to us as flowers belong to a garden.
Each opening drinks in its share.
Then each like a mother cat carries a baby in its mouth,
taking it to the grandmother of roses.
Can you see them?

Now a bird with elegantly colored wings lights in a nearby tree
to sing the mystery of beginning again.
What a fine song that is.

SOUL SPRING

Everything visible has an invisible archetype.
Forms wear down and die. No matter.
The original and the origin do not.

Every fragile beauty, every perfect forgotten sentence,
you grieve their going away, but that is not how it is.
Where they come from never goes dry.
It is an always flowing spring.

Imagine soul as a fountain, a source,
and these visible forms as rivers that build
from an aquifer that is an infinite water.

The moment you come into being here
a ladder, a means of escape, is set up.

First, you are mineral, then plant, then animal.
This much is obvious, surely. You go on
to be a human developing reason and subtle intuitions.

Look at your body, what an intricate beauty
it has grown to be in this dustpit.

And you have yet more traveling to do,
the move into spirit,
where eventually you will be done with this earthplace.
There is an ocean where your drop
becomes a hundred Indian Oceans.

Where *Son* becomes *One*. Be sure of two things.
The body grows old,
and your soul stays fresh and young.

2.
Al-Jami, The Gatherer

The impulse comes to gather. The quality of how we are together, how we talk, this is our gift to the world, a breezy assembly of friends passing quickly through themselves into absence. We feel continuously amazed by the company we keep and how it keeps changing. The purpose of every gathering is discovered: to recognize beauty and to love what is beautiful. Conversation rises out of every particle. It is all alive. We live within love, and yet we run away. We do not know why. This is no ordinary friendship. Come to this empty table, a cleared place where something new can happen. When you take the hand of someone you love, what do those hands become? Waterbirds rise from one lake to find another. What does it mean *to give up the soul?* A river in spring flood, and we are the sun, all those varieties of light. Rumi's invitation is still current:

Come, come, whoever you are,
wanderer, fire worshiper, lover of leaving.
This is not a caravan of despair.
It does not matter that you have broken your vow
a thousand times, still come,
and yet again come.

EVERYONE OUTDOORS TALKING

First day of spring, beginning a whole year of spring.
Everyone outdoors talking.

Rose to narcissus.
Have you seen that ugly raven's face?

No. He has no interest in us.
That's good news!

Pomegranate asks the apple tree for a peach.
All you loafers down at that end of the orchard,
you're always wanting peaches.

You got to have a soul like Jesus
to be handed a peach.

Inside this ordinary banter come messages from the source,
from absolute absence.

The plants stretch new wings in the sun.
Cloud and fog burn off. *Bless your heart.*
That's enough.

Sun moves into Aries permanently!
Come see me.
I will.
I'd like that.
But I can't leave this!

Ground, soaked; sky full of candles.
Visions of fire and water alternating.

Drag your feet off the boat.
Look at him standing there.

I used to have mountain ranges in my chest.
Now it's smooth plain.

Grief lives between the cat paws.
You can say *eek-eek* or *gehk-gehk,*
but there's no way to escape.

Throw this cloth-making equipment into the fire,
the alphabet spindle that is stuck in your throat,
the cleft stick of your neck wrapped with thread.

A STORY THEY KNOW

It is time for us to join the line of your madmen
all chained together.
Time to be totally free, and estranged. Time to give up our souls,
to set fire to structures and run out in the street.

Time to ferment.
How else can we leave the world-vat and go to the lip?
We must die to become true human beings.

We must turn completely upsidedown
like a comb in the top of a beautiful woman's hair.

Spread your wings as a tree lifts in the orchard.
A seed scattered on the road,
a stone melting to wax, candle becoming moth.
On the chessboard the king is blessed again with his queen.

With our faces so close to the love mirror,
we must not breathe,
but rather change to a cleared place where the building was
and feel the treasure hiding in us.

With no beginning or end,
we live in lovers as a story they know.

If you will be the key,
we will be tumblers in the lock.

THE MEETING

When the friend opens the door and says,
You are here, please come in.
It is such a pleasure to give up talking
and listen to his long story about Khidr,
the guide of souls.

A tailor cuts cloth uniquely for each person.
Springs open in the center of the lake.
Trees move in the breeze that comes before dawn.

A nightingale sits in the rosebush and asks,
Who do you love? Tell me.
No one else is here.

The rose, So long as you are you, I cannot.
This is the passionate demand,
the one the burning bush made of Moses.

I am a sacred pool. Take off your shoes.
Wade in.
You are the essence of place and placelessness,
honored one. Take my hand.

The needle's eye will not accept
a strand of thread that is folded double.

So it is with you.
You find yourself holding the royal bowl
and welcoming all to the banquet.

The sun stands in fire up to its chin,
so that we can have daylight.

When you take the hand of someone you love,
what happens to those hands?

Your darling comes, and you ask,
How can I help? Come here.

Reason wonders, *Should I go?*
And your loving, *Should I run?*

The one you love signals,
Yes. I want both of you.

The table is there. Sit down.
Choose the bright company.
Do not worry about food.

Now I pass to you this silence,
so that the alternations of night and day
with their flaming language
may finish the story.

LEAVING

Every moment love arrives from all sides,
but no more sightseeing.

We are leaving for pure emptiness,
traveling with friends we once lived with,
beyond angels, beyond spirit, to our home city of majesty.

Load up. Say goodbye to this dusty place.
A young luck rides at the head of us.

Giving up the soul is the main business of this caravan,
with the chosen one leading,
the one the moon came begging to.

A humble, delicate girl is following the fragrance of his hair.
The moon splits open. We move through,
waterbirds rising to look for another lake.

Or say we are living in a love-ocean,
where trust works to caulk our body-boat,
to make it last a little while,
until the inevitable shipwreck,
the total marriage, the death-union.

Dissolve in friendship like two drunkards fighting.

Do not look for justice here
in the jungle where your animal soul
gives you bad advice.

Drink enough wine so that you stop talking.
You are a lover, and love is a tavern
where no one makes much sense.

Even if the things you say are poems
as dense as sacks of Solomon's gold,
they become pointless.

WE ARE THE SUN

We are a warm spell
that comes in a relentless winter.

We are the sun, with all the different kinds of light.
We are wind.

Doves when they call *coo, where,*
are looking for us.

Nightingales and parrots change their perches
hoping to be nearer to us.

Word of us reached the fish.
They swerved and leapt.

Waves from that stirring keep coming in.
The soul has been given its own ears to hear things
that the mind does not understand.

In the great spirit world Muhammad's name
is called with his four friends,
Abu Bakr, Omar, Uthman, and Ali.

Those are our names too.
We have come out of slavery with bales of sugarcane.
No need to mention Egypt.

The sweetness of how we talk together
is what we crush and bring the world.

UNCLE OF THE JAR

Some talk of cup and jar and river
and how they depend on each other.

What flows in the river fills the jar,
but only a potter knows the state of the cup.
One drinks from the other.

We know what was in what by the residue.
Some naive people have not gotten close enough
to smell the musk, so they cannot judge.

But still they do, and others repeat
their lack of knowledge. What shall we call that?

Another time fragrance from a jar
drives thousands of Turks mad, and Hindus too,
or a witch rides the jar town to town
witch-laughing at the jarless witches.

It is best to follow some fragrance you catch
on your own, alone.

Let that take you to the face of someone
who has escaped from jars and cups.

You have heard the old saying among drunks,
I am the uncle of the jar.

Find one like that and sit down beside him.
There will be no inexperienced gossip,
no words at all maybe.

A silence resides in an empty jar as fragrance,
as a river in spring flood.
That is the jar you have been looking for.

ASYLUM

You that pour, ease up.
Our minds have moved to the asylum.

The jar's rim, dark red, the town burning.
This comb has no handle, all teeth.

Each candle-moment there is a new moth.
Some people, when they hear
how the mind goes crazy in love, close down.

Their hearts contract. There is a confusion in surrender
that the intellect so hates it devises a key made of fire
to destroy the lock, the door, and the whole house.

But love's madness has gone before,
and there is nothing left, no rooms, no door, no lock,
just this airy falling asylum of friends
that we call Shams.

A DELICATE GIRL

The terrible grief of being human,
let us drink it all, but with a difference.

We sit with Junnaiyd and Bestami.
The moon rising here cannot be covered with cloud.

There are no deaths for lovers.
Who is the self? A delicate girl that flows out
when we draw the sword of selfless action.

This earth eats men and women,
and yet we are sent to eat the world,
this place that tries to fool us with *tomorrow*.
Wait until tomorrow,
which we outwit by enjoying only this *now*.

We gather at night to celebrate being human.
Sometimes we call out low to the tambourine.

Fish drink the sea, but the sea does not get smaller.
We eat the clouds and evening light.
We are slaves tasting the royal wine.

BLADE

The soul of this community is coming toward us,
the sun on his forehead, wine jar in right hand, stride by stride.

Do not ruin this chance with politeness and easy promises.
The help we called for is here,
the invitation to join with great souls.

Any place we gather becomes a ceremony
on the way to the Kaaba, which means:
Pass quickly through your own being into absence.

The self of your name and fame secures you
with a new knot every moment.

Personal identity is a sheath. The creator of that, a sword.
The blade slides in and unites, worn covering
over bright steel, love purifying love.

STRANGE GATHERING

This man holds up a tambourine,
and an entire musical mode comes out into the air.

Prepare to travel. Tie the pack, loosen the reins.
John the Baptist and David and Joseph
are turning somersaults.

Jesus and Moses watch Gabriel
by the door casting spells.

Abraham looks lost in his longing,
holding a sword over Ishmael *and* Isaac.
They bow down.

Muhammad says to God, My true brothers
are those who believe, though they do not see me.
I wish I could see them.

Abu Bakr, True. It is true.

Layla and Majnun, Husrev and Shirin
stay glass-bright in the world of pleasure.

Rustam, warrior. Hamza, Muhammad's uncle.
Arrows, shield, and Ali's sword,
who could stand against that blade,
or throw it and split the moon?

Hallaj here is love's king.
He bows at the name of Shams Tabriz
and says again, *I am the truth.*

The soul is tremendously honored by that.

KEEP MOVING

Do you hear what the stringed instrument says about longing?

The same as the stick, I was once a green branch in the wind.

We are all far from home.
Language is our caravan bell.

Do not stop anywhere.
The moment you are attracted to a place,
you grow bored with it.

Think of the big moves you have already made,
from a single cell to a human being.
Stay light-footed, and keep moving.

Turkish, Arabic, Greek,
any tongue is a wind that was formerly water.

As a breeze carries the ocean inside it,
so underneath every sentence is, *Come back to the source.*

A moth does not avoid flame.
A king lives in the city.

Why should I keep company with owls
out here in the empty buildings?

If your donkey acts crazy and will not work,
apply the bullwhip to his head.
He will understand.

Do not try to love him back to his senses.
Whack him.

TREES

Spring, and no one can be still,
with all the messages coming through.

We walk outside as though going to meet visitors,
wild roses, trilliums by the water.

A tight knot loosens.
Something that died in December
lifts a head out, and opens.

Trees, the tribe gathers.
Who has a chance against such an elegant assemblage?

Before this power,
human beings are chives to be chopped,
gnats to be waved away.

WALKING OUT OF THE TREASURY BUILDING

Lord, the air smells good today,
straight from the mysteries of the inner courtyard,
a grace like new clothes thrown across the garden,
free medicine for everybody.

The trees in their prayer, the birds in praise,
the first blue violets kneeling.
Whatever came from Being is caught up in being,
bewildered, forgetting the way back.

One man turns and sees his birth
pulling separate from the others.

He fills with light, and colors change here.
He drinks it in, and everyone is shining with his beauty.
I cannot really say that I feel the pain of others,
when the whole world seems so sweet.

Face to face with a lion, I grow leonine.
Walking out of the treasury building, I feel generous.
Anyone still sober in this weather must be afraid of people,
afraid what they will say.

Enough talking. If we eat too much greenery,
we are going to smell like vegetables.

KEEPER OF SECRETS

You came here to tell my secret to everyone,
what I give no sign of.
Last night in a dream you offered a cup.
I said, I will not drink wine.
Do not. The loss is yours.
I am afraid of being shamed.
I will reach for you and you will not be there.

It is astonishing to me
that someone offers you his innermost life,
and you frown.
Will you be deceptive with me as you are with others?
I am the keeper of secrets. You cannot hide from me.
I am the beauty of the perceived world,
but you lay back on the ground.
I am the true direction of the spirit,
but you glance around at clouds.

If you turn away now,
you will do the same on the day you die.
Be pale for the one who created color.
Do not put saffron on your face for the sake of shadows.
Be a rooster, conscious of time and the leader.
Do not change your rooster to a hen.
Bend and sit crookedly, but tell the straight truth.
Truth is enough. I am the friend, your spirit.
Why look for someone else?

If you like the verse about lending to God,
lend a clipping from a counterfeit coin

and get back the deed to a diamond mine.
If for two or three days you bandage your eyes with awe,
you make your sensible eyes a fountain for the other ocean.
If only for a second you go straight for this target,
that arrowy intention becomes your bow and your bowstring.
There is no generosity better than this.
That with your sins and your forgetfulness
I am telling you how to pray.

So much for words, which have to be written down,
or not contained in the mouth.
If you were to open every living particle,
you could make a mouth of each.

THE SHOP

Lightning falling on the helpless,
a surge of pearl out of the rock, covering the rock,
this life torn into a hundred pieces,
and one of those pieces a ticket to let me back into my life.

A spirit world divided into eight sections, one a scroll.
Eight scrolls in the parchment of your face.
What kind of bird am I becoming,
kneeling like a camel, pecking at the fire like an ostrich?

You and I have worked in the same shop for years.
Our loves are great fellow workers.
Friends cluster there, and every moment
we notice a new light coming out in the sky,
invisible, yet taking form,
like Christ coming through Mary.
In the cradle, God.

Shams, why this inconsistency?
That we live within love
and yet we run away?

THE WINE VAT'S LID

I go to the one who can cure me and say,
I have a hundred things wrong.
Can you combine them to one?

I thought you were dead.
I was, but then I caught your fragrance again
and came back to life.

Gently, his hand on my chest.
Which tribe are you from?
This tribe.

He begins to treat my illness.
If I am angry and aggressive, he gives me wine.
I quit fighting. I take off my clothes and lie down.
I sing in the circle of singers.
I roar and break cups, even big jars.

Some people worship golden calves.
I am the mangy calf that worships love.

A healing presence has called me from the hole I hid in.
My soul, if I am agile or stumbling,
confused or in my true being, it is still you.

Sometimes the sleek arrow.
Other times, a worn leather thumbguard.

You bring me where everything circles.
And now as you put the lid back on the wine vat, pure quiet.

THE WATERWHEEL

Stay together, friends.
Don't scatter and sleep.
Our friendship is made of being awake.

The waterwheel accepts water and turns
and gives it away, weeping.

That way it stays in the garden.
Whereas another roundness rolls
through a dry riverbed
looking for what it thinks it wants.

Stay here, quivering with each moment
like a drop of mercury.

A COMMUNITY OF THE SPIRIT

There is a community of the spirit.
Join it, and feel the delight
of walking in the noisy street
and *being* the noise.

Drink all your passion and be a disgrace.
Close both eyes to see with the other eye.
Open your hands if you want to be held.

Consider what you have been doing.
Why do you stay
with such a mean-spirited and dangerous partner?

For the security of having food. Admit it.
Here is a better arrangement.
Give up this life, and get a hundred new lives.

Sit down in this circle.

Quit acting like a wolf,
and feel the shepherd's love filling you.

At night, your beloved wanders.
Do not take painkillers.

Tonight, no consolations.
And do not eat.

Close your mouth against food.
Taste the lover's mouth in yours.

You moan, But she left me. He left me.
Twenty more will come.

Be empty of worrying.
Think of who created thought.

Why do you stay in prison
when the door is so wide open?

Move outside the tangle of fear-thinking.
Live in silence.

Flow down and down
in always widening rings of being.

NO ORDINARY FRIENDSHIP

Soul so close, whatever you think of I know,
but I want more convincing proof.

Do not arrive and say, Now I am here.
Our closeness is not like that.

I am a support column in your house,
a waterspout on your roof.

I share with you the secrets
that others will tell on their last day.

This is no ordinary friendship.
I attend your banquet as wine is passed around the table.

Like lightning, I am an expert at dying.
Like lightning, this beauty has no language.
It makes no difference whether I win or lose.

You sit with us in a congregation of the dead,
where one handful of dirt says, I was once a head of hair.
Another, I was a backbone.
You say nothing.

Love comes in saying,
I can deliver you from yourself in *this* moment.

Now lover and beloved grow quiet.
My mouth is burning with sweetness.

AT HOME IN BOTH PLACES

I never get enough of laughing with you, this wild humor.
Thirsty and dry, I complain,
but everything is made of water.
Lonely, yet my head leans against your shirt.
My wounded hands are your hands.

Do something drastic.

You say, Come and sit in the innermost room,
where you will be safe from the love-thief.

I reply, But I have tried to be the ring knocker on your door,
so you will not have to be always letting me in and out.

You say, No. You stand on the threshold waiting,
and you are here in the inner chamber too.
You are at home in both places.

I love the quietness of such an answer.
Come to this table of quietness.

3.
Al-Batin, The Hidden

There are invisible aspects to being sentient and embodied. Consciousness is invisible. Love is invisible. Both are immeasurable. Placed and passionate, cool and in motion, we move along, earthy and pure soul. There is a voice inside the green. What have you *not* seen? We change, and see differently. Mystery is everywhere. Do not try to find the meanings. There is a hiding implicit in creation. Something is always being concealed. Never think you know what that is, though laughter says a lot about it. The heart is the secret inside the secret. You can never say, or know, what is concealed inside you.

THE LIVING DOUBLENESS

I ask my heart, Why do you keep looking
for the delights of love?

I hear the answer back, Why will you not join me
in this companionship?

This is the conversation of being a human being,
the living doubleness.

Cool and in motion like water,
placed and passionate like fire.

Subtle as wind, yet obvious
as a wine glass poured to the brim,
spilled over and drunk down
all at once for a toast.

Like rain, you make any image more vivid.
Like a mirror, you can be trusted to hold beauty.

There are mean people who see only meanness
reflected in your beauty, but they are wrong.

You are pure soul
and made of the ground.

You are eyeshadow
and the kindness in eyelight.

A ruby from no telling which mine,
let yourself be set in a seal ring.

Lift the sword-discernment
that rules a thousand compassions.

Shams in the lovely shape of Shams,
spring-source of invisible meaning.

GREEN FROM INSIDE

The moon comes to visit as a guest of the night.
Rose sits down by thorn.
Someone washing clothes asks for the sun's forgiveness.

Compass leg circles the point.
Muhammad arrives here a stranger,

spring to this dry tree. Hallaj smiles at his cross.
The pomegranate flowers.

Everyone talks about greenery, not with words,
but quietly, as green itself talks from inside,
as we begin to live our love.

SALADIN

The heart sees the joy of early dawn, the breeze.
What have you seen? What have you not seen?

Sometimes to plunge into a bewilderment ocean.
Sometimes, to find the gray amber of whales
deep in the mountains. Hundreds of windows.
Haze returns into the sea.

My weeping eyes, wave by wave, mix with the ocean.
It becomes an eye.

Both worlds, a single corn grain in front of a great rooster.
One who wants, one who is wanted, the same.

Who knows God? Someone through with *La*. No.
The broken lover knows about this.
Nobody in this robe but God.

Appear as you truly are, Saladin.
You are my soul, the eye that sees God.

HARVEST

As the sun goes down in the well,
lovers enter the seclusion of God.

Later at night we meet like thieves
who have stolen gold, our candlelit faces.

A pawn has become king.
We sit secretly inside the presence
like a Turk in a tent among Hindus,
and yet we are traveling past a hundred watchmen,
night-faring, drowned in an ocean of longing.

Sometimes a body rises to the surface
like Joseph coming out of his well of abandonment

to be the clarity that divides Egypt's wheat fairly
and interprets the royal dreaming.

Some people say about human beings, *Dust to dust,*
But how can that be true of one
who changes road dust to doorway?

The crop appears to be one thing
when it is still in the field.

Then the transformation time comes,
and we see how it is half chaff, half grain.

SEE WHAT YOU HAVE DESPISED IN YOURSELF

They are here with us now,
those who saddle a new unbroken colt every morning
and ride the seven levels of the sky,
who lay down at night with the sun and moon for pillows.

Each of these fish has a Jonah inside.
They sweeten the bitter sea.
They shape-shift the mountains,
but with their actions neither bless nor curse.

They are more obvious,
and yet more secret than that.

Mix grains from the ground they walk with streamwater.
Put that salve on your eyes and you will see
what you have despised in yourself
as a thorn opens into a rose.

CLIMB TO THE EXECUTION PLACE

Grief settles thick in the throat and lungs:
thousands of sorrows being suffered, clouds of cruelty,
all somehow from love.

Wail and be thirsty for your own blood.
Climb to the execution place. It is time.

The Nile flows red. The Nile flows pure.
Dry thorns and aloes wood are the same,
until fire touches.

A warrior and a mean coward stand here similar,
until arrows rain.

Warriors love battle. A subtle lion with strategy
gets the prey to run *toward* him saying, *Kill me again*.

Dead eyes look into living eyes.
Do not try to figure this out.

Love's work looks absurd,
but trying to find a meaning will hide it more.
Silence.

TO THE EXTENT THEY CAN DIE

A Chinese mirror shows all sides of a human being.
That is the one for you.

Someone born deaf has no more use for high notes
than newborn babies for a fine merlot.

What would a land bird be doing out over open sea?
We are rinds thrown out by the tavern of absolute absence,
unconcerned about profits, or dowry, or what to wear.

We are a hundred thousand years beyond insanity.
Plato does not speak of this.

The physical beauty of men and women is not an image here.
Lovers are alive to the extent that they can die.

A great soul approaches Shams, What are you doing here?
Answer: What is there to do?

BROOM WORK

If every heart had such a private road into the friend as this,
there would be a garden bench on the tip of every thorn.
Every grief would be an exuberance.

Flame-colored souls enjoy each other.
Lightning stands doorkeeper for the full moon.

If it did not, the sky's shifting
would start to occur on the ground.

If legs and feet and wings took us to the beloved,
every atom would become such transportation.

If everyone could see what love is,
each would set up a tentpole in the ocean.

The world's population pitched and living
easily within the sea.

What if inside every lover's tear you saw the face of the friend,
Muhammad, Jesus, Buddha, the impossible-possible
philosopher, the glass diamond one, Shams Tabriz?

A friendship fire dissolves divisions.
Yesterday becomes tomorrow.
Stay low and lower under the green roof.
Keep sweeping the floor.

That broom work keeps a brilliance covered
that would confuse us more than we can stand.

BACK INTO THE REEDBED

Time to ignore sensible advice,
to untie the knots our culture ties us with.

Cut to the quick.
Put cotton in both sentimental ears.

Go back into the reedbed.
Let cane sugar rise again in you.

No rules or daily duties.
Those do not bring the peace of silence.

BOWLS OF FOOD

Moon and evening star
do their slow tambourine dance to praise this universe.

The purpose of every gathering is discovered:
To recognize beauty and to love what is beautiful.

Once it was like that. Now it is like this.
So the saying goes around town,
and serious consequences too.

Men and women turn their faces to the wall in grief.
They lose appetite.

Then they start eating the fire of pleasure,
as camels chew pungent grass for the sake of their souls.

Winter blocks the road. Flowers are taken prisoner underground.
Then green justice tenders a spear.

Go outside to the orchard.
These visitors came a long way, past all the houses of the zodiac,
learning something new at each stop.

And they are here for such a short time,
sitting at these tables set on the prow of the wind.

Bowls of food are brought out as answers,
but still no one knows the answer.

Food for the soul stays secret.
Body food gets put out in the open like us.

Those who work at a bakery do not know the taste of bread
like the hungry beggars do.

Because the beloved wants to know,
unseen things become manifest.

Hiding is the hidden purpose of creation.
Bury your seed and wait.

After you die, all the thoughts you had
will throng around like children.

The heart is the secret inside the secret.
Call the secret *language*, and never be sure what you conceal.

It is the unsure people who get the blessing.
The lifting limbs of the cypress, opening rose, nightingale song,
fruit, these are *inside* the chill November wind.
They are its secret.

We climb and fall so often. Plants have an inner being,
and separate ways of talking and feeling.

An ear of corn bends in thought. Tulip, so embarrassed.
Pink rose deciding to open a competing store.

A bunch of grapes sits with its feet stuck out.
Narcissus gossiping about iris.

Willow, what do you learn from running water? Humility.
Red apple, what has the friend taught you? To be sour.

Peach tree, why so low? To let you reach.
Look at the poplar, tall, but without fruit or flower.

Yes, if I had those, I would be self-absorbed like you.
I gave up self to watch the enlightened ones.

Pomegranate questions quince. Why so pale?
For the pearl you hid inside me.
How did you discover my secret? Your laugh.

The core of the seen and the unseen universes smiles,
but remember, smiles come best from those who weep.

Lightning, then the rain-laughter.
Dark earth receives that clear, then grows a trunk.

Melon and cucumber come dragging along on pilgrimage.
You have to *be* to be blessed.

Pumpkin begins climbing a rope. Where did he learn that?
Grass, thorns, a thousand ants and snakes,
everything is looking for food. Don't you hear the noise?

Every herb cures some illness. Camels delight to eat thorns.
We prefer the inside of a walnut, not the shell.

The inside of an egg, the outside of a date.
What about your inside and outside?

The same way a branch draws water up many feet,
God is pulling your soul along.

Wind carries pollen from blossom to ground.
Wings and Arabian stallions gallop toward the warmth of spring.

They visit. They sing and tell what they think they know.
So-and-so will travel to such-and-such.

The hoopoe carries a letter to Solomon.
The wise stork says *lek-lek*. Please translate.

It is time to go to the high plain, to leave the winter house.
Be your own watchman as birds are.

Let the remembering beads encircle you.
I make promises to myself and break them.

Words are coins. The veins of ore and the mineshaft,
what they speak of. Now consider the sun.

It is neither oriental nor occidental.
Only the soul knows what love is.

This moment in time and space is an eggshell
with an embryo crumpled inside, soaked in belief-yolk,

under the wing of grace, until it breaks free of mind
to become the song of an actual bird, and God.

YOU SO HIDDEN

You so subtle that you enter silently our souls,
how would it be if you for a time were here on earth?

You so hidden you are hidden from hidden things,
when you enter me, my hiddenness shines like a lantern.

You Solomon, who understands bird language,
and can speak it, what will you say through me?

King whose bow no one can draw,
use me for an arrow.

Shams, you are the way I know God.
Walk into this copper mine and turn it to gold.

THE TENT

Outside, the freezing desert night.
This other night grows warm, kindling.
Let the landscape be covered with thorny crust.
We have a soft garden in here.

The continents blasted, cities and little towns,
everything become a scorched blacked ball.
The news we hear is full of grief for that future,
but the real news inside here is
there is no news at all.

PRIVACY

Who is this standing in my house?
He signals with his hand,
What do you want from me?
Nourishment, and the privacy of one truth.

There are so many deceptive people
pretending to be faithful.
Do not sit among them,
eyes shut like a bud, mouth open like a rose.

The world is a mirror, an imaging of love's perfection.
No man has ever seen a part greater than the whole.
Go on foot through this garden like the grass does.
Only the rose is riding, all the rest on foot.
Rose, both sword and swordsman.
Reason in the abstract, and reasoning in each of us.

Generous Saladin, let your hand be
a constant necklace on my neck.

THIS SPLASHING AROUND

There are people with rooms full of gold.
You can see how rich they are,
but how is it when mystical wealth shows in the face?

A lover moans for the friend,
and a rosebush leaps from the ground
to see what is happening.

Take off your clothes and jump in the pool.
Escape the forehead pressure of mind.

We used to think this splashing around was foolish.
Then came a wink, and we were done for.
How long do you stay jealous and angry?

Let two or three sad songs rise from your chest.
Or just keep doing as you are now.

Maybe in your loud confusion
the world will disappear and the curtain will lift.

Passion breaks loose. Now silence.
The love-king says, It takes courage to keep the deep self quiet.

DRUM

In this drumbeat moment of red flowers opening
and grapes being crushed,
the soul and luminous clarity sit together.

All desire wants is a taste of you, this moment
that is like two small mountain villages
where everyone longs for presence.

We start to step up. A step appears.
You say, I am more compassionate than your father and mother.
I make medicine out of your pain.
From your chimney smoke I shape new constellations.

I tell everything, but I do not say it,
because, my friend,
it is better that your secret be spoken by you.

WHEREVER HE IS MOVING

Lovers turn to fire and a circulating star.
The sun rises. Stars disappear.
We cannot see the sun's face today.
Wandering, not worth much,
every morning we hear a call and go toward that,
divided into thirty parts,
drowned in our own embryo blood,
ground fine in the mill of experience.

There are no rules in this valley,
no mind but madness within madness,
with all of it inside Shams-love,
wherever he is moving.

THIS SOUP

You have that quality that God has,
when you enter a house at night,
it glows with many lamps being lit.

When you come into a human being, the same thing.
You have the quality of wine.
The assembly kindles as you are being passed around.

And when passion is gone,
the first excited flush over,

you are there carrying water quietly
to the grasses and the rosebush.

When the visible world freezes,
you open the other.

You give urgency to longing.
How else would the dark ground ever meet the sky radiance
that serves it by bringing water and by constantly sifting,
but not as prospectors sift for metals.

You are the mine and the touchstone.
We point our prayer rugs toward you.
Why do you worship us?

It is no wonder when a beggar visits a king,
but this is the king begging the beggar,
so that the beggar thinks he is king.

Sky, why are you night and day
constantly attending this lowliness?

The sky answers, All motion has a reason.
I am being drawn.

This poetry nourishes the angels.
When I am silent, they come hungry to me,
Speak. Feed us, please.

But you are not an angel.
Why are you listening?
Is this your food too?

Would you like some chives with it?
How could you possibly want this soup
that the mystery keeps simmering all day
in the kitchen of my brain, chopping and adding things to it.

Shams, turn your face here.
No. I have said that wrong.

The sun is all face,
always facing everywhere.

There is no back
of the head to Shams.

WHAT THE SUN SAYS RISING

A love for what is unseen has taken my mind away.
That horse has carried me here, but where am I?

I come to an archway
through which I see a world with no sun and no moon.

Let me rest a minute,
to let my mind come back and help me describe it to you.

Listen carefully,
for I shall speak of the soul,
and you *are* the soul.

Come closer.
Put your ear against my mouth.
The most secret mystery is this love.
And the next is how lamps of vision are lit through the ear.

Khidr the guide goes with you to the clear spring,
so that like water you too may scatter light.

Zuleikha grew young in her love for Joseph.
The old world gets energy from this star.

Taste for a moment a piece of the whole
and understand who you are.

You have fallen into mouths.
People are chewing you.
You are delicious well-baked bread.

Dance, when light takes your hand.
Do not stay cold and heavy like wet sand.
The sun comes up saying,

You are not a goat standing on its hindlegs
about to butt a rival.
You are the shepherd of lions.
Light the candles of your five senses
from the fire that is in your heart.

Those senses are the five players you control.
Your love is a deeply memorized verse,
something you will never forget.

In every dawn a voice comes that says,

Let the road dust settle.
Now, be led.

Do not be afraid of the horse,
like someone who does not want to go anywhere.

Sweetness says,
Open your mouth.
Do not stay shut.
Enjoy the taste.

Do not just talk about joy,
as you tell other people's stories.

Worship the sun in this friendship with Shams,
who is a master of spirit science,
and the sun within the light of daylit places.

4.
Al-Khabir,
The Aware, The Knowing

The names of God are qualities that live in the core of our being. *Khabir* is the aspect that knows we will live through death, the part that burns and becomes fragrance for a while, then disappears into absence. Dying gives the soul more range, allows it to perch on a cliff of the wind with an awareness that is deeper than love. Shams Tabriz carries *this* in his presence. A profound gladness fills the human psyche when it knows the part of the self that does not die. A moth builds with its surrender a house to live in made of candlelight. Education and custom dissolve to a piece of a rosy shell.

THE KNOTS UNTIE

Fire is whispering a secret in smoke's ear,
This aloes wood loves me,
because I help it live out its purpose.
With me it becomes fragrance,
and then disappears altogether.

The knots untie and open into absence,
as you do with me, my friend,
eaten by flame and smoked out into the sky.

This is most fortunate. What is unlucky
is not to change and disappear.

The black soil must crumble to give itself to plants.
Think how sperm and egg become a smiling face.

Bread must dissolve to turn into thought.
Gold and silver in their raw forms are not worth much.

This way leads through humiliation and contempt.
We have tried the fullness of presence.
Now it is time for desolation.

Love is pulling us out by the ears to school.
Love wants us clean of resentment
and those impulses that misguide our souls.

We are asleep, but Khidr keeps sprinkling water
on our faces. Love will tell us the rest
of what we need to know soon.

Then we will be deeply asleep and profoundly awake
simultaneously like the cave companions.

SOLOMON ANT

This feverish desiring does not calm down,
because God does not want it to.
Wishes and wantings come from there.

When my shirt is wet, blame the sea.
We soul-fish swim among the fishing lines
of what we want, unable to imagine
the beauty of the fisherpeople jiggling the hooks.

God was here before the universe.
What desire brought us into being?
I do not know. It is enough that we go straight
for what and whom we are drawn to.

No. There is no crooked or straight with this,
though we persist in judging actions and their source:
Bad, bad, good, bad, good.

Think of an ant that wants to fly. Wonderful.
He digs at the palace wall. He claims to be Solomon.
He demands a crown. This is how we are.

We are not what we are wanting,
and yet somehow the longings are not apart from us.

Shams, will you untie this knot?

WATER FROM THE WELL OF THE SOUL

This world-river has no water in it.
Come back, spring.

Bring water more fresh than Khidr or Elijah knew,
from the fountain that pulses in the well of the soul.

Where water is, there bread arrives.
But not the reverse.
Water never comes from loaves.

You are the honored guest.
Do not weep like a beggar for pieces of the world.

The river vanishes because of that desiring.
Swim out of your pond.

Go where all the fish are Khidrs,
where there are no secondary causes.

That water rises in the date tree,
and in the roses in your cheek.

When it flows toward you,
you will feel deep contentment.

The nightwatchman shakes his rattle
as part of his fear.

You will not need him anymore.
Water itself guards the fish that are in it.

TALKING TO THE LUCK-BIRD

Your jasmine body shrugs a signal to me.
My soul flies against the constraining cage.

Now the luck-bird's shadow is overhead.
I shout, Go away. You are not part of this.

Oh really? Says the bird of good and bad circumstances.
You refuse happiness? You anticipate no troubles?

These wittering worries and wishes
keep human beings apart from the friend.

I want the face itself.
As I say that, the luck-bird goes wild for jasmine.

Now the fortune-teller and the enlightened teacher,
the body and the soul, are as crazed as I am.

A BEAUTIFUL WALK INSIDE YOU

Through this blood veil the lover sees a beautiful walk.
Reason says, There are only six directions.
North, east, south, west, up, and down.
There is no way out of those limits.

Love says, But I have many times escaped.

Reason comes to a marketplace and begins haggling prices.
Love wanders away with other business to transact,
something to do with incomparable beauty.

There are secret things happening.
Hallaj listens to whispers
and walks off the speaker's platform onto a scaffold.

Dreg-drinkers have love perceptions
that reasonable men fiercely deny.

They say, We cannot go barefooted in that courtyard.
There is nothing but thorns through there.

Love answers, The thorns are inside you.
Be silent, and pull what hurts out of your loving's foot.

Then you will see gardens and secluded rose bowers,
and they will all be inside you.

Shams is the sun obscured by this cloud of words.
Maybe he will burn the overcast off
and let love clear and brighten.

MORE RANGE

We are friends with the one who kills us,
who gives us to the ocean waves.

We love this death. Only ignorance would say,
Put it off a while, day after tomorrow.

Do not avoid the knife.
This friend only seems fierce,
bringing your soul more range,
perching your falcon on a cliff of the wind.

Jesus on his cross, Hallaj on his—
those absurd killings hold a secret.

Cautious cynics *know* what they are doing
every moment and why.

Submit to love without thinking,
as the sun this morning rose recklessly
extinguishing our star-candle minds.

KNOWLEDGE BEYOND LOVE

Shams has knowledge beyond love,
an emptiness like air.

This saddens and confuses me.
Wandering bits of wood in ocean water.

There is a change that lets Jesus be born every breath.
Mention Shams and your talking and writing
will be lit from within.

You believe that this I say and write is blood
and must not be spilled, a lonely circulation.

My intellect lies in the hallway listening to language
as if there were a group playing music outside.

I do not say that my mind ignores my soul,
but this was their conversation yesterday:

Mind. What will happen?
Soul. You must forget me completely.
What I feel does not occur in time.

Fires have been set on the mountain
to help us with the night passage.

Mind dissolves. You see Joseph everywhere.
The tide comes in. Sometimes the sea becomes one drop.

If Moses, we learn about the Kabbalah.
If Jesus, the Christian sacrament.

If soul, we turn vast and airy.
If earth, we are grounded and dancing and hungry.
We expand like bread from within.

Ego does not forgive.
It stands and shouts coarse commands.

But the morning breeze
and one handful of earth from somewhere near Tabriz
will heal my eyes and show what to do.

CUP

The cup wants to be lifted and used,
not broken, but carried carefully to the next.

The cup knows there is a state for you beyond this,
one that comes with more vast awareness.

The cup looks still, but it acts in secret to help.
Sometimes you pour cup to cup. Nothing happens.

Pour instead into your deep ocean-self without calculation.
If eyesight blurs, find a railing to follow.

SOUR, DOUGHY, NUMB, AND RAW

If we are not together in the heart, what's the point?
When body and soul are not dancing,
there is no pleasure in colorful clothing.

Why have cooking pans when there is no food in the house?
In this world full of fresh bread, amber, and musk,
so many different fragrances,
what are they to someone with no sense of smell?

If you stay away from fire,
you will remain sour, doughy, numb, and raw.

You may have lovely, just-baked loaves around you,
but those friends cannot help.

You have to *feel* the oven's fire.

SOMEONE BEING DRAWN TO YOU

Today we pull you back.
You swore you would not come,
then you broke that oath.
Now you are keeping it again.

You give us this need.
The ocean makes a flounder flounder
when it is not in the ocean.

How should someone act who is being drawn to you?
Completely submissive.

Does that frighten you?
The pearl of silence is not for sale.

A NEW-GREEN BRANCH

Every day is Friday,
the beginning of holidays, holy days.

Isn't last Friday remembered now with a festival?
You have on the right clothes for this festival,
your light, your clear trust,
your inside and outside the same,
not a sweet walnut filled with garlic.

Go around in this ring
like a lover on the doorstep of a lover.
How can straw be still on a river?
How can a mystic stay angry?

To some eyes these words are a new-green branch.
To sensual eyes, they are old matters
carved on a building.

THE OLDEST THIRST THERE IS

Give us gladness that connects with the friend,
a taste of the quick,
you that make a cypress strong and jasmine jasmine.

Give us the inner listening that is a way in itself
and the oldest thirst there is.

Do not measure it out with a cup.
I am a fish. You are the moon.
You cannot touch me,
but your light fills the ocean where I live.

THE REED FLUTE'S WORK

I say to the reed flute, You do the work,
but you know sweet secrets too.

You share the friend's breathing.
What could you need from me?

The reed replies, Knowledge is for total destruction.
I say, Burn me completely then and leave no knowing.

How could I, when it is knowledge that leads us?

But that knowledge has lost compassion
and grown disgusted with itself.
It has forgotten about silence and emptiness.

A reed flute has nine holes
and is a model of human consciousness,
beheaded, though still in love with lips.

This is your disgrace, this moaning.
Weep for the sounds you make.

ROSELIT PIECE OF SHELL

Say the moth is building a house of candlelight.
That is how heart and soul live together.
One is a lion hunter. The other, a drunk.
One is clear and awake.
The other, mad with loneliness,
an angry face that is peaceful inside.

There has never been anyone so intimate with this world,
nor ever such an itinerant observer.
Confused by attraction, a field of grain catches fire.
That is what it is like to say things openly.

What should I call you?
More than candle and moth,
a pagan cypress tree,
an old man doing a small foot-tap dance,
ocean, no teeth in his mouth, mirror.

I grow old inside your light.
Listen, you say, to the sound of *philoso*-phy, *philoso*-pher,
education and custom dissolving
to a roselit piece of shell.

That is all we get,
a bit of a look into where there is no beginning
to what is always constantly starting out.

No belonging,
only daring and courage,
the beauty of those.

A BOWL

Imagine the time the particle you are
returns where it came from.

The family darling comes home.
Wine without being contained in cups is handed around.
A red glint appears in a granite outcrop
and suddenly the whole cliff turns to ruby.

At dawn I was walking along with a monk
on his way to the monastery.
We do the same work, I told him. We suffer the same.

He gave me a bowl, and I saw:
The soul has *this* shape.

You that teach us, Shams Tabriz,
and actual sunlight, help me now,
being in the middle of being
partly in myself, and partly outside.

UNFOLD YOUR OWN MYTH

Who gets up early to discover the moment light begins?
Who finds us here circling, bewildered like atoms?
Who comes to a spring thirsty
and sees the moon reflected in it?
Who like Jacob, blind with grief and age,
smells the shirt of his lost son and can see again?
Who lets a bucket down and brings up a flowing prophet?
Or, like Moses, goes for fire and finds what burns inside the
    sunrise?

Jesus slips into a house to escape enemies
and opens a door to the other world.
Solomon cuts open a fish, and there is a gold ring.
Omar storms in to kill the Prophet and leaves with blessings.
Chase a deer and end up everywhere.
An oyster opens his mouth to swallow one drop.
Now there is a pearl.
A vagrant wanders empty ruins.
Suddenly he is wealthy.

But do not be satisfied with stories,
how things have gone with others.
Unfold your own myth,
without complicated explanations,
so everyone will understand the passage,
We have opened you.

Start walking toward Shams, the teacher, the sun.
Your legs will get heavy and tired.
Then comes a moment of feeling the wings you have grown,
lifting.

BISMILLAH

It is a habit of yours to walk slowly.
You hold a grudge for years. With such heaviness,
how can you be modest? With such attachments,
do you expect to arrive anywhere?

Be wide as the air to learn a secret.
Right now you are equal portions clay and water, thick mud.

Abraham learned how the sun and the moon and the stars all set.
He said, No longer will I try to assign partners for God.

You are so weak. Give up to grace.
The ocean takes care of each wave until it gets to shore.
You need more help than you know.
You are trying to live your life in open scaffolding.

Say *Bismillah*, In the Name of God,
as a priest does with a knife when he offers an animal.
Bismillah your old self to find your real name.

5.

Al-Bari,
The Maker from Nothing

These bodies we inhabit came out of nowhere. Every spring, all the green fabric appears. The water in Fightingtown Creek keeps going by. The amazement is that we are here at all. Fresh-baked bread, branches put on the bonfire. The source of what calls us into a new friendship remains a big secret. These qualities we call God's names take the shapes of people in a landscape. They walk around and meet each other by chance. Say this full moon tonight is a pearl that grew in some galactic ocean. A gourd vine sprout shows itself, just barely. What *is* nonexistence? Is it more real than this dream? The miller's intelligence invents a way to let the river help with grinding grain. Ego, and the heart, must be ground fine before they become useful for breadmaking. These are mysterious matters, and so lovely, the playing of souls as they become whole. Now consider the elegant alternation from speech to silence, the balance of the two and what that is like.

TWO DAYS OF SILENCE

This wonderful moment, the taste of nothing,
in the company of the poor and the empty.

Sit with Bestami, not some fortune-teller.
There are more than two holidays a year.
We celebrate a birthday and a solstice every second.

Newborns, we need fresh bread.
Life grows from the dead,
as the living get led into death.

Dry branches go to the fire
as green limbs bend to the ground with fruit.

Pleasure fills a mother's breast.
Put your mouth there and suck. You must.

I have made many elegant speeches to the assembly.
Now it is time to walk outside and be quiet.

Shams draws me to words,
then two days of silence.

SOUL HOUSES

Who is this king
that forms another king out of the ground,
who for the sake of two beggars
makes himself a beggar?

Who is this with his hand out saying,
Please, give just a little, so I can give you a kingdom.

He heals. He enlivens.
He tells the water to boil
and the steam to fade into air.

He makes this dying world eternal.
His greatest alchemy is how he undoes the binding
that keeps love from breathing deep.
He loosens the chest.

With no tool he fashions where we live.
Do not grieve for your rusty, iron heart.
He will polish it to a steel mirror.

And as you are being lowered into the ground,
closed away from friends, don't cry.

He turns the ants and the snakes
into beautiful new companions.

Every second he changes cruelty
to loyal friendship.

Remember the proverb, *Eat the grapes.*
Do not keep talking about the garden.
Eat the grapes.

From a rough stone ledge
come a hundred marble fountains.

Out of unconditioned emptiness
comes this planet with all its qualities.

Lakewater over there.
Out of one huge NO come a chorus of yeses.

Rivers of light flow from human eyes,
and consider your ears,
where language alchemizes into amber.

He gives the soul a house,
then another and another.

He descends into the ground
and makes it majesty.

Be silent now.
Say fewer and fewer praise poems.
Let yourself become living poetry.

ONE BEING INSIDE ALL

Lovers, it is time for the taste of fire.
Let sadness and your fears of death
sit in the corner and sulk.

The sky itself reels with love.
There is one being inside all of us, one peace.

Poet, let every word tremble in its wind bell.
Saddle the horse with great anticipation.

Flute notes are calling us into friendship.
Begin again.
Play the melody all the way through this time.

Sun-presence floods over.
Quietness is an empty cup.
Accept that you must hide your secret.

YOU MAKE YOUR OWN OIL AS YOU COOK

Your kindness cannot be said.
You open doors in the sky.

You ease the heart
and make God's qualities visible.

We taste your honey
and fly around as happy as bumblebees.

You remember what was agreed upon
before the universe began.

You hear the sound of those praise words,
Am I not (Yes!) your lord?

Poisonous people you have little to do with,
only what is necessary.

You make your own oil as you cook,
beyond any recipe or idea of soul growth.

You look to meet another someone like Shams Tabriz.
You will not find that.

WHAT IS INSIDE THE GROUND

Whatever gives pleasure is the fragrance of the friend.
Whatever makes us wonder comes from that light.

What is inside the ground begins to sprout
because you spilled wine there.

What dies in autumn comes up in spring
because this way of saying *no*
becomes in spring your praise song *yes*.

TWO DONKEYS

Friend, there is a sweetness to the moon's one pearl,
but consider the ocean it grew in,
and the soul's great turning wheel.

Grafitti people on bathhouse walls have intelligent origins,
but think of who drew the mind.

It does take know-how to make oil from suet.
These suet-jelly eyes we see with were also skillfully devised.

There is a donkey who likes to be fed barley with other donkeys,
and there is a donkey that loves the changes
that happen in the soul.

Now silence lets the one behind your eyes talk.

SPRING DRUMMING AGAIN

Again, the new moon's sharp sickle.
Again, we form in procession.
Again, March makes the ground a garden.
Again, the lily talks slyly.
Again, this green satin no tailor sews.
Again, the trees put on their hats.

Spring drumming begins.
We play along on the drums of our stomachs.

The lake that was iron ice
is now ridged in the breeze like David's gentle chainmail.

A voice in nonexistence says, Herbs, it is time to reach up.
The mystic crane returns from wherever he goes,
and all the other birds *shreek* praise.

The humiliated ones get dressed up
and put their heads out the windows again.

It is a public concert on the tomb of January.
The willow shakes her head,
and I have this to say to language, *Leave me alone*.
But language keeps chasing me, arguing.

I do not want to talk anymore about lovers
with this landscape so bathed in green light.

The ones we thought were lost have come back.
The work of resurrection is clear.
There must be decaying, then re-creation.
The sun and these plants are evidence enough,
a dazzle of paradise within paradise.

Live here, where souls do what they do.
One achieves union. Another plays the part of Pharaoh.
Now be silent. Speak to souls with silence.
Silence reveals more than language.

GO BEHIND THE SCREEN

Suddenly I fall from the pavilion into a place
where I can see the world's ugliness and fake beauty,
rouge on a diseased face, a thorn sunk in a kidney
the blind crone holding out a winner's wreath,
her black ribbons loose, eyes darkened with purple.

Do not look at her anklets.
Look at her legs.

The puppet show is charming,
but go behind the screen and see who runs it.
Wash your hands and face of all this.

Someone who tries for these prizes
burns up quickly like wood chips.

There is a friend who will help you,
the one who turned the wheel
and brought us out of nonexistence,
the sweet-breathing one.

These words are ways of just adding up our breaths.
It is better to be silent inside the friend's breathing.

THE MILL

The heart is a wheat grain.
We are the mill where this body is the millstone
and thought, the moving river.

The body asks the river why it runs on so.
The river says, Ask the miller who made the millrace
that directs my falling that turns your stone.

The miller says, You that love bread,
if this turning were not happening,
what would you dip in your broth?

So a lot of questioning goes on
around the milling of wheat.
But what, really, is this breadmaking work?

Let silence now speak about wheat and the river,
about the heart and the intellect,
about the miller and his millstone-body,
about the taste of bread dipped in soup,
and this delicious listening we do at the mill.

THE ELUSIVE ONES

They are lovers again. Sugar dissolving in milk.
Day and night, no difference.
The sun is the moon, an amalgam.
Their gold and silver melt together.
This is the season when the dead branch
and the green branch are the same branch.

The cynic bites his finger because he cannot understand.
Omar and Ali on the same throne, two kings in one belt.
Nightmares fill with light like a holiday.
Men and angels speak one language.
The elusive ones finally meet.

The essence and the evolving forms
run to meet each other
like children to their father and mother.
Good and evil, dead and alive,
everything blooms from one natural stem.

You know this already. I'll stop.
Any direction you turn it is one vision.
Shams, my body is a candle touched with fire.

A GARDEN WHERE THE HOUSE WAS

I am lost in your face, in your lost eyes.
The drunk and the madman inside me
take a liking to each other.
They sit down on the ground together.

Look at this mess of a life
as the sun looks fondly into ruins.

With one glance many trees grow from a single seed.
Your two eyes are like a Turk born in Persia.
He is on a rampage, a Persian shooting Turkish arrows.
He has ransacked my house,
so that no one lives here anymore,
just a boy running barefooted all through it.

Your face is a garden that comes up where the house was.
With our hands we tear down houses and make bare places.
The moon has no desire to be described.
No one needs this poetry.
The loose hair strands of a beautiful woman
do not have to be combed.

AFTER BEING IN LOVE, THE NEXT RESPONSIBILITY

Turn me like a waterwheel turning a millstone.
Plenty of water, a living river.
Keep me in one place and scatter the love.
Leaf-moves in wind, straw drawn toward amber,
all parts of the world are in love,
but they do not tell their secrets.

Cows grazing on a sacramental table,
ants whispering in Solomon's ear.
Mountains mumbling an echo. Sky, calm.

If the sun were not in love,
he would have no brightness,
the side of the hill no grass on it.
The ocean would come to rest somewhere.

Be a lover as they are,
that you may come to know your beloved.
Be faithful that you may know faith.
The other parts of the universe
did not accept the next responsibility as you can.
They were afraid they might make a mistake with it,
the inspired knowing that springs from being in love.

THORNBUSH MUSIC

Jasmine comes up where you step.
You breathe on dirt, it sails off like a kite.

You wash your hands,
and the water you throw out shines with gold.

You say the first line of the Qur'an,
and all the dead commentators lift their heads.

Your robe brushes a thornbush,
and a deep chord of music comes.

Whatever you break
finds itself more intelligent for being broken.

Every second a new being
stands in the courtyard of your chest like Adam,
without a mother or a father,
but the beginning of many generations to come.

I should rhyme that fifty times.

The beginning of many generations to come,
a line without any inclination to end.

But I won't. I close my mouth
in hopes that you will open yours.

SPINDRIFT

Do not worry about saving these songs.
And if one of our instruments breaks,
it does not matter.

We have fallen into the place
where everything is music.

The strumming and the flute notes
rise into the atmosphere,

and even if the whole world's harp should burn up,
there will still be hidden instruments playing.

So the candle flickers and goes out.
We have a piece of flint and a spark.

This singing art is sea foam.
The graceful movements come from a pearl
somewhere on the ocean floor.

Poems reach up like spindrift
and the edge of driftwood along the beach, wanting.

They derive
from a slow and powerful root
that we cannot see.

Stop the words now.
Open the window in the center of your chest,
and let the spirits fly in and out.

SPILLINGS

This mirror inside me shows
I cannot say what, but I cannot not know.

I run from body. I run from spirit.
I do not belong anywhere.

I am not alive.
Do you smell the decay?

You talk about my craziness.
Listen rather to the honed-blade sanity I say.

This gourd head on top of a dervish robe,
do I look like someone you know?

This dipper gourd full of liquid,
upside down and not spilling a drop.

Or if it spills, it drops into God and rounds into pearls.
I form a cloud over that ocean and gather the spillings.

When Shams is here, I rain.
After a day or two, lilies sprout, the shape of my tongue.

6.
Al-Hayy, The Living

When those who love meet each other's eyes, an expansion comes that cannot be contained in what the pronouns refer to, *you* and *I* and *we*, those imaginary beings. A livingness comes that is beyond pronouns, a vitality with a lot of laughter in it, and limitless motion. Lovers keep moving. Even as they seem to settle down, they are really being borne along aloft like a flock of gnats inside the wind. Music, a variety of roses in conversation, lute strings resonating with ocean-sound. These are some of the images that Rumi explores for how it is to be alive. The poet Bill Stafford, in his writing classes, tried to get each individual to decide *on his or her own* what it was in their writing that they liked, without any interference from a teacher or other students. He responded with a lot of "Uh-huh" and "I see," but no judgment. He could outwait you. He had such tremendous respect for the student writer's independence and integrity. That was a deeply settled thing in him. The living river of your life is continuously changing. Drink from it. Let that taste tell you how to move.

THE VERGE OF TEARS

You make our souls tasty like rose marmalade.
You cause us to fall flat on the ground
like the shadow of a cypress still growing at its tip.

Rainwater through a mountain forest,
we run after you in different ways.

We live like the verge of tears inside your eyes.
Don't cry. You trick some people with gold ropes.
You tie them up and leave them.

Others you pull near at dawn.
You are the one within every attraction. All silence.

You are never alone, never that,
but you must be distracted, because look,

you have taken the food you were going to give Jesus
out to the stable and put it down in front of the donkey.

ENTERING THE SHELL

Love is *alive*, and someone borne along by it
is more alive than lions roaring
or men in their fierce courage.

Bandits ambush others on the road.
They get wealth, but they stay in one place.

Lovers keep moving, never the same, not for a second.
What makes others grieve they enjoy.

When they look angry, do not believe their faces.
It is spring lightning, a joke before the rain.

They chew thorns thoughtfully along with pasture grass.
Gazelle and lioness, having dinner.

Love is invisible except here, in us.
Sometimes I praise love; sometimes love praises me.

Love, a little shell somewhere on the ocean floor,
opens its mouth.

You and *I* and *we*, those imaginary beings,
enter that shell as a single sip of seawater.

A MIXED-BREED APPLE

A little mixed-breed apple,
half red, half yellow, tells this story.

A lover and beloved get separated.
Their being apart was one thing,
but they have opposite responses.

The lover feels pain and grows pale.
The beloved flushes and feels proud.

I am a thorn next to my master's rose.
We seem to be two, but we are not.

WHAT YOU GAVE

Why are you lying in the middle of the road?

From the love-wine you poured.

I may be excessive with my giveaway impulses,
but I still have what you gave
when you held my head against your chest.

You pour what you pour
without a flask, without a cup.

That mastery and generosity
washes away all restraint.

Reason burst just for the joy of it
when you gave me the bowl.

Something flows from your eyes
that is beyond a thousand false desires.

DESOLATION

From the left and from the right
come vilification and blame,
but you stay filled with compassion.

The moon gives light so generously
that the dogs bay at it.
They do not affect the moon.
They are like critics, each with a certain specialty.

A lover is a mountain,
not flecks of dead grass blown about.

A lover is a flock of gnats,
alive and lost inside the wind.

If it is true that rules rise from love,
it is also true that lovers pay no attention to rules.

Desolation everywhere is true cultivation.
Ignoring benefits is a benefit in love.

Jesus calls from the fourth heaven,
where communion is celebrated.

Welcome. Wash your hands and face.
It is time to sit at the table together.

CHOOSE A SUFFERING

Yesterday in the assembly I saw my soul
inside the jar of the one who pours.

Do not forget your job, I said.
He came with his lighted face, kissed the full glass,
and as he handed it to me,
it became a red-gold oven taking me in,
a ruby mine, a greening garden.

Everyone chooses a suffering that will change
him or her to a well-baked loaf.

Abu Lahab, biting his hand, chose doubt.
Abu Huraya, his love for cats!

One searches a confused mind for evidence.
The other has a leather sack full of what he needs.

If we could be silent now,
the master would tell us some stories
that they hear in the high council.

THE DEATH OF SALADIN

You left ground and sky weeping,
mind and soul full of grief.

No one can take your place in existence or in absence.
Both mourn, the angels, the prophets,
and this sadness I feel
has taken from me the taste of language,
so that I cannot say the flavor of my being apart.

The roof of the *kingdom within* has collapsed.
When I say the word *you*, I mean a hundred universes.

Pouring grief-water or secret dripping in the heart,
eyes in the head or eyes of the soul,
I saw yesterday that all of these
flow out to find you when you are not here.

That bright firebird Saladin went like an arrow,
and now the bow trembles and sobs.

If you know how to weep for human beings,
weep for Saladin.

THE MUSIC WE ARE

Did you hear that winter is over?
The basil and carnation cannot control their laughter.

The nightingale, back from his wandering,
has been made singing master over all the birds.
The trees reach out their congratulations.

The soul goes dancing through the king's doorway.
Anemones blush because they have seen the rose naked.

Spring, the only fair judge, walks in the courtroom,
and several December thieves steal away.

Last year's miracles will soon be forgotten.
New creatures whirl in from nonexistence,
galaxies scattered around their feet.

Have you met them?
Do you hear the bud of Jesus crooning in the cradle?

A single narcissus flower has been appointed
Inspector of Kingdoms. A feast is set.
Listen. The wind is pouring wine.

Love used to hide inside images. No more.
The orchard hangs out its lanterns.

The dead come stumbling by in shrouds.
Nothing can stay bound or be imprisoned.

You say, End this poem here, and wait for what is next.
I will. Poems are rough notations for the music we are.

GLORY TO MUTABILIS

Spring is how the soul renews and refreshes itself.
Fields damp and sprouting, roses glowing,
birds learning to talk.

Morning wind animating everything.
Cypress bends to iris, Tell me dear . . .

Iris to tulip, Show me how you are faithful.
Plane trees play their tambourines.

Pine trees clap hands. Doves do
their one-note question, *Coo, Where?*

Which means, Be visibly here with us.
A pink rose stands straight. Violets kneel.

Grape leaves do full prostration.
A new kind of poetry is coming.

Glory makes promises again to *Mutabilis*.
Thunder says, Wash your face in this,
and your hands and your feet.

Narcissus blinks and comes near the nightingale to say,
We need a new song.

Reply: This is for love's emptiness.
Now the green ones dress like Khidr.

It is time to hear the secrets dervishes know.
No. The *Penelope* and the jasmine agree.

Silence is the best alchemy.

THE MOST ALIVE MOMENT

The most alive moment comes when those who love each other
meet each other's eyes and in what flows between them then.

To see your face in a crowd of others,
or alone on a frightening street, I weep for that.

Our tears improve the earth. The time you scolded me,
your gratitude, your laughing,
always your qualities increase the soul.

Seeing you is a wine that does not muddle or numb.

We sit inside the cypress shadow where amazement
and clear thought twine their slow growth into us.

IT IS ALL LAUGHING

Let your laughing face keep laughing,
like a moon, not born out of anyone,
but if it had been,
it would have been born laughing.

Joseph is elevated to the judgment chambers in Egypt.
Listen to the laughter from in there.

Locked double doors blow open.
Water pours. Fire catches. Wind breaks up.
Spring ground lifts a little finger.
It is all laughing.

THE REPLY

Water opens the garden like a new friendship.
Leaf says to fruit, Quit scratching your ear,
and come outside.

The sweet grape makes the deepest teacher,
because its trunk is spindly.

Lust is a winter the garden contracts in.
For how long? Too long.

Wash your face with springwater.
Now a branch of blooms talks to the basil, Lie down.

Birds say to trees, Hold us.

A rose to God, Do not let winter come again.

The reply: Do not grieve over December,
or Mongol tribes that raid Khorasan.
Those are my concern.

Juice does not flow from fruit
until you squeeze them.

I give unnumbered life
when I take away the numbers.
I serve wine that gives no headache
when I withhold the headache wine.

But you go on painting pictures
and blackening pages with print,
like smoke obscuring light.
Read the day instead of books.

Get off your horse and let him ride away,
the perfect equestrian.

THE DIVER'S CLOTHES LYING EMPTY

You are sitting here with us, but you are also
out walking in a field at dawn.
You are yourself the animal we hunt
when you come with us on the hunt.
You are in your body like a plant
is solid in the ground, yet you are wind.
You are the diver's clothes lying empty
on the beach. You are the fish.

In the ocean are many bright strands and dark strands
like veins that are seen when a wing is lifted up.
Your hidden self is blood in those, those veins
that are lute strings that make ocean music,
not the sad edge of surf, but the sound of no shore.

DECORATING THE CELL

The drum we hear inside us now
we may not hear tomorrow.

We have such fear of what comes next. Death.
These loves are like pieces of cotton.
Throw them in the fire.

Death will be a meeting like that flaring up,
a presence you have always wanted to be with.

This body and this universe keep us from being free.
Those of you decorating your cells so beautifully,
do you think they will not be torn down?

The eventual demolishing of prisons is a given.
Fire-change, disaster-change,
you can trust that those will come around to you.

WITH YOU HERE BETWEEN

Lovers work,
so that when body and soul are no longer together,
their loving will be free.

Wash in wisdom-water,
so you will have no regrets about the time here.

Love is the vital core of the soul,
and of all you see, only love is infinite.

Your nonexistence before you were born
is the sky in the east.

Your death is the western horizon,
with you here between.
Your way leads neither east nor west, but in.

Test your love-wings and make them strong.
Forget the idea of religious ladders.
Love is the roof. Your senses are waterspouts.

Drink rain directly off the roof.
Waterspouts are easily damaged
and often must be replaced.

Say this poem in your chest.
Do not worry how it sounds going through your mouth.

A human body is a bow.
Breathing and speech are arrows.

When quiver and arrows are used up or lost,
there is nothing more for the bow to do.

A BIT OF EMBROIDERY

You have heard how the night is wide and long
for the sake of lovers and thieves.
We do the work of both.

I steal pearls from the king's vault.
Why be content with a piece of cloth?

I am one of those subtle thieves
who find a way up to the roof this night
when everything human beings love is here for the taking.

There is nothing but your presence.
Let this subject rest.

Here is another story, strange and rare.
If you have not seen Christ, listen to this
as a white hawk hearing the drum
flies back to the king.

As a circle of gold gets stamped with the royal crest
and becomes a useful coin.

When you first became treasure,
you did not know that there is an informer
who tells where every treasure is hidden.

Bring your value here openly.
Do not pretend with prostrations,
or special commemorations, or abstinence.

Do not borrow a fancy shawl
and sit wrapped in a corner saying, *I am Junnaiyd.*
I am the Bestami of this age.

Give back what is not yours.
No excuses, no pretext.

Take in simple sunlight.
Be a bit of embroidery on Shams's sleeve.

YOUR LOVE REVEALS YOUR BEAUTY

Give yourself a kiss.
If you live in China, do not look somewhere else,
in Tibet or in Mongolia.

If you want to hold the beautiful one,
hold yourself to yourself.

When you kiss the beloved,
touch your own lips with your fingers.

The beauty of every woman and every man is your beauty.
The confusion of your hair obscures that sometimes.

An artist comes to paint you
and stands there with his mouth open.

Your love reveals your beauty,
but all coverings would disappear if only for a moment
your holding back would stand before your generosity,
and ask, Sir, who are you?

At that, Shams's life-changing face
gives you a wink.

THE WOOD AND THE FLAMES, STILL TALKING

No more wine for me.
I am past delighting in the thick red and the clear white.
I am thirsty for my own blood as it moves into a field of action.

Draw the keenest blade you have and strike,
until the head circles around the body.

Make a mountain of skulls like that.
Split me apart.

Do not stop at the mouth.
Do not listen to anything I say.
I must enter the center of the fire.

Fire is my child,
but I must be consumed and become fire.

Why is there crackling and smoke?
Because the wood and the flames are still talking.

You are too dense. Go away.

You are too wavering. I have solid form.

In the blackness those two friends keep arguing.
Like a wanderer with no face.
Like the most powerful bird in existence
sitting on its perch, refusing to move.

What can I say to someone so curled up with wanting,
so constricted in his love.

Break your pitcher against a rock.
We do not need any longer
to haul pieces of the ocean around.

We must drown, away from heroism,
and descriptions of heroism.

Like a pure spirit lying down,
pulling its body over it like a bride
her husband for a cover to keep her warm.

THE DAY I DIE

On the day I die,
when I am being carried toward the grave,
don't weep.

Don't say, He's gone. He's gone.
Death has nothing to do with going away.

The sun sets and the moon sets,
but they are not gone.

Death is a coming together.
The tomb looks like a prison,
but it is really release into union.

The human seed goes down in the ground
like a bucket into the well where Joseph is.

It grows and comes up full
of some unimagined beauty.

Your mouth closes here
and immediately opens
with a shout of joy there.

OLD, YET FRESHLY BEGUN

Here is where you live. Come inside.
Touch what is not, and then this is.

Raise dust in both worlds.
Then the going goes the same:
pain, difficulty; peace, pleasure.

But you are beyond those four,
beyond the winding way.

Old as what has no starting out, yet freshly begun,
wound and salve for the dervish.

All religions bow to you at the sky's table,
where the sun sits down just as the moon leaves.

But at the autumn feast of Shams's love
you will not be chosen for sacrifice.
You are too lean a lamb for that.

NEVER QUITE AS ALIVE

You are the winged one set free and flying,
while a hundred others stay confined.
You are the clear-eyed hawk, the low-murmuring dove,
the red-and-green-spike-of-color parrot,
friend to both high and low,
wonder with no sadness about existence or nonexistence,
source of courageous enthusiasm.

I was shut tight in something like grief.
You opened the door.
But now you have turned your face and gone away.
You put my life in danger with this going.
Like Isaac you are the friend of every soul.
Whoever loses such a friend will never be quite as alive
as they were when they were with you.

7.

Al-Haqq, The Truth

The strength of the quality of truth is that of letting the mystery remain in itself, intact, not reduced to formula. Let the logical and the linear take forms. Truth remains formless and free. I asked a Tibetan monk once for help with my writing. "Quit being a writer," he said as he opened his arms to the sky. Rumi had a flute player named Hamza. When Hamza played, it was as though Nothing were playing anonymous music. Everything in nature is begging you to die before you die, to follow the moth's example. You have an Egypt within you, miles of riverside canebrake, the source of all sweetness, yet you reach for external forms. You are yourself the desired one, Joseph. Close your eyes and gaze in the mirror at the flame that lit your senses. The Unseen One said once on Sinai, "You shall not see me." But even though he said that, I have filled the essence of that *he* with my soul,

the Christian Trinity, the Zoroastrian light-and-dark, old Taoist poems
about floating and watching the changing light, Zen haiku, and much
else. So union finds a new way to be, recklessly exposed. Every soul is
a king with no flag and no parapet to shield him from the sun.

HAMZA'S NOTHING

A moth, flying into the flames, says with its wing fire, *Try this.*
The wick with its knotted neck broken tells you the same.

A candle as it diminishes, explains, *Gathering more and more*
is not the way. Burn, become light and heat. Melt.

The ocean sits in the sand
letting its lap fill with pearls and shells,
then empty. The bitter taste hums, *This.*

The phoenix gives up on good-and-bad, flies to nest on Mt. Qaf,
no more burning and rising from ash. It sends out one message.

The rose purifies its face, drops the soft petals, shows its thorn,
and points. Wine abandons thousands of famous names,
the vintage years and delightful bouquets,
to run wild and anonymous through your brain.

Empty, the flute closes its eyes to Hamza's nothing.
Everything begs with the silent rocks for you to be flung out
like light over this plain, the presence of Shams Tabriz.

ANOTHER INVITATION

My mouth, my entire body, laughs.
A rose is all rose.

My loving is here with you.
You come before dawn with a torch, and you take me,
but my soul remains back there alone.

Issue another invitation.
Do not ask for one without the other.

If you do not go tonight and bring my soul to me,
I will become a loud, disruptive noise,
and I will not be making it alone.

MILES OF RIVERSIDE CANEBRAKE

The news has come, but you must not have heard.
Jealousy has changed to love.
Do you have any love left?

The moon has opened its face and its wings made of light.
Borrow eyes to see this, if yours cannot.

Night and day an arrow comes toward you
from a hidden bow.
If you have no shield and nowhere to hide
from the death that is always coming closer,
you may as well yield.

The copper of your being
has already been transmuted to gold by Moses' alchemy,
and yet you fumble in a money bag for coins.

You have within you an Egypt,
miles of riverside canebrake, the source of all sweetness,
yet you worry whether candy will come
from a store outside yourself.

External form, you reach for shapes,
yet *you* are the Joseph.

Close your eyes and gaze in the mirror
at the flame that lit your senses.

Your body is a camel
going swift and straight to the Kaaba.

You think you are idling around town on a donkey,
or heading off the opposite way, but you are not.

This caravan is a triumph
being drawn directly into God's reality.

ALIVE WITH SCRIPTURE

Every moment a voice comes out of the sky,
a verse, Creation is ample and full of grace.
Sura 51:47

Those who hear this in the soul respond.
They turn to God. They praise.

They bow down all the way with gratitude.
Sura 9:112

To the lord of ladders
by which the spirit ascends.
Sura 70:4

The carpenter of the imagination
has no way to make such a ladder.
Only the one who says, *All are returning*.
Sura 21:93

But the patient adze blade can help.
To receive what is given, be diligent.
Sura 28:80

Watch someone working with an adze.
Dissolve in that steady work.
Do not jump to some expected outcome,
saying, We will surely win.
Sura 26:44

Stay stubborn, as the adze blade nicks hardwood.
If you move up two rungs,
the people on the right will claim you.
If you reach the roof, they will say,
Above the above, on the star highways.
Sura 51:10

Sufi of the world's community,
rise to the circle of Sura 37:165,
the blessed arranged in adoration.
Listen. Be so empty
that nothing but God is left.
Purify the learning
that keeps you from knowing.
Sura 59:13

Bow like *nun*, the twenty-fifth Arabic letter,
like the gerund sound *-ing* at the end of a word.
Lie flat. Become soul-writ,
Sura 68, which begins with *nun*,
so alive with scripture
that you stand for those who have no hypocrisy.

Root like a lotus, plunging deep in the mud,
that does not mind a death wind in its leaves.
Wait, for I am waiting too.
Sura 52:30

Study the orchard of some soul
that has lost the power to grow anything.
Sura 68:20

That stays in its disastrous sleep,
a morning black as midnight.
Sura 68:19

YOU SHALL NOT SEE ME

You are rest for my soul,
a surprising joy for my bitterness.

Imagination has never imagined
what you give to me.

The sound of someone whistling in the street,
or asking questions, if that person brings word of you,
those sounds are worth more than all the world's poetry.

There is nothing I want but your presence.
In friendship, time dissolves.

Life is a cup. This connection is pure wine.
What else are cups for?
I used to have twenty thousand different desires.

The unseen king said once on Sinai,
You shall not see me.

But even though he said that he was not,
I have filled the essence of that *he* with my soul.

The Christian Trinity, the Zoroastrian light-and-dark,
I absorb them all.

Though my body has not noticed,
union has begun to see a new way to be.

Grown old with grief and longing,
when someone says *Tabriz,*
I am young again.

A BRIGHTENING FLOOR

There is a soul spring that adds to everyone's awareness,
a friend who brings peace and healing silence to death.

I work for the kindness that touches stone and pearl the same,
that sees a garden peacock equal with the road raven.

Form dissolves, but wisdom remains.
Your soul and your loving mix with the mud of your body,
but they have their pleasures apart.

Shams steps into the room bringing blessings,
a brightening floor and a star decorating the roof.

WIND THAT MIXES WITH YOUR FIRE

I see myself as a thorn. I move near the rose.
As vineyard, I remember the vintner's skill.

As a cup of poison, I long to be the antidote.
I am a glass of wine with dark sediment.
I pour it all in the river.

I am sick. I reach for Jesus' hand.
Immature, I look for one who knows.

Out of the ground a poem grows eye medicine.
Now love says to me, *Good*.
But you cannot see your own beauty.

I am the wind that mixes with your fire,
that stirs and brightens, then makes you gutter out.

NOT INTRIGUED WITH EVENING

What the material world values
does not shine the same in the truth of the soul.

You have been interested in your shadow.
Look instead directly at the sun.

What can we know by just watching
the time-and-space shapes of each other?

Someone half awake in the night sees imaginary dangers.
The morning star rises. The horizon grows defined.

People become friends in a moving caravan.
Nightbirds may think daybreak a kind of darkness,
because that is all they know.

It is a fortunate bird who is not intrigued with evening,
who flies in the sun we call Shams.

A LION LOOKING FOR LAUGHTER

Your face here suddenly like spring.
Applause, laughter.
You sit in the pomegranate branches
so tickled with the beauty.

This town would disappear
without the sound of your opening,
your creek-noise laughing,
like the deep redness of hundreds of roses.

Inside the love-forest a lion walks looking for laughter.
Dawn. The sun comes up from a different direction.
The Lord is tricky today. No one knows what next.

Shams and God's qualities in Shams
compose an ocean in us
where laughter pearls plump into being.

THE FACE

So the frowning teacher came and left.
He is very consistent with that vinegar face.

But maybe he shows that to us and smiles with others.
Such a beautiful teacher, but so sour.
He is a pure standard for tartness.

Consider how your face is a source of light.
If you enter a grieving room with the friend in your eyes,
light will bloom there according to the laws of sweet and sour.

Locked in a cell, you grow bitter,
but out walking in morning sunlight with friends,
how does that taste?

There are exceptions.
Joseph caught the rose fragrance
down in his abandoned wellhole.

In this quietness now
I feel someone seated on my right
like a kindness that will never leave.

GREED AND GENEROSITY

Look at this face.
Open your eyes into these eyes.
When you laugh, everyone falls in love.
Lift your head up off the table.
See, there are no edges to this garden.
Sweet fruits, every kind you can think of,
branches green, and always slightly moving.

How long should you look at the earth's face?
Come back and look again.
Now you see the nervous greed,
deep inside plants and animals.
Now you see them constantly giving themselves away.

Greed and generosity are evidence of love.
If you cannot see love itself, see the results.
If you cannot find the love-colors in anything,
look for the pale, tired face of a lover.

Take this town with its stores
and everyone running around,
some with a lot of money, some without any.

THE RIGHTS OF CRYING

Why so fugitive?
I have some right to be with you,
the rights of crying.

If there were laughter all around me,
I would still feel closed in if you were not there.
With my children and everyone else I loved,
I would still be distracted.

How can I tie down one of your feet?
I do not have enough strength or patience.

No matter how far you go,
even beyond sunlight into where Jesus is visible,
I will come and wait to be told
why you go away from me.

THE OTHER THING

There are a few resistance pockets left,
patches of shade the sun has not struck,
but mostly this universe is transformed.
Every star has become the evening star.

Every soul is a king with no flag and no parapet
to shield him from direct light.

Go within, and discover this land
where everyone is a living soul under a wide sky-field
with a king entering from the other side, a jubilee,
a singing where wine and dessert and *the other thing*
are given away.

Last night I was out of myself.
If I were that way again,
I could finish this poem, but I am not.

My poet-self is a protective pawn put before the king,
who is Shams,
who changes every being to an ocean,
and every body to a coral reef.

MY WORST HABIT

My worst habit is I get so tired of winter
I become a torture to those I am with.

If you are not here, nothing grows.
I lack clarity. My words tangle and knot up.

How to cure bad water? Send it back to the river.
How to cure bad habits? Send me back to you.

When water gets caught in habitual whirlpools,
dig a way out through the bottom to the ocean.
There is a secret medicine given only to those
who hurt so hard they cannot hope.

The hopers would feel slighted if they knew.

Look as long as you can at the friend you love,
no matter whether that friend is moving away from you,
or coming back toward you.

SOUL AND FRIEND

Soul: where this tree grows
and learns to drink without getting drunk.

Soul soaks into existence everywhere
except my rough, contemptuous personality.

Friend: intelligence, sometimes the soul,
water, bread, a cave where we sit with friends.

Invisible bowl to drink from,
health coming back to a patient.

Definite statement, pulsing spring, cloud.
I'll stop, not because words have become tedious,
but to keep that bird sitting on its branch.

8.

As-Salaam, Peace

Being fully alive in the moment has a peace to it, a continuous begin-
ning. The tailor, settled among his shop goods, quietly sewing, sitting
tailor-fashion, as though in meditation. Repose inside work is deep
nourishment. There is a clarity inside surrender. It is like what comes
with the restraint from food and words during Ramadan. The sky is a
lens to look through. We are finding new ways to wander within this
majestic imagination. The holiday we have been waiting for is here.
The friends we have wanted to be with have come. One of Rumi's
metaphors for what it is like to be a *lover* is a fish in the sea. You have
seen the way fish seem to be enjoying the ocean? That is how a *lover*
moves through the intelligence of this life that we are inside.

CALM IN THE MIDST OF LIGHTNING

When the love lion wants to drink our blood,
we let him.

Every moment we offer up a new soul.
Someone comes to collect the turban and the shoes.

Calm in the midst of lightning
stands the cause of lightning.

The way I look is so fragile,
yet here in my hand is an assurance of eternity.

A snake drags along looking for the ocean.
What would it do with it?

If for penance, you crush grapes,
you may as well drink the wine.

You imagine that the old Sufis
had dark sediment in their cups.
It does not matter what you think.

The flower that does not smile at the branch
withers.

Shams Tabriz rises as the sun.
It is night now.
What is the point of counting stars?

A MOUNTAIN NEST

Have you seen a fish dissatisfied with the ocean?
Have you seen a lover?

Have you seen an image
that tries to avoid the engraver?
Have you seen a word emptied of meaning?

You need no name.
You are the ocean. I am held in your sway.

Fire in your presence turns to a rosebush.
When I am outside of you, life is a torment.

Then Solomon walks back into Jerusalem,
and a thousand lanterns illuminate.
The divine glory settles into a mountain nest.

The emperor and the source of light, Shams Tabriz,
lives here with no location in my chest.

FULL SUN

There is one who teaches the moon
and the evening star their beauty.

Muslims, I am so mingled with that
that no one can mingle with me.

I was born of this love,
so now I hang from this branch.

Shadows are always changing, fleeing.
I feel that fear.

There is no peace except in full sun.

A voice says, Quick, the rope trick,
and, Where did the moth go?

When you hear that,
coil the rope and begin to climb.

Fly straight into the candle, this burning so dear
no coolness can tempt us out of its flame.

BEGIN

This is now. Now is.
Do not postpone till then.
Spend the spark of iron on stone.
Sit at the head of the table.
Dip your spoon in the bowl.

Seat yourself next to your joy,
and have your awakened soul pour wine.

Branches in the spring wind,
easy dance of jasmine and cypress.

Cloth for green robes
has been cut from pure absence.

You are the tailor,
settled among his shop goods, quietly sewing.

A CLEAN SANDY SPOT

You blame and give advice,
and recommend medicinal spells.

You make detailed analyses and loud public conclusions
about this company of lovers.

Do you really consider yourself a lover?
A flat, clean, sandy spot gives wheat to the barn for nothing.
No particle can grow to seedling from anything but the whole.
You know this.

Why this continuous personal critique?
Love's fire puts a sad smile on.
Advice rarely brings the coolness of peace.

The moon's ashy light covers this world
as love waits quietly for a bird in the branches of some town,
say Tabriz, to begin.

A VAGUE TRACE

Soul gave me this box of emptiness.
What I say is one truth I know.

I go to neither side of any argument.
I stay in the center, letting explanations rise from failure,
this weeping witness face, this saffron tulip,
a vague trace.

Whoever understands me like Saladin does,
this is for you, this opening.

TALKING THROUGH THE DOOR

You say, Who is at the door?
I say, Your slave.

You say, What do you want?
To see you and bow.

How long will you wait?
Until you call.

How long will you cook?
Until the resurrection.

We talk through the door.
I claim a great love and that I had given up
what the world gives to be in that love.

You say, Such claims require a witness.
I say, This longing, these tears.

You say, Discredited witnesses.
I say, *Surely not.*

You say, Who did you come with?
I say, This majestic imagination that you gave me.

Why did you come?
The musk of your wine was in the air.

What is your intention?
Friendship.

What do you want from me?
Grace.

Then you ask, Where have you been most comfortable?
In the palace.

What did you see there?
Amazing things.

Then why is it so desolate?
Because all that can be taken away in a second.

Who can do that?
This clear discernment.

Where can you live safely then?
In surrender.

What is this giving up?
A peace that saves us.

Is there no threat of disaster?
Only what comes in your street, inside your love.

How do you walk there?
In perfection.

Now silence. If I tell more of this conversation,
those listening will leave themselves.

There will be no door,
no roof or window either.

LOOK, FISH

I saw the friend clearly,
and I stopped reading books and memorizing poems.
I quit going to church and fasting
to be a better person.
I quit worrying about when I should be praying.
I saw how I was undisciplined and toxic.
I saw how lovely and strong.
No mercy for the drunk, a full sentence.

Let the beautiful one come out in fine clothes.
Wind his hair into God's rope.
Twist the braids into a cross for Christians to see.
His light is better than the sun's.
How could he have gotten so withered and weak?
Now he jokes and pounds the table.
He was wine under a lid, Joseph at the bottom of the well.
Know yourself in the light of the true ones,
as the ground sees its face in a garden,
as rock knows its own secret when put next to a ruby,
iron next to polished steel. Come into existence.

Flies go round to every pile of dung,
and finally out of that compost comes the Anya bird,
the true man. When a person is born
of this new moment, it does not wear off tomorrow.
Sit with lovers and be useful. Do not wander away.
Look, fish, at the ocean behind you.
Go back where you came from, sea creature.

You hear the sound of water,
and you know where you want to be.
Why wait? You have gone places that you regret going
for money and other reasons. Do not do that again.
Water says, Live here.
Do not carry me around in buckets and pans.
Those are false duties. Rest and be quiet.

IN PRISON

Do not despair in prison.
The king who freed Joseph is on his way to let you out.

Joseph himself is coming too,
who tore Zuleikha's veil and let her see.

You cry *Lord* all night.
Now that lord is here.

You have grown so used to the old pain.
Now there is a cure.

A key enters your stiff lock.
You have stayed away from the companions
you most wanted to be with. No longer.

This is a feast day,
but keep quiet in the resonance
that brings this wondering silence
that is growing larger than all speaking.

RUMI'S DEATHBED POEM

Go to your pillow and sleep, my son.
Leave me alone in the passion of this death night.

Let the mill turn with your grieving.
But stay clear. Do not fall in the river with me.
There is no way out, no cure but death.

Last night in a dream I saw an old man in a garden.
It was all love.
He held out his hand and said, *Come toward me.*

If there is a dragon on this path,
that man has the emerald face than can deflect it.

This is enough. I am leaving my self.

Sultan Velad, my son,
if you want to be impressively learned,
memorize a famous historian,
and quote him as someone else.

THE BELOVED NIGHT

This is the night of union,
when the stars scatter their rice over us.
The sky is excited.

Venus cannot stop singing the little songs she is making up.
Pisces is stirring milky dust from the ocean floor.
Jupiter rides his horse over to Saturn,
Old man, jump up behind me. The juice is coming back.
Think of something happy to shout as we go.

Mars washes his bloody sword, and puts it up,
and starts building things.
The Aquarian jar fills,
and the virgin pours from it generously.

The Pleiades and Libra and Aries
have no trembling in them anymore.

Scorpio walks out looking for a lover,
and so does Sagitarius.

This is not crooked walking like the crab.
This is the holiday we have been waiting for.

It is finally time to sacrifice Taurus
and learn how the sky is a lens to look through.
Listen to what is inside whatever I say.

Shams will appear at dawn,
and then even this night will change
from its beloved darkness
to a day beyond any ordinary sweet daylight.

QUIETNESS

Inside this new love, die.
Your way begins on the other side.
Become the sky.
Take an axe to the prison wall.
Escape.
Walk out like someone suddenly born into color.
Do it now.
You are covered with thick cloud.
Slide out the side. Die,

and be quiet. Quietness is the surest sign
that you have died.
Your old life was a frantic running
from silence.

The speechless full moon
comes out now.

SANAI

Someone says, Sanai is dead.
No small thing to say.

He was not bits of husk,
or a puddle that freezes overnight,
or a comb that cracks when you use it,
or a pod crushed open on the ground.

He was fine powder in a rough clay dish.
He knew what both worlds were worth:
A grain of barley.

One he slung down, the other up.

The inner soul, that presence of which most know nothing,
about which poets are so ambiguous,
he married that one to the beloved.

His pure gold wine pours on the thick wine dregs.
They mix and rise and separate again
to meet down the road.

Dear friend from Marghaz,
who lived in Rayy, in Rum, Kurd from the mountains,
each of us returns home.

Silk must not be compared with striped canvas.

Be quiet and clear now
like the final touch points of calligraphy.

Your name has been erased
from the roaring volume of speech.

SPRING IS CHRIST

Everyone has eaten and fallen to sleep. The house is empty.
We walk out to the garden to let the apple meet the peach,
to carry messages between rose and jasmine.

Spring is Christ,
raising martyred plants from their shrouds.
Their mouths open in gratitude, wanting to be kissed.
The glow of the rose and the tulip means a lamp is inside.
A leaf trembles. I tremble in the wind-beauty
like silk from Turkestan.
The censor fans into flame.

This wind is the Holy Spirit.
The trees are Mary.
Watch how husband and wife play subtle games with their
    hands.
Cloudy pearls from Aden are thrown across the lovers,
as is the marriage custom.

The scent of Joseph's shirt comes to Jacob.
A red carnelian of Yemeni laughter
is heard by Muhammad in Mecca.

We talk about this and that.
There is no rest except on these branching moments.

RED SHIRT

Has anyone seen the boy that used to come here?
Round-faced troublemaker, quick to find a joke,
slow to be serious. Red shirt, perfect coordination,
sly, strong muscles, with things always in his pocket:
reed flute, ivory pick, polished and ready for his talent.
You know that one.

Have you heard stories about him?
Pharaoh and the whole Egyptian world
collapsed for such a Joseph.
I would gladly spend years getting word of him,
even third- or fourthhand.

NOT A DAY ON ANY CALENDAR

Spring, and everything outside is growing,
even the tall cypress tree. We must not leave this place.
Around the lip of the cup we share, these words:
My life is not mine.

If someone were to play music, it would have to be very sweet.
We are drinking wine, but not through the lips.
We are sleeping it off, but not in bed.
Rub the cup across your forehead.
This day is outside of living and dying.

Give up wanting what other people have.
That way you are safe.
"Where, where can I be safe?" you ask.

This is not a day for asking questions,
not a day on any calendar.
This day is conscious of itself.
This day is a lover, bread and gentleness,
more manifest than saying can say.

Thoughts take form with words,
but this daylight is beyond and before thinking and imagining.
Those two, they are so thirsty,
but this gives smoothness to water.
Their mouths are dry, and they are tired.
The rest of this poem is too blurry for them to read.

THE LEAST FIGURE

I tried to think of some way to let my face become his.

Could I whisper in your ear a dream I have had?
You are the only one I have told this to.

He tilts his head laughing, as if,
I know the trick you are hatching, but go ahead.

I am an image he stitches
with gold thread on a tapestry,
the least figure, a playful addition,
but nothing he works on is dull.
I am part of the beauty.

9.

Ar-Rahim, The Compassionate

We come upon evidence of presence. We jiggle a battered saucepan. There is a shredding that makes us more alive. Word-bunches and music bring in new compassion. The shadow has been of great service. Things that have hurt us bring blessings. We made an agreement before we came to these lives. We responded to a question, and the wave of that answer (Yes!) carries us along. The body's boat contains the motion that will break open and set us free. We know this, and we forget. The evening sky turns dark garnet red. We turn that way to worship. Nothing belongs to anyone. Like lightning, we become expert at dying, our mouths burning with sweetness.

I SEE MY BEAUTY IN YOU

I see my beauty in you.
I become a mirror that cannot close its eyes to your longing.
My eyes wet with yours in the early light.
My mind every moment giving birth,
always conceiving, always in the ninth month,
always the come-point. How do I stand this?

We become these words we say,
a wailing sound moving out into the air.

These thousands of worlds that rise from nowhere,
how does your face contain them?

I am a fly in your honey,
then closer, a moth caught in flame's allure,
then empty sky stretched out in homage.

YOUR MORNING SHADE

You are the dawn that arrives in the middle of the night,
dark hair strands of music filling the reed,
understanding entering through ear and eye,
the fragrant steam of soup.

Signs and specific instructions articulate from you,
teaching us new ways to wander.

Asking *why* and *how* are no longer right.
Say soul is like the feet of an ant, or oceanwater,
bitter and salty, or a snake that has the antidote
for its poison also in its skull.

We push through these puzzling forms
to sit in your morning shade.

THE WAVE OF THAT AGREEMENT

Every second a voice of love comes from every side.
Who needs to go sightseeing?

We came from a majesty, and we go back there.
Load up. What is this place?

Muhammad leads our caravan.
It is lucky to start out in such a fresh breeze.

Like ocean birds, human beings come out of the ocean.
Do not expect to live inland.

We hear a surging inside our chests,
an agreement we made in eternity.

The wave of that agreement
rolled in and caulked our body's boat.

Another wave will smash us.
Then the meeting we have wanted will occur.

THE FAINT LAMENT OF FORM

Friend, I am a mirror
holding all six directions,
but I cannot contain you.

You shine here because you polished the surface.
The sun once asked your sun, *When will I see you?*

As you set, I rise, was the answer.

This is not reasonable.
Reason cannot walk where this poem is going.

The great splendor of intellectual clarity
becomes a grain of corn in love's bag,
waiting to be thrown out around the fowler's snare.

You are the bird that plunges into the ocean of mystery,
and that ocean becomes your turning center.

The joy of questions
becomes a thousand answering earring bells.

All day we revolve around your tree
like limb shadows.

Night comes, a weary sleep.
Then again at dawn the faint lament of form.

With you the body's dog-soul becomes a fox.
Because of you a lion bows down before a jackal.

More and more concentric skies appear
with the earth as their center.

You call for us to start out, and we do.
This is the journey Adam left paradise on.

The love-ocean roils with praise,
and that sound increases now as I end this
and wait for your discourse to begin.

EVIDENCE

Here is evidence of presence.
Eight times we feel it going out from behind the veil,
catching outsiders, then back in,
confusing even those with no mind.

Open book, awareness dispersed, shut.
A shiver of change, picture-making quill tip,
a note from an empty flute, face that lights a candle.

Some sleep. Others lie awake.
The friend gets up in the early dawn and goes outdoors.

The light-form of our teacher leaves,
but the glistening of his courage remains.

EVENING SKY GARNET RED

Morning opens a door with help for those
who do not ask for any.

Love tears its shirt. Mind begins the sewing repair.
You come and both run off.
I burn with aloes wood to touch the one who set this.

Dressed sometimes like disaster, sometimes like a guide,
the ox of the self sweetens his mouth in a pasture.

A parrot falls in love with an Arabian colt.
Fish want linen shirts.
The drunken lions want drunken gazelles.

It cannot be said how you take form.
One man asks for spoiled cheese.

The prayer rugs all point different ways.
If you would soak again the evening sky your garnet red,
the *qibla* tips would all point that way.

THIS BATTERED SAUCEPAN

Whatever you feel is *yours* the friend pulls you away from.
That one does not heal your wounds or torment you more.
Neither sure, nor uncertain, that one keeps you *moving*.

Decisions made at night seem strange the next day.
Where *are* you when you sleep?

A trickster curls on the headboard.
Restless in the valley, you go to the ocean.

Then turning toward the light, you fall in the fire.
Who jiggles this battered saucepan?

The sky puts a yoke on you to help with turning around a pole.
Teachers get dizzy like students.

The lion that killed you now wonders
whether to drag you off or tear you to pieces here.

There is a shredding that is really a healing,
that makes you more *alive*.

A lion holds you in his arms.
Fingers rake the fretbridge for music.

A compass revolves around the metal foot point.
Some grow fond of battle armor, some, satin clothing.
Others, like me, love the word-bunches called poetry.

THE MYSTERY OF THE WAY

The musician draws his hand across the strings,
so that the idlers will come in off the street.
Those who have been waiting start to work.
The thieves of inner qualities no longer threaten.
They are brought to justice.
The figurers cannot read their own columns of figures.
Friend calls friend to the secret cave.
Saddle the nimble horses with gold-inlaid leather.
Let the packhorses continue with their loads.

Comfort the grieving,
not those who think only of how to sell things.
The sensualities they live for
are sharp points pushing into their flesh.

Those who walk into fire feel refreshed.
Those who run to water scald themselves.
The dusty face of Moses moves toward light.
Pharaoh parades into stupidity and humiliation.

The mystery of the way
is the old trick of reversing horseshoes.
Moses bends to pick up a stick. It's alive.

CHAMPION LOVEMAKER AND LEADER OF MEN

If you could not feel tenderness and hurt,
if you could live in the poorhouse of not-wanting
and never be indignant,
if you could take two steps away from the beautiful one
you want so much to lie down with,
if you could trust that there is a spirit wife for you somewhere,
a nest, a jewel setting where when you sit down
you know you have always wanted to be,
if you could quit living here and go there,
if you could remember clearly what you have done.

But strong hooks hold you in this wind.
So many people love you.
You mix with the color and the smell and the taste
of your surroundings, champion lovemaker and leader of men.
You cannot give up your public fascination
or your compassion for the dying.

There is another compassion
that you do not know yet, but you may,
when griefs disappear.

It is a place,
with no questioning thorns in the pasture grass.
If you could remember that you are not a crow,
but the mystic osprey that never needs to light,
you could be walking there now with Shams.

THE BUDDHIST SUFI

Last night my soul asked a question of existence,
Why are you upsidedown with flames in your belly?
Happy, unhappy, indigo-orange like the sky?

Why are you an off-balance wobbling millstone
like the Buddhist Sufi, Ibrahim Balkhi,
who was king, beggar, buddha, and dervish.

Existence answers,
all this was made by the one who hides inside you.
You are like a beautiful bride,
quick to anger, stubborn, hot, naked,
but still veiled.

Reason and patience like well-meaning uncles
come to rail about how difficult this world is.

Love helps you to see into the invisible.
Water washes your hands.
Earth sits quiet like a childhood friend.

Watch the ocean circling your body-ship.
Stare into the holy Zamzam well at Mecca.
Within it you will see more Meccas and more Kaabas.

The king breaks in,
Stay quiet now, and do not jump into that well,
unless you know how to make a bucket and a rope
from my severed arm-stumps.

UP TO THE NECK

I sat long enough in fire.
Now I am up to the neck in the water of union.

You say, Up to the neck is not enough.
Make your head your foot and descend into love.
There is no up-to-the-neck union.

I say, But for the sake of your garden
I sat up to my neck in blood.

You say, Yes, you escaped the alluring world,
but not yourself.

You are the magician caught in his own trickery.
Cut the breath of self and be silent.

Language cannot come from your throat
as you choke and go under.

OPEN YOUR MOUTH TO THIS WIND

Science and theology would be just whims of the wind,
if you knew full surrender.

These beautiful world-birds would seem like flies,
if that wing-shadow fell across you.

The famous drums would sound like tapping sticks.
If that dawn rose, you would be released
from whatever is holding you.

What you thought was ahead would be behind.
One word, one *letter*, from that book
and you would understand.

Your fire wavers with the thought of death,
but if it burned in eternity, it would not tremble.

Those you are traveling with keep you distracted.

Open your mouth to this wind,
and let a straw catch in your throat.

Choke and die
of the worthlessness you value.

Your childish intelligence got stuck at *He frowned*,
that part of the Qur'an where Muhammad's revelations
are interrupted by a wandering blind man.

Muhammad frowns,
then turns to the man's true intention.

After frowning, comes *Blessed is he*.
Reach through your worrying to that.

This silence. This moment. Every *moment*,
if it is genuinely inside you, brings what you need.

WETNESS AND WATER

How does a part of the world leave the world?
How can wetness leave water?

Do not try to put out a fire
by throwing on more fire.
Do not wash a wound with blood.

No matter how fast you run,
your shadow more than keeps up.
Sometimes it's in front.

Only full, overhead sun
diminishes your shadow.

But that shadow has been serving you.
What hurts you blesses you.
Darkness is your candle.
Your boundaries are your quest.

I can explain this,
but it would break the glass cover on your heart,
and there is no fixing that.

You must have shadow and light source both.
Listen, and lay your head under the tree of awe.

When from that tree, feathers and wings sprout on you,
be quieter than a dove.
Do not open your mouth for even a *cooooooooo*.

When a frog slips into the water,
the snake cannot get it.

Then the frog climbs back out and croaks,
and the snake moves toward him again.

Even if the frog learns to hiss,
still the snake will hear through the hiss
the information he needs, the frog-voice underneath.

But if the frog could be completely silent,
then the snake would go back to sleeping,
and the frog could reach the barley.

The soul lives there in the silent breath.
And that grain of barley is such that,
when you put it in the ground, it grows.

Are these enough words,
or shall I squeeze more juice from this?

Who am I, my friend?

OUT OF THE IMAGE-MAKING BUSINESS

I used to want buyers for my words.
Now I wish someone would buy me away from words.

I have made a lot of charmingly profound images,
scenes with Abraham and Abraham's father, Azar,
who was also famous for icons.

I am so tired of what I have been doing.
Then one image without form came, and I quit.

Look for someone else to tend the shop.
I am out of the image-making business.
Finally I know the freedom of madness.

A random image arrives.
I scream, *Get out!* It disintegrates.

Only love.
Only the holder the flag fits into, and wind.
No flag.

FLUTES FOR DANCING

It is lucky to hear the flutes for dancing
coming down the road. The ground is glowing.
The table is set in the yard.

We will drink all this wine tonight
because it is spring. It is.
It is a growing sea. We are clouds over the sea,
or flecks of matter in the ocean
when the ocean seems lit from within.
I know I am drunk when I start this ocean talk.

Would you like to see the moon
split in half with one throw?

WAX

When I see you and how you are,
I close my eyes to the other.
For your Solomon's seal I become wax throughout my body.
I wait to be light.
I give up opinions on all matters.
I become the reed flute for your breath.

You were inside my hand.
I kept reaching around for something.
I was inside your hand,
but I kept asking questions of those who know very little.

I must have been incredibly stupid or insane
to sneak into my own house and steal money,
to climb over the fence and steal my own vegetables.
But no more. I have gotten free of that ignorant fist
that was pinching and twisting my secret self.

The universe and the light of the stars come through me.
I am the crescent moon put up over the gate to the festival.

THE MANY APPEALS OF THE COLOR RED

Red with shyness,
the red that became all the rose-garden reds.

The red distance.
Red of the stove and boiling water,
red of the mountain turning bloodred now.

Mountain holding rubies secretly inside,
should I love more you,
or your modesty?

10.
An-Nur, Light

The heart and the face are deeply connected. You can see the heart's light in the face. Ligaments of light hold the world together. This is an ocean of light with walking flames inside each individual. Eventually the light of the soul and the light of actual sunlight become the same. The light of your childhood. I experienced this once. After a long flight to south India, I woke into the light of my childhood. As you start out on a journey, the passageways of the self keep changing. We hope to arrive where reason cannot go, where dry sticks are full of light. The stars truly *are* suns, and Shams Tabriz is everywhere. Let your face be open to the light and clearly here.

THE LIGHT INSIDE THE FACE

The soul gives off a light. You are that beauty.
How does the soul stand such light?

Great elegant-feathered, many-colored bird
inside whose stretching wing-shadow
even crows become stately messengers,
you grace this unforgivable place with kindness.
You help those who hurt, loosening their knotted hearts.

Oceans disappear and reappear
inside this pearl that you are.

I weep when we meet, asking,
How unfaithful have you been, my friend?

And I cry outloud when we leave each other,
Is *this* how you stay faithful?

Yet there is a joy in being apart,
pleasure even here.

When loving goes truly insane, you are the cause,
because you once lived there in the controlling mind,
and then you left and took all coherence away.

A face opens. You are the face
within the face, the light. Forgive me.

A WALKING FIRE

Today, now, this is when
we can meet the friend,
now, as the sun comes up.

The beloved, who yesterday was so distant,
today is kind and bringing food.

Someone who knows this one
and is not demolished and completely reborn,
that one is made of marble,
not blood and bone and brain and eyes and hair.

Gabriel knocks on the friend's door.
Who is it? *Your servant.*
Who came with you? *Your love.*
Where? *In my arms.*

But the whole world is in love with me.
What you have brought is a common thing.
Go away.

Now Shams comes along,
a walking fire beyond anything I can say.

THE SHINE IN THE FIELDS

The shine in the fields and in the orchard
has become the light of your face.

No home now, no loved occupation,
no belongings, no figuring profit and loss.

When this love comes, it is impossible
to worry about honor or reputation,
what the community gives, the more and the less.

There is no longer any demarcation line
between the worlds. Hats fly off.

A pack of dogs snarl and bite each other
around a carcass. We are not those dogs.

Only God knows our secrets, and that is enough.
We have no more arguments over doctrine.

What is planted in each person's soul will sprout.
We surrender to however that happens.

Companions used to be magnets that drew us
together to talk. No more. No more even the sun.

It has turned itself into the face
of Shams Tabriz, the sanctity and the praise.

MORE OF YOUR NAMES

To say more of your names.
You are the one who was with us in the beginning,
telling secrets in the first house.

We were afraid of fire, but then we found your flame.
You are also a wind that puts out the mind's candle,
that city leveled.

With friends, friendship.
With enemies, the standing apart,
or right in the middle, resembling both.

Knowledgeable ones sigh their disdain,
Oh the stories lovers tell.

But you are those stories,
you that bring dawn to the end of night.

Beauty that originates,
the look and the presence inside the look,
majesty of Shamsuddin, praise,
and the light-connecting ligaments that hold this earth.

DARING ENOUGH TO FINISH

Face that lights my face,
you spin intelligence into these particles I am.

Your wind shivers my tree.
My mouth tastes sweet with your name in it.

You make my dance daring enough to *finish*.
No more timidity!

Let fruit fall
and wind turn my roots up in the air,
done with patient waiting.

INHALE AUTUMN, LONG FOR SPRING

Union is a watery way.
In an eye, a point of light.
In the chest, the soul.

The place where ecstatic lovers go is called the tavern,
where everyone gambles,
and whoever loses has to live there.

So, my love,
even if you are the pattern of time's orderly passage,
do not go, or if you go, wear a disguise.

But do not cover your chest.
Stay open there.

Someone asks me, *What is love?*
Do not look for an explanation.
Dissolve into me,
and you will know when it calls.
Respond.

Walk out as a lion, as a rose.
Inhale autumn, long for spring.

You that change the dull field,
who give conversation to damaged ears,
make dying alive,
award guardianship to the wandering mind,

You who erase the five senses at night,
who give eyes allure and a blood clot wisdom,
who give the lover heroic strength,
you who hear what Sanai said,
Lose your life, if you seek eternity.

The master who teaches us is absolute light,
not this visibility.

OCEAN LIGHT

The moon at dawn stooped like a hawk
and took me and flew across the sky.

Traveling inside that light, so close,
my body turned to spirit.

I saw nothing but light.
The secret of revelation came clear
with my ship submerged in that.

As it moved, consciousness rose into being,
and the voice of consciousness
made every foam fleck a new bodying.

Matter receives a signal from the sea it floats in,
but without the sun,
without the majesty of Shams,
no one would see the moon,
or ever dissolve in ocean light.

SOUL LIGHT AND SUN THE SAME

If a lover is not continually burning,
he should sit and crack his knuckles with the old men.

A lover does not fit in groups very well, or with himself.
He rides away quickly from doubt and appearances.

A spring, a green branch, every day new,
the first time you feel held,
curved like a lute playing grief music.

Gazelle and lioness walking together,
soul light and sun the same.

THE GENERATIONS I PRAISE

Yesterday the beauty of early dawn came over me,
and I wondered who my heart would reach toward.

Then this morning again and you.
Who am I?

Wind and fire and watery ground move me mightily
because they are pregnant with love, love pregnant with God.

These are the early morning generations I praise.

SNEEZING OUT ANIMALS

I look for the light I used to see.
The key is hidden here somewhere.
I face toward India, then Turkestan.

I am the ground you walked on.
There is an old story about Noah's ark,
when the garbage began piling up.

Yes. That scow was in trouble.
Noah scratched a pig's back.
The pig sneezed out a rat, two rats.

The rats ate the garbage.
Then Noah scratched a lion,
who sneezed out cats, who ate the rats.

I was sneezed out by a lion and put in a bag,
where I heard, If you are a lion cub, tear the bag.

I did. Shams Tabriz lives beyond
the blue bag of the sky.

THE IMPORTANCE OF SETTING OUT

If a tree could fly off, it would not suffer the saw.
The sun hurries all night to be back for morning.
Salty water rises in the air,
so the garden will be drenched with fresh rain.

A drop leaves home,
enters a certain shell, and becomes a pearl.
Joseph turns from his weeping father, toward Egypt.
Remember how that turned out.

Journeys bring power and love back into you.
If you cannot go somewhere,
move in the passageways of the self.

They are like shafts of light, always changing,
and you change when you explore them.

WAKING UP, DAWN MUSIC

Wake up with the morning breeze, and ask for a change.
Open and fill yourself with the wine that is your life.
Pass it around. Pass it to me first.
Revive me with your waking.

Listen to the harp sound, and sing.
Dawn music is your joy.

Give me your excitement,
but let it ground me, so I do not wander.
Watch the ripples on the surface.
Then launch me like a ship.

Once I was only a piece of wood.
Then Moses threw me down.
Now I am a powerful dragon.
I was dead. Jesus raised me.
Muhammad spoke, and this tree shimmered.

Say the word again, Shams, so we can feel you,
your light within everything.

MOVE INTO THE SUN

You who have done great things, listen to the reed,
the reed, the voice of the reed.

What is the reed? The lover's place to kiss,
place to kiss, the lover's place to kiss.

With no hands and feet it serves.
It brings what you want,
hand and foot, hand and foot.

The reed is pretext. That is not its fault.
A sound of wings, nothing seen.

We are beggars. Everything a beggar has
was given to him by the Rich and All-Sufficient.
We are total darkness. God is light.

Sun comes into our houses and mixes with shadows.
Climb out on the roof if you want more light.

If you do not want to live depressed any longer,
move into the sun. The sun.

THE OCEAN MOVING ALL NIGHT

Stay with us. Do not sink to the bottom
like a fish going to sleep.
Be with the ocean moving steadily all night,
not scattered like a rainstorm.

The spring we are looking for
is somewhere in this murkiness.
See the night lights up there traveling together,
the candle awake in its gold dish.

Do not slide into the cracks of ground like spilled mercury.
When the full moon comes out, look around.

A CLEARED SITE

The presence rolling through again
clears the shelves and shuts down shops.

Friend of the soul, enemy of the soul,
why do you want mine?

Bring tribute from the village.
But the village is gone in your flood.

That cleared site is what I want.
Live in the opening where there is no door to hide behind.
Be pure absence.
In that state everything is essential.

The rest of this must be said in silence
because of the enormous difference between light
and words that try to say *light*.

SOME KISS

There is some kiss we want with our whole lives,
the touch of spirit on the body.

Seawater begs the pearl to break its shell,
and the lily, how passionately
it needs some wild darling.

At night, I open the window
and ask the moon to come and press its face
against mine, Breathe into me.

Close the language-door, and open the love-window.
The moon won't use the door, only the window.

STICKS FULL OF LIGHT

I am a cup in the friend's hand.
Look in my eyes if you do not believe that.
A cup filled with blood, a cup with a slender stem.

The one who holds me is none of this,
but this that is so filled with images
belongs to that one, the one with no form,
who knows what is best for a sand grain or a drop of water,
who opens and closes our ability to love.

Like a donkey, we are being taught.
The donkey thinks whoever unties him and brings hay is God.

In the same way, we are gnostics,
each with a unique experience of what binds and what releases us.

We hear that voice and our ears twitch
like the donkey who hears his trainer coming.
Oats may be on the way, and water.
What have you been given like that?

Confinement, you complain.
Stick your head out.
That is all that will fit through the five-senses opening.

So. You have a wonderful view,
but no way *into* the prospect.

I have no wings, you mutter, depressed,
but your looking outside the senses is a fire that kindles the
    body.

Small sticks and dry grasses catch to a burning light,
and here is an odd bit: even if not on fire and shining,
the sticks are still light.

To those who will come after I say,
Life is not for waiting.

Do not postpone. Love is bringing everyone by the ear
into a place where reason cannot go,
where Muhammad's eyes close in sleep
and instruments grow quiet.

Truth does not sleep.
Sunlight does not go away.
The stars are suns. Shams is everywhere.

SUNLIGHT

Sunlight, fill this house again,
delighting friends, blinding enemies.
Come from behind the mountain.
Turn all stones red.
Ripen back the grapes gone sour.
Dress the fields, the garden, and the pasture,
with strands of every color.
Cure the lovers.
Let your face be openly here,
not covered with cloud.
Clarify what is
with direct, unfiltered, light.

WET AND DRY

When you are out walking in sunlight,
see the love covering all.

When you look up at clouds, remember grief,
friends that are gone.

When you see the new moon, behold this fresh burning
that I am, here still alive,
near your sky-wandering spirit.

The world darkens into night,
and some lovers feel so deeply hurt.

Then this flying fire-presence disintegrates across another day,
giving away its burning feathers, generous eagle.

And now a bloodshot, blood-thirsty planet rises red,
for which we close. We dry up.

On our lips there is wet, then dry.
When you look into my eyes, see both dry and wet.

ONE DROP

One drop of wine falls on the ground, soaks in.
All this commotion of intelligence and feeling
comes from that intentional spilling.
Your sadness so concerned with itself, how it's going,
secrets rising out of the soil, thorns wrapped with petals.
Only someone sickened by fall can rise now from the bed.
What is the fall wind?
A clear refusal.
What is spring?
Your opening heart.

PASSAGE INTO SILENCE

The essence of darkness is light,
as oil is the essence of this light.

You are the origin of all the jasmine, narcissi, and irises to come.
You are sunlight moving through houses,
David's hand molding smooth chainmail,
September moon over the unharvested crop.

You *set* the grain in the husk.

A rose torn open,
my head not worrying about debt,
you, soul and body mortared together in bed,
you saying, You are, you are,
then stopping to twist the strings to sweeten the voice.

When I give this body to the ground, you will find another way.
These words are an alternate existence.
Hear the passage into silence and be that.

SHREDS OF STEAM

Light again, and the one who brings light.
Change the way you live.

From the ocean-vat, wine-fire in each cup.
Two or three of the long-dead wake up.
Two or three drunks become lion hunters.

Sunlight washes a dark face.
The flower of what is true opens in the face.
Meadow grass and garden ground grow damp again.
A strong light like fingers massages our heads.
No dividing these fingers from those.

Draw back the lockbolt.
One level flows into another.
Heat seeps into everything.
The passionate pots boil.
Clothing tears into the air.
Poets fume shreds of steam,
never so happy as out in the light.

11.

Ash-Shakur, The Grateful

What we most want comes through how we fail and get humbled. Then there is an herb garden with many delicate and pungent plants. Sometimes a good friend will quietly show how what you thought you were doing well, like teaching a class, is not really very valuable to anyone, a waste of time. That is a very good friend, and I am grateful, Andrew. Gratitude is a quality I am good at. It wells up. It wants me to be more careful, more diligent, not impeccable, never claiming that. There is one who is made of all these qualities. It is *you*, the one unable to describe itself. Be grateful for that.

UNDERWATER IN THE FOUNTAIN

When you die into the soul,
you lift the lid on the cooking pot.
You see the truth of what you have been doing.

It looks sad and terrible before the crossover move
that lets nine levels of ascension turn to ordinary ground:

Silence, a conversation with Khidr,
blind and deaf, underwater in the fountain.

DROWSY

Drowsy, awake to everything,
out of myself, inside you, the work of your wine vat
where the grapes are invisible.

All one sees is stained feet tromping about,
making a juice different from ordinary grapes.

This wine gives no hangover,
but do not condemn yourself for living in leftover stupor.

Someone built and set the hangover trap
you find yourself in.

It is the bottom of Joseph's pit,
where he becomes medicine, a clean tent,
a field of stubble and shine.

Shams is winter daylight.
I more resemble the long night coming after.

SO WE CAN HAVE WHAT WE WANT

You wear coarse wool, but you are a king,
as the soul's energy hides, as love remembers.

You enter this room in a human shape
and as the atmosphere we breathe.

You are the central pole through the nine levels
connecting them and us to absolute absence.

So that we can have what we want
you give failure and frustration.

You want only the company of the lion
and the lion cub, no wobbly legs.

That man there, you suggest,
might remove his head before entering the temple.
Then he could listen without ears
to a voice that says, *My creature.*

A month of walking the road,
you make that distance in one day.

Never mind gold and silver payments.
The one who follows and the one who leads are inseparable,
as the moon and the circle around it.

An Arab drags his camel to town.
You go through your troubles and changing beliefs,
both no different from the moon moving across
or basil grown and getting cut for a bouquet.

It does not matter that you have been lost.
The hoopoe is still looking for you.

It is another beginning, my friend,
this waking in a morning with no haze,
and help coming without your asking.

A glass submerged is turning inside the wine.
With grief waved away, sweet gratefulness arrives.

EVERY TREE

Every tree, every growing thing as it grows,
says this truth, *You harvest what you sow.*

With life as short as a half-taken breath,
do not plant anything but love.

The value of a human being can be measured
by what he or she most deeply wants.

Be free of possessing things.
Sit at an empty table.
Be pleased with water, the taste of being home.

People travel the world looking for the friend,
but that one is always at home.

Jesus moves quickly to Mary.
A donkey stops to smell the urine of another donkey.
There are simple reasons for what happens.

You will not stay clear if you sit for long
with the one who pours the wine.

Someone with a cup of honey in his hand
rarely has a sour face.

If someone says a eulogy,
there must be a funeral nearby.

A rose opens because she is the fragrance she loves.
We speak poems,
and lovers down the centuries will keep saying them.
The cloth God weaves does not wear out.

DOORSILL

Ordeal. The time of testing is here.
Words like *fortitude* and *valor*
mean something among people again.

Old agreements weaken and break.
When the knife reaches bone,
your life must change.

Be glad the refining fire is around you.
Laugh as you stand on this doorsill.
Out of your dry thorn opens a rose garden.

I point to you,
because you give me joy that cannot be said.

Heavy blows beat about my head.
I need your compassion.

Muhammad's warriors have come from the Kaaba
to help me in this fight.

My reason says, *Be quiet. What can you know?*
I try to be silent, but my weeping comes anyway.

Muhammad says, *You did not throw when you threw.*

This I feel in my body
is like an arrow suddenly released to its moment.

WHAT FEAR OF LOSS?

When we are with you,
what fear of loss could we possibly have?

You change every grief to gold.
You give us the key to each world we come to.

You sweeten the lips of those we love
and open their mouths in desire.

You are beyond all guessing,
yet within each guess.
Hidden, yet beginning to be revealed.

We have fallen into the sugar shaker.
We are the ground beneath you.
Let someone else describe the sky.

Hold us in silence.
Do not throw us back into some discussion.

IS THIS A PLACE WHERE STORIES ARE ACTED OUT?

Ask someone whose house this is
where music continues to flow out.

Is this the Kaaba or a temple of light?
Is something here that the universe cannot hold?

Or is this a place where stories are acted out?
Do not tear it down. And do not try to talk to the owner.

He is asleep. Make perfume of the dust
and other thrown-away matters here,
where the framing is poetry
and the kitchen talk pure praise.

Whoever enters this room becomes wise.
This is the house of love, where no one can distinguish
leaf from blossom, or trap from bait.
Everything mirrors everything.

The hair tip sinks through the comb.
No one knows anyone's name.

Do not wait on the doorsill. Walk this forest
full of lions and do not consider the danger.

No need to set fires everywhere you go.
The lion's thicket is silence.

Anything you say will be flame enough
to draw them from where they rest.

THE SUN'S GLOWING CASTIRON MOLD

Today your beauty has another dimension.
Today, another rose,
a higher lift into the cypress.

The sun's glowing castiron mold
grows wider than the universe.

No one knows where this commotion comes from,
only that it is here.

Look in the eyes of the deer
as it pounces on the lion.
There is a wide desert plain in those eyes
that is beyond the two worlds,
a madness freer than anything anyone has felt.

A lover empties the ocean.
Today is love. Tomorrow the friend.

A lover holds in himself or herself
tomorrows farther than any future.

Saladin is not here.
It is no wonder.

A jealous king thinks he must keep changing every moment
the one in charge of his harem.

PREPARING THE PEN

I become a pen in the friend's hand,
tonight writing say, tomorrow ray.
You trim the pen for fine calligraphy.
The pen says, *I am here, but who am I?*

You blacken the pen's face.
You wipe it in your hair. You hold it upside down.
Now you begin to write.

On one sheet you cancel everything.
On another you add a dangerous conjunction.
The writing depends entirely on the scribe
who knows how to split the head of the pen.

Galen knows what a patient needs.
The pen cannot speak for itself,
or know what to disapprove of in its own nature.

Whether I say *pen or flag*,
it is with this wonderful conscious unconsciousness,
the mind unable to include its own description,
composing blindly, held in a hand, yet free.

HOW YOU BECAME WHAT YOU ARE NOW

How did you get away?
You were the pet falcon of an old woman.
Did you hear the king's falcon drum?
You were a drunken songbird put in with owls.
Did you smell the fragrance of a garden?

You got tired of sour fermenting
and left the tavern.
You went like an arrow to the target
from the bow of time and place.

The man who stays at the cemetery pointed the way,
but you did not go.
You became light and gave up wanting to be famous.
You do not care about what you are going to eat,
so why buy an engraved belt?

I have heard of living at the center,
but what about *leaving* the center of the center?
Flying toward thankfulness,
you become the rare bird with one wing made of fear and one of
    hope.

In autumn, a rose crawling along the ground in the cold wind.
Rain on the roof runs down and out by the spout as fast as it can.

Talking is pain. Lie down and rest,
now that you have found a friend to be with.

BONFIRE AT MIDNIGHT

A shout comes out of my room
where I have been cooped up.
After all my lust and dead living I can still live with you.
You want me to.
You fix and bring me food.
You forget the way I have been.

The ocean moves and surges in the heat
of the middle of the day,
in the heat of this thought I am having.
Why are not all human resistances
burning up with this thought?

It is a drum and arms waving.
It is a bonfire at midnight on the top edge of a hill,
this meeting again with you.

A RIPE FIG

Now that you live in my chest
anywhere we sit is a mountaintop.

Those other images,
which entice people like porcelain dolls from China,
which have made men and women weep for centuries,
even those are changing now.

What used to be pain is now a lovely bench,
where we rest under the roses.

A left hand has become a right.
A dark wall, a window.
A cushion in a shoe heel, the leader of the assembly.

Intelligence and silence.
What we say is poison to some,
and nourishing to others.

What we say is a ripe fig,
but not all birds that fly eat figs.

THE DEEPEST REST

Death is a wedding feast,
and the secret of that is that God is one.

Sunlight comes in through the windows
and gets reflected around the room.

Then the windows are closed.
Individual grapes become one dark wine.

For someone who lives in the light of God,
death is nourishment.

Do not judge those who are beyond judgment.
Do not speak of anything you have not experienced.

There is another light.
Try to see by that.

The *Qutb* watches for you.
Allow him to see you.

Let your eyes fill with tears.
Let your eyes sleep while you stay awake.
That is the deepest rest.

Be clear and thoughtful in sleep.
Interpret your dreams. If you are not lucid there,
you are just boiling and cooking unconsciously
in the love stew of *wanting oneness* all your life.

STINGY ALOES WOOD

A lion is devouring a sheep.
A little, lame, blind, blue fox comes along
and steals the sheep's tail.

The lion allows this when one swing of the lion's paw
could obliterate the fox.

Remember the brothers
who came with the ridiculous news,
A wolf has eaten Joseph.

The lion of the sky could not harm such a favorite.
Your hearts are guarded like that.
Give everything to the one who protects.

When someone humiliates you,
turn your face there.

Fear and hurt are lassoes
drawing you through a door.

Lord, lord, you say, weeping.
Green herbs sprout where those tears fall.

Dawn comes, and blindness drains away.
Each day is eternity.

Do not avoid your suffering.
Plunge it in the Nile.

Purify your stubbornness.
Drown it. Burn it.

Your body is a stingy piece of aloes wood
that will not let go its healing smoke
until you put it in the fire.

Now Shams leans near to remind me,
That is enough sourness. No more vinegar.

SWEET OUTLAWS

You say, My sweetness is worth many pearls.
I say I have no pearls.

You say, Borrow some.
You must make a net of pearls to catch me in.

Or maybe you came to the wrong address.
This is a gambling house.
Here you must have valuables to risk.

If you do not want to do that, leave.
We are outlaws.
Whatever you bring we tear to pieces.

We are kinder than anyone you have ever met,
but we do destroy what you own,
your fine clothes, even your mustache.

There are those who collect things
and those who disperse them.

Your body must become soul,
every hair tip quivering with spontaneous life.

Recognize lovers by how they tremble.
How much is a tear worth? A look.
We are servants to that, not born of father or mother.

If you do not live inside this face,
sit behind like the nape of the neck,
or advance in front like a blunt shield,
noticing how grateful people are
for a single glance from the friend.

A GRAPE

I come with excuses. You plug your ears.
So I accept every difficulty.

If you would say I do not exist,
I would be grateful.

When this longing makes me disreputable,
then I have a little self-respect.

This vine begins to become wine
when you say, *Pressure is necessary*
for you to burst open under my foot.

SHAMS'S AIR

Some say you are thorn; others, jasmine.
Some say you have no belief; others, that you are devout.
Pay no attention to such opinions. You are a lover.

Open your soul's eyes.
See the four rivers moving through you—
wine, milk, honey, and ordinary riverwater.

The archangel Gabriel bows to you.
A fly falls in buttermilk, hoping next time for honey.

Satan gets exiled from grace,
because he will not honor the first lover, Adam.
Your heart is a rose garden and a river.
You accept what is good and what is foolish in humanity.

You get entangled with both,
like the one who gave freewill,
who trusted people when even the sky refused to.

Shams Tabriz has spread an airiness
around the earth. We call it *freedom*.

CONTENT WITH IGNORANCE

I did not know that love would make me this crazy,
with my eyes like the River Ceyhun
carrying me in its rapids to the sea,
where every bit of my shattered boat sinks to the bottom.

An alligator lifts its head and swallows the ocean,
then the ocean floor becomes a desert
covering the alligator in sand drifts.

Changes do happen. I do not know how,
or what remains of what has disappeared into the absolute.

I hear so many stories and explanations,
but I keep quiet,
because I do not know anything,
and because something I swallowed in the ocean
has made me completely content with ignorance.

THE NEW MOON

A human being being human, out of breath,
burns the strangeness to ash,
and breathes deeper.

Completely gone, the new moon
is able then to become the new moon.

Autumn anger turns wistful in early spring.
Language-headaches smoothe their brows.

Let the military hero fight barehanded
with lions and elephants.

When you drift *up*, remember: Fold in on yourself
as clouds do to open downward
their water bags of rain.

12.
Al-Latif,
The Subtle, The Intricate

I saw a television program once with a young woman, a scientist, kneeling on a California beach saying that, since the Hubble telescope, it can be said *for certain* that there are more suns in the universe than there are grains of sand on all the beaches in the world. She was letting sand pour from the cone of her hand like an hourglass. The grains ran out. She brushed her hands together and looked down at the world of sand around her, then out into the sky: "That's amazing." The intricacy of the universe can hardly be overstated, or stated at all. Never mind the inner world of consciousness, language, mysticism, prayer, the *physics* of telepathy. These days, with all the discoveries being made, *Al-Latif* is a powerfully unfolding name for the Mystery. Hamza Yusef, in his wonderful book *The Purification of the Heart,* gives some astonishing, and extravagantly intricate, *Latifian* statistics about the human heart. It pumps one hundred gallons every hour through a closed vascular system, the human body. The length of that system of veins and arteries and all the little capillaries is equal to sixty thousand miles, two times the circumference of the earth! And it has recently been discovered, he says, that the heart has forty thousand neurons in it, with which it and the brain communicate. Interestingly, though, as we all know, the heart does not always obey the commands of the brain.

WHAT IS NOT HERE

I start out on this road, call it *love or emptiness*.
I only know what is not here.

Resentment seeds, back-scratching greed,
worrying about outcome, fear of people.

When a bird gets free, it does not go back
for remnants left on the bottom of the cage.

Close by, I am rain. Far off, a cloud of fire.
I seem restless, but I am deeply at ease.
Branches tremble. The roots are still.

I am a universe in a handful of dirt,
whole when totally demolished.

Talk about choices does not apply to me.
While intelligence considers options,
I am somewhere lost in the wind.

RAW, WELL-COOKED, AND BURNT

You ask, Why do you cry with such sweetness all around?

I weep as I make the honey, wearing the shirt of a bee,
and I refuse to share this suffering.

I play the sky's harp.
I curl around my treasure like a snake.

You say, What is this I business?

Friend, I have been a long time away from that.
What you see here is your own reflection.

I am still raw, and at the same time well-cooked,
and burnt to a crisp.

No one can tell if I am laughing or weeping.
I wonder myself.
How can I be separated and yet in union?

WHY AND WHERE WE GO

You are more beautiful than soul,
more useful than eyes.

Whatever I have seen in myself,
I did not see it. You saw. You chose me.

I say this poem to honor that choice.
I choose to lie down in a burning coffin-bed.

Ask my eyes, Why do you flow?
Ask my back, Why so bent?

Ask my soul, Why do you wear iron shoes on the road?
Also ask my soul if it has met another like you,
or heard of such a thing in any language.

You are the sun dissolving dull overcast,
the fragrance of a field. Joseph entering *this* room.

Peeling oranges with a knife,
we see you and nick our hands.

Without touching the ground, you draw a line.
We turn that way. You are why
and where we go and what we do there.

WORD FOG

Words, even if they come from the soul, hide the soul,
as fog rising off the sea covers the sea,
the coast, the fish, the pearls.

It is noble work to build coherent philosophical discourses,
but they do block out the sun of truth.

See God's qualities as an ocean.
This world is foam on the purity of that.
Brush it away and look through the alphabet to essence,
as you do the hair covering your beloved's eyes.

Here is the mystery:
This intricate, astonishing world is proof
of God's presence even as it covers the beauty.

One flake from the wall of a gold mine
does not give much idea what it is like
when the sun shines down inside
and turns the air and the workers golden.

LEAVES ABOUT TO LET GO

This world of two gardens, both so beautiful.
This world, a street where a funeral is passing.

Let us rise together and leave *this world*,
as water goes bowing itself down to the sea.

From gardens to the gardener,
from grieving to a wedding feast.

We tremble like leaves about to let go.
There is no avoiding pain,
or feeling exiled, or the taste of dust.

But also we have a green-winged longing
for the sweetness of the friend.

These forms are evidence of what cannot be shown.
Here is how it is to go into that.

Rain that has been leaking into the house
decides to use the downspout.

The bent bowstring straining at our throats
releases and becomes the arrow.

Mice quivering in fear of the housecat suddenly change
to half-grown lion cubs, afraid of nothing.

So let us begin the journey home,
with love and compassion for guides,
and grace protecting.

Let your soul turn into a mirror
that passionately wants to reflect Joseph.
Hand him your present.

Now let silence speak.
As that begins, we will start out.

SPILLED SPEECH

As everyone drifts off to sleep,
I am still staring at the stars.

Separation from you *does* have a cure.
There is a way inside the sealed room.

If you will not pour wine,
at least allow me half a mouthful of leftover dregs.

Secretly I fill my sleeve with pearls.
When the love-police detain me,
let your moon come down and hold me in its arms.

Officer, I know this man.
I will take him home.

Let my wandering end as the story does
of the Kurd who loses his camel.
Then the full moon comes out, and he finds what he lost.

These rock and earth forms
were originally sun-warmed water, were they not?
Then the planet cooled and settled to what we are now.

The blood in our bodies carries a living luminous flow,
but watch when it spills out and soaks into the ground.

That is how speech does,
overflowing from silence.

Silk on one side,
cheap, striped canvas on the other.

THE DANCE OF YOUR HIDDEN LIFE

Move your hair in the light.
Let it scatter amber,
as the souls of Sufis begin a dance,
sun, moon, and stars in a circle.

We are dancing their dance.
A slight melody enters the great wheel
and helps it turn.

A spring breeze makes everyone laugh.
Autumn wakes from his dead sleep.

Rose and thorn pair up.
Many people are dancing with snakes.

The orchard king from his secret center says,
Welcome to your hidden life.

They move together,
the cypress and the bud of the lily,
the willow and the flowering judas.

Ladders have been set up around the garden,
so that everyone's eyes lift.

A songbird sits on a branch
like the kind man who guards the treasury,
and has just been paid from it.

Shoots emerge from a dark core.
The new leaves are tongues.
The fruit, our growing, collective heart.

As they begin to form,
these apples, peaches, pears, and plums,
we understand what our tongues have been doing.

HUNT MUSIC

Musk and amber remind us of the air of sunrise,
when any small motion seems part of one elaborate making.

The body's harp gets handed to the soul to play.
The strings are rage, love, and jealousy.
All the wantings mix their energy-music.

Who *tuned* this instrument where wind is one string,
and Shams's eyes another,
in which a gazelle turns to stalk the hunting lioness?

AN OINTMENT MIXED WITH EARTH

I was a thorn rushing to be with a rose,
vinegar blending with honey,
a pot of poison turning to healing salve,
pasty wine dregs thrown in the millrace.

I was a diseased eye reaching for Jesus' robe,
raw meat cooking in the fire.

Then I found some earth to make an ointment with
that would honor my soul, and in mixing that,
I found poetry. Love says, *You are right.*
But do not claim credit for those changes.

Remember. I am wind.
You are the ember I ignite.

IF YOU WANT TO LIVE IN YOUR SOUL

The soul within our individual souls
loves the one who runs and falls down
more than the one who sits and watches.

The soul within soul lives in a lover.

Consider this metaphor. How you love is the open sky.
These personal selves are the separate roofs of a town.

Your tongue, the guttering where words flow.
If the roof is not clean, the words get thick and murky.

Some people have elaborate systems that drain water
from other roofs. This is not wise.
There is a false eloquence to it.

A lover is one who waters a garden from a rain barrel
that fills under his own roof.
Roses that grow from that have tears in them.

Sometimes the scale pans may weigh correctly,
but the balancer is off.

A sweet doctor may give bitter medicine.
A foot finds the right shoe in the dark.
Love moves on its way through the pleasure it feels.

Even though the time you live in is violent
and frightening, you are safe in Noah's boat.

If you want to know who someone is,
hang around with those close by. They know.

The rule that covers everything is,
How you are with others, expect that back.

If you want to know God,
enjoy the company of lovers.

If you want to be thought a great person,
learn some subtle point and say it with many variations
as the answer to every question.

If you want to live in your soul,
find a friend like Shams and stay near.

SPRING

Again, the violet bows to the lily.
Again, the rose is tearing off her gown.

The green ones have come from the other world,
tipsy, like the breeze up to some new foolishness.

Again, near the top of the mountain
the anemone's sweet features appear.

The hyacinth speaks formally to the jasmine,
Peace be with you.

And peace to you, lad.
Come walk with me in this meadow.

Again, there are Sufis everywhere.

The bud is shy, but the wind removes her veil
suddenly, My friend.

The friend is here like water in the stream,
like a lotus on the water.

The narcissus winks at the wisteria, Whenever you say.
And the clove to the willow, You are the one I hope for.
The willow replies, Consider these chambers of mine yours.
Welcome.

The apple, Orange, why the frown?
So that those who mean harm will not see my beauty.

The ringdove comes asking, Where? Where is the friend?
With one note the nightingale indicates the rose.

Again, the season of spring has come,
and a spring-source rises under everything,
a moon sliding from the shadows.

Many things must be left unsaid because it is late,
and whatever conversation we have not had tonight,
we will have tomorrow.

LOST CAMEL

I have heard that a certain man lost his camel.
He goes everywhere, not finding that camel.
He falls asleep in the desert by the side of the road,
tired and thinking now he is through looking.

Late in the night he wakes up full of that loss.
The moon comes rolling out like a white ball
on the huge, empty polo field of the sky. By that light
he sees his camel standing in the middle of the road.
His tears come easily like a quick rain.

He turns his face up, wet and shining.
How can I say what you are with your light?

Let this be a night like that one.
Each second the moon tells us, *Be more passionate.*
We should shine back and tell it the same thing.

It makes us restless. It grieves for us.
Take it inside you, that one whose presence is water.
We are the stream, searching along.
That one is musk. We are the way musk smells.
Why not spray ourselves?

GOLDSMITHING

By Saladin's shop suddenly I hear the music
of gold being hammered, gold and God.

As gold thins out,
the presence becomes a sheer, gold-leaf light
on this goldbeater's face, in his eyes as he works.

As the love-secret of Jacob becomes Joseph's smile,
as lovers leave what keeps them confined,
as Job's patience dissolves to nothing,
you are the friend coming toward this touching.

You are the soul,
and when you hear yourself in some hypocrisy,
cut free. Quickly, cut.

THE NIGHTWATCHMAN

I sit by the side of one who watches
like the stars at night without sleeping watch.

My friend sits on the roof at night.
I attend that watching.

During the day I help with the gardening.
He is both a tender of flowers and flowering trees.

It is no shame to be in this friendship,
or if it is, it is.

I was on my way elsewhere
when I saw the nightwatchman
sitting on the sky's roof like a guard.

Like a king, like a gardener in his garden,
rain-wet stones, like the body's hand-me-down.

The nightwatchman knows the way from body to soul,
how soul moves in stomach bile, in blood and semen, in saliva.

Soul works inside those fluids
to keep the body fresh and full of energy.

So the stars and the planets and this world are moving
to bring grace here through the cold night-clarity.

Events like battle arrows crisscross from every direction.
There is only one archer.

The skill of the sheepdog comes from the shepherd.
A city has a collective intelligence,
and each person there has a unique knowing.

Sometimes random bits pretend to be a caravan,
but it was a good messenger
who brought us the order out on the road
to Come back. Come back.

STRANGE BUSINESS

If you do not have a woman who lives with you,
why are you not looking?
If you have one, why are you not satisfied?
You have no resistance to your friend.

Why don't you become the friend?
If the flute is too quiet to say,
teach it manners.
Someone is holding you back. Break off.

You sit here for days saying, *This is strange business.*
You are the strange business.
You have the energy of the sun in you,
but you keep knotting it up at the base of your spine.
You are some weird kind of gold
that wants to stay melted in the furnace,
so you won't have to be coins.
Say ONE in your lonesome house.
Loving two is hiding inside yourself.

You have gotten drunk on so many kinds of wine.
Taste this. It will not make you wild.
It is fire. Give up,
if you do not understand by this time
that your living is firewood.

This wave of talking builds.
Better we should not speak it,
but let it grow within.

PHRASE YOUR QUESTION

Why doesn't a soul fly when it hears the call?
Fish on the beach always move toward wave sound.

A falcon hears the drum and brings the quarry home.
Why is not every dervish dancing in the sun?

You have escaped the cage.
Your wings are stretched out.
Now, fly.

You have slept in sheds and outbuildings
so long that you think you live there.

How many years, like children,
do we have to collect sticks and pieces of broken pottery
and pretend that they are valuable?

Leave childhood. Go to the banquet of true human beings.
Split open the cultural mold.
Put your head up out of the sack.

Hold this book in the air with your right hand.
Are you old enough to know right from left?

A voice says to your clarity, *Walk.*
Move into the moment of your death.
Learn some discipline there.

To the soul, Move into the invisible,
and take what's given. You are the king.
Phrase your question and expect an answer.

LIES FROM EACH OTHER

The way of lovers is different.
To them, lies from each other
are better than truth from others.

Impossibilities occur.
Synagogue becomes Kaaba.

Bitter is sweet and exhaustion, love.
The moment the friend waves you away,
water comes from Khidr's spring.

No is a thousand *yeses*
in the code of emptiness.
Criminality fills with forgiveness.

There is no describing the windings of this road.
I have talked enough.

When dear Lord Shams pours himself,
everything I say tastes like the presence.

I AM THE GROUND

I am the slave who frees the master.
I teach the teacher.
I am essence born freshly every day.
I built the ancient civilizations.
I brush medicine on fading eyesight.

I relight intelligence.
In grief, I am pitchblack darkness.
On a feast day, I am the children's excitement.
I am the ground who fills the sky's brain
with fiery lightning-love, air, and wind.

You could not sleep last night,
too happy with how I was remembering you.

No one is to blame that sometimes I am a scandal,
or obviously unfair.

The surface is rusting over. I had better go into silence.
I am breathing too close to this mirror's face.

WE ARE THREE

My love wanders the rooms,
melodious flute notes, plucked wires,
full of a wine the Magi drank on the way to Bethlehem.

We are three.
The moon comes from its quiet corner,
puts a pitcher of water down in the center.
The circle of surface flames.

One of us kneels to kiss the threshold.
One drinks, with wine-flames playing over his face.
One watches the gathering,
and says to any cold onlookers,

This dance is the joy of existence.

13.
Bawa Muhaiyaddeen

I was especially lucky with this name of God. I got to be in his presence. I sat in his room and sometimes helped with the food preparations. He taught me how to cut an onion. Now every time I do that, I remember how it was in his presence. Bawa was asked one day what it was like for him to be alive. "It is like driving a car," he said. "You are making certain decisions, going here and there, and yet you are the landscape you are driving through. You are a separate being and yet you are everything too."

I cannot say that I know what he is talking about. I have not had that experience, not that I am conscious of. But I have been so blessed to be able to sit in the same room with one of these names for Mystery off and on for nine years (1977–86). I met Bawa Muhaiyaddeen in a dream on May 2, 1977, a year and a half before I met him in this visible reality. He talked about many things with me. But his real influence was in the radiance and compassion, the depth and humor of his presence. Sufis would visit and say, "The light of God is on him." It was true. That is how it felt to be in his room. I just wanted to *be* there. Questions gradually fell away.

He liked to paint the Beautiful Names of Allah as a rosebush with ninety-nine roses of various shades of red, yellow, orange. He once told me that the cosmos, the tangible, apparent universe, was very tiny, a dot. One can go anywhere in it as fast as a thought. The great world is the world of awareness, the inner, which is somehow also the outer.

A TRANSPARENT TREE

I have traded my soul for the universe.
Don't speak.

The jeweler who thought he was buying gold
to work with now owns the mine.
But commerce metaphors are wrong.

What has happened in me is more profound,
like a fish underwater beginning to say words.

A transparent tree grows in the nightsky orchard
where I have found a little corner to be in,
as when two planets intersect.
I have met Shams.

SILKWORMS

The hurt you embrace becomes joy.
Call it to your arms where it can change.

A silkworm eating leaves makes a cocoon.
Each of us weaves a chamber of leaves and sticks.

Silkworms begin to truly exist
as they disappear inside that room.

Without legs, we fly.
When I stop speaking, this poem will close,
and open its silent wings. . . .

A VOICE THROUGH THE DOOR

Sometimes you hear a voice through the door calling you,
as fish out of water hear the waves,
or a hunting falcon hears the drum's *Come back. Come back.*

This turning toward what you deeply love saves you.

Children fill their shirts with rocks and carry them around.
We are not children anymore.

Read the book of your life which has been given you.
A voice comes to your soul saying,
Lift your foot, cross over, move into the emptiness
of question and answer and question.

A GREAT ROSE TREE

This is the day and the year of the rose.
The whole garden is opening with laughter.

Iris whispering to cypress.
The rose is the joy of meeting someone.

The rose is a world imagination cannot imagine.
A messenger from the orchard where the soul lives.

A small seed that points to a great rose tree.
Hold its hand and walk like a child.

A rose is what grows from the work the prophets do.
Full moon, new moon.

Accept the invitation spring extends,
four birds flying toward a master.

A rose is all these,
and the silence that closes and sits in the shade, a bud.

A LIGHT WITHIN HIS LIGHT

I circled awhile with each of the intelligences,
the nine fathers that control the levels of spirit growth.

I revolved for years with the stars
through each astrological sign.

I disappeared into the kingdom of nearness.
I saw what I have seen,
receiving nourishment as a child does in the womb.

Personalities are born once.
A mystic many times.

Wearing the body-robe, I have been busy in the market,
weighing and arguing prices.

Sometimes I have torn the robe off
with my own hands and thrown it away.

I have spent long nights in monasteries,
and I have slept with those who claim to believe nothing
on the porches of pagodas, just traveling through.

When someone feels jealous,
I am inside the hurt and the need to possess.
When anyone is sick, I feel feverish and dizzy.

I am cloud and rain being released,
then the meadow as it soaks in.

I wash the grains of mortality
from the cloth around a dervish.

I am the rose of eternity, not made of water or fire,
not of the wandering wind, or even earth.
I play with those.

I am not Shams Tabriz,
but a light within his light.

If you see me, be careful.
Tell no one what you have seen.

PURE SILENCE

I have come this time to burn my thorns,
to purify my life,
to take up service again in the garden.

I come weeping to these waters
to rise free of passion and belief.

Look at my face.
These tears are traces of you.

I will shorten this poem,
because the rest of it is being said
in the world within our eyes.

Do you know this silence?
It is not the same as in your room
when you have no one to talk to.

This is pure silence,
not the kind that happens
when living dogs are eating a dead one.

A WAKING TOWN

The taste of this life comes from you,
soul moving like a mountain stream under a sky of flowers.
Seeing such beauty makes me expect the dregs tomorrow.

I call you *moon*, but that is not right.
Does anything resemble you?

The noise of a waking town fills my chest.
Shams is saying this.

WALKINGSTICK DRAGON

I want to dance *here* in *this* music,
not in spirit, where there is no time.

I circle the sun like shadow.
My head becomes my feet.

Covered with existence, Pharaoh.
Annihilated, I am Moses.

A pen between God-fingers, a walkingstick dragon,
my blind mind taps along its cane of thought.

Love does no thinking.
It waits with soul, with me, weeping in this corner.

We are strangers here where we never hear *yes*.
We must be from some other town.

LET THE WAY ITSELF ARRIVE

Desires come, my wishes and my longing.
I am tied up, knot on top of knot.

Then you that untie me come.
Enough talk of being on some "path."

Let the *way* itself arrive.
You picked up a handful of earth.
I was in that handful.

I can say the difference between good and bad,
but not how I know your beauty.

Mind refuses to burn with love.
Saladin is central, yet hidden.

The *Qutb*, the pole of love,
reaches *here*, to this ground.

MOUNTED MAN

Look at this figure of a man on horseback,
his turban with gold thread, striking a gallant pose
and asking, Where is death? Show me.

He seems powerful, but he is a fake.
Death attacks from six sides. *Hello, jackass.*

Where is your magnetism now, the famous temperament?
The jokes you told, the carpets you gave relatives?

It is not enough to spend your life turning bread into dung.
We are pawing through manure to find pearls.

There are people with the light of God on them.
Serve those. Do not trivialize any suffering.

I say this to myself. I am that mounted man, his illusion.
How long shall I keep pointing to others?

Shams Tabriz is a fountain.
We wash in the water of his eyes.

CLOUDS

Every dustgrain shines in the sun.
I turn, remembering that.

Be finely ground in the love-mortar,
as pearls and coral are for medicine.
Beauty now is particulate, granular.

A light-spirit lives in you for your whole life.
When it leaves, it leaves completely.
You can call, but it will not come.

Only if your soul learns some spirit magic
will it choose to rest anywhere for a while.

Remember those arrogant angels, Harut and Marut,
who thought they were superior to Adam.
They were given lust and passion and sent down into the world,
where they tried to seduce a beautiful woman.

She resisted. She wanted to learn from them
the magic power-word
by which they could ascend back to the spirit world.

In their blind desire they told it to her,
and she immediately rose to become the planet Venus,
the evening star, while they, to show their passionate distraction,
and to be forgiven, chose to hang head down
in a pit in Babylon.

That well, the Babylonian angel prison,
was a momentary stopping place.

Now remember Tabriz,
the town that glows from within.
Even the clouds there are read for their astrological meanings.

LANGUAGE IS A TAILOR'S SHOP WHERE NOTHING FITS

The sun comes up out of the water.
Dust motes fill with music.
La'illaha il'Allah,
There is no reality but God.

Why mention flecks of dust?
When the sun of the soul's intelligence arrives,

it wears no cloak and no hat.
Then the moon, the soul's love, rises out of watery hills,
and the sun goes down, Joseph into his well.

Point your head out of the ground like an ant.
Walk onto the threshing floor with new information.
We have been so happy with rotten bits of grain,
because we did not know about these sweet green ears.

It is so simple to say, We have hands and feet.
We can walk out into the open.

Why mention ants?
Solomon himself tears his robe with wanting this
that we try to say with useless imagery.

Language is a tailor's shop where nothing fits.
They have cut and sewn a gown to fit the figure of the buyer.
The gown is too long. The buyer is too short.

Bring a taller person.
The tape measure is a bowstring
as long as from here to the moon.
Bring someone that tall.

Now maybe I will be quiet
and let silence separate what is true from what are lies,
as threshing does.

ONLY ONE SUNRISE A DAY

You will not find another friend like me.
You spend your days in all directions.
No one accepts your money but me.
You are the dry ditch. I am rain.
You are the rubble of a building.
I am the architect.

There is only one sunrise a day.
In your sleep you see many shapes and people.
When you wake, you see nothing.
Close those eyes and open these eyes.

What you have been wanting is a donkey lying sick on the ground.
What you have been doing is the bit and halter on that donkey.

There is sweet syrup here where you have been buying vinegar,
and unripened fruit. Walk into the hospital.
There is no shame in going where everyone has to go.
Without that healing you are a body with no head.
Be a turban wound around the head.

The mirror is black and rusty.
Who is the lucky man doing business with?
Think of the one who gave you thought.
Walk toward whoever gave you feet.
Look for the one behind your seeing.

Sing and clap because the whole ocean is a bit of foam.
No accidents are happening here.

Listen within your ear.
Speak without forming words.
Language turns against itself and is likely to cause injury.

THAT MOMENT AGAIN

Light going dim. Is it my eyes or a cloud,
or the sun itself, or the window?

I cannot see the point of the needle,
or the other end of the thread.

I want that moment again
when I spread out like olive oil in the skillet.
The same heat makes iron steel.
Abraham, a bed of jasmine sitting quietly, or talking.

Unmanned, I am a true person,
or at least the ring knocker on the door where they live.
The prophet says, *Fasting protects.* Do that.
On dry land a fish needs to be wrapped in something.
In the ocean, as you see, it grows a coat of mail.

I HAVE SUCH A TEACHER

Last night my teacher taught me the lesson of poverty,
having nothing and wanting nothing.

I am a naked man standing inside a mine of rubies,
clothed in red silk.

I absorb the shining, and now I see the ocean,
billions of simultaneous motions moving in me.

A circle of lovely, quiet people
becomes the ring on my finger.

Then the wind and thunder of rain on the way.
I have such a teacher.

THE SNOW-WORLD MELTS

Think of the phoenix coming up out of the ashes,
but not flying off.
For a moment we have form. We cannot see.
How can we be conscious and you be conscious
at the same time and separate?
Copper when an alchemist works on it
loses its copper qualities.
Seeds in spring begin to be trees. No longer seed.
Brushwood put in the fire changes.
The snow-world melts.
You step in my footprint, and it is gone.

It is not that I have done anything
to deserve this attention from you.
Predestination and freewill, we can argue them,
but they are only ideas.
What is real is a presence, like Shams.

WIND THAT TASTES OF BREAD AND SALT

There is no more wine. My bowl is broken.
I am terribly sick, and only Shams can cure me.

Do you know Shams, the prince of seeing,
who lifts the utterly drowned up out of the ocean
and revives them, so that the shore
looks like multiple marriages are going on,
easy laughing, a formal toast, a procession with music.

Shams is a trumpet note of light that sets the atoms spinning,
a wind that comes at dawn tasting of bread and salt.

Move to the edge and over. Fly with the wings he gives,
and if you get tired, lie down, but keep opening inside your soul.

A THIRSTY FISH

I do not get tired of you.
Do not grow weary of being compassionate toward me.

All this thirst-equipment must surely be *tired* of me,
the waterjar and the water-carrier.

I have a thirsty fish in me
that can never find enough of what it is thirsty for.

Show me the way to the ocean.
Break these half measures, these small containers.
All this fantasy and grief.

Let my house be drowned in the wave that rose last night
out of the courtyard hidden in the center of my chest.

Joseph fell like a moon into my well.
The harvest I expected was washed away.
But no matter.

A fire has risen above my tombstone hat.
I do not want learning, or dignity, or respectability.

I want this music and this dawn
and the warmth of your cheek against mine.

The grief-armies assemble, but I am not going with them.

This is how it always is when I finish a poem.
A great silence overcomes me,
and I wonder why I ever thought to use language.

A WATERBIRD FLYING INTO THE SUN

What I want is to see your face,
in a tree, in the sun coming out, in the air.

What I want
is to hear the falcon drum
and light again on your forearm.

You say, Tell him I am not here.
The sound of that brusque dismissal becomes what I want.

To see in every palm your elegant silver coin-shavings,
to turn with the wheel of the rain,

to fall with the falling bread of every experience,
to swim like a huge fish in ocean water.

To be Jacob recognizing Joseph,
to be a desert mountain instead of a city.

I am tired of cowards.
I want to live with lions, with Moses.
Not whining teary people.
I want the ranting of drunkards.

I want to sing like birds sing,
not worrying who hears, or what they think.

Last night a great teacher went door to door with a lamp,
He who is not to be found is the one I am looking for.

Beyond wanting, beyond place, inside form, that one.
A flute says, I have no hope of finding that.

But love plays and is the music played.
Let that musician finish this poem.

Shams, I am a waterbird
flying into the sun.

14.
Osho

Osho was very generous with his genius. When I went to Poona in 1988, he answered a question of mine. "Rumi says, 'I want burning, burning.' What does this burning have to do with my own possible enlightenment?"

"You have asked a very dangerous question, Coleman. Burning has nothing to do with your enlightenment. This work you have done with Rumi is beautiful. It has to be, because it is coming out of Rumi's love. But for you these poems can become ecstatic self-hypnosis."

He pretty much nailed me to the floor with that one. *Sufism is good, but end up with Zen.* It was a fine hit he gave me. I am still drawn to the Sufi longing and love-madness, but clarity is coming up strong on the inside. I have not assimilated his wisdom yet, but I mean to. I am very grateful to him. But it is not wisdom for everyone. Osho crafted his words to suit the individual. Ecstatic self-hypnosis might be just the thing for someone else. He was showing me a daylight beyond any beloved darkness, an ecstatic sobriety beyond any drunkenness.

FRIDAY

For a dervish every day feels like Friday,
the beginning of a holiday,
a fresh setting out that will not find an end.

Dressed in the soul's handsomeness,
you are a whole month of Fridays,
sweet outside, sweet in.

Your mind and your deep being walk together
as friends walk along inside their friendship.

Debris does not stay in place on a fast-running creek.
Let grudges wash out into the sea.

Your soul's eye watches a spring-green branch moving,
while these other eyes love the old stories.

MUSK IN A SMALL BOX

Two things that are impossible:
To fill a saddlebag with air,
and to make a lover of God repent.

If guilt and atonement were an ocean,
I would not be wet.

If I were buried in the ground,
the earth would start smoking and catch fire.

Particles keep turning,
and my soul keeps imagining and desiring.

That is its work, my livelihood.
A saddle maker rides to another town,
but he still makes saddles.

Everything alive goes to the grave.
Be a slave to the ground.

Musk in a small box stays musky.
Whenever your heart grows light
inside your chest, your chest is not a dungeon,
but a sky, a great pasture.

Babies get very happy in the womb.
Blood is better than wine for them.
The smallness is a rose garden.

I hesitate to say this,
because it might be misunderstood.

A HUNDRED AND ONE

Your life has been a mad gamble. Make it moreso.
You have lost now a hundred times running.
Roll the dice a hundred and one.

You have become a single string stretched on the fret.
Expect to be struck.

Falcon's claw on the dove's soft side,
you cannot find your home again?
Hire a guide.

You have carved a pretend piece of wood.
This is my horse, you say.
Fine. Ride it to the next level.

You do not hear God talking to you?
You pray instead.
That is prayer without worship, brother.
You must bow completely down to be beheaded.

Garlic and onion smell wonderful,
but try to catch the fragrance of amber.

When Shams accepts you as companion,
sit near him and listen.

A MAN TALKING TO HIS HOUSE

I say that no one in this caravan is awake
and that while you sleep a thief is stealing
the signs and symbols of what you thought was your life.

Now you are angry with me for telling you this.
Pay attention to those who hurt your feelings
telling you the truth.

Giving and absorbing compliments
is like trying to paint on water,
that insubstantial.

Here is how a man once talked to his house.
Please, if you are ever about to collapse, let me know.

One night without a word the house fell.
What happened to our agreement?

The house answered, Day and night I have been telling you
with cracks and broken boards and holes appearing
like mouths opening. But you kept patching
and filling those with mud, so proud
of your stopgap masonry you did not listen.

This house is your body, which is always saying,
I am leaving. I'm going soon.

Do not hide from one who knows the secret.
Drink the wine of turning toward God.

Do not examine your urine.
Examine instead how you praise, what you wish for,
this longing we have been given.

Fall turns pale light yellow wanting spring,
and spring arrives. Seeds blossom.

Come to the orchard, and see what comes to you,
a silent conversation with your soul.

THE TIME OF DIVULGING

December is gone, along with January and February.
Spring is here. Tulip buds appear.

The empty trees stagger and flail
like drunks going home.

The wind recites a spell.
The rose arbor trembles.

The dark blue water lotus, niluphar, says to the jasmine,
Look how twisted together we are.

Clover blossom to meadow grass,
This is the grace we have wanted.

The violets bow, responding to the hyacinths,
and the narcissus winks, An interesting development.

The willow slings her light-headed hair around,
saying nothing, and the cypress grows even more still.

Everybody is so beautifully becoming themselves.
Artists go outdoors
to let the beauty move through their hands and brushes.

Sweet-feathered birds light on the pulpit.
The soul sings, *Ya Hu*. The dove sings, *Coo, coo*.

The roses open their shirts. It is not right
to stay closed when the time of divulging comes.

One rosebud remarks to the nightingale,
Lilies have hundreds of tongues,
but they do not tell their secrets.

No more holding back. Be reckless.
Tell your love to everybody.

And so the nightingale does.
The plane tree bends to the vine,
Stand up. The prostrating part of prayer is over.

The vine, This prostration is not voluntary.
I have that in me that makes me always like this,
burning with surrender, flat on my face.
It is the same power that makes you plane.

The rose asks the saffron, Why so pale?

The plump red apple replies,
Because saffron does not understand
that the beloved is absence as well as this fullness.

Just then stones begin bombarding him,
but he laughs, knowing how lover calls to lover.

Zuleikha tears Joseph's shirt,
but that is love-play to make him naked.

The apple absorbs a direct hit but stays on the tree.
I hang here like Hallaj, feeling those lips on me,
the honor of being lifted up on a crucifixion apple tree.

Now the kissing is over.
Fold your love in. Hide it like pastry filling.
Whisper within with a shy girl's tenderness.

HOLIDAY WITHOUT LIMITS

Going into battle, we carry no shield.
Playing in concert, unaware of the beat or the melody.

We have become grains on the ground underfoot,
fold on fold, layers of love, nothing else.

Obliterated, as when the eye medicine
is no longer even a powder.
Then it cures sight.

An accident gradually gets accepted
as the thing that needed to happen.
Sickness melts into health.

There is nothing worse than staying congealed.
Let your liver dissolve into blood.
Let your heart break into such tiny pieces
that it cannot be found.

The moon orb wanes. Then for three days
you could say there is no moon.

That is the moon that has drawn so close to the sun,
it is nowhere, and everywhere.

Send us someone who can sing music for the soul,
though we know such longing cannot rise from a lute
or a tambourine, not from the sun,
or Venus, or any star.

As day comes, give back the night-fantasy things you stole.
Admit your arrogance as the stars do at dawn.

When the sun goes down, Venus begins bragging,
claiming light, arguing her loveliness over the moon.

Jupiter lifts a gold coin from his bag.
Mars shows his blade to Saturn.
Mercury sits on a high throne
and gives himself successive titles.

That is how it goes in the middle of the night.
Then dawn. Jupiter is suddenly poor.
Mars and Saturn have no plans.
Venus and the moon run away, broken and terrified.

Then the sun within the sun enters,
and this night-and-day talk
seems a meaningless convention,
the lighting business.

A true holy day for a man or a woman is the one
when they bring themselves as the sacrifice.

When Shams shone his light from nowhere,
I felt a holiday without limits begin
where once was just a person.

WE CANNOT DECIDE

There has never been beauty like yours.
Your face, your eyes, your presence.

We cannot decide which we love most,
your gracefulness or your generosity.

I came with many knots in my heart,
like the magician's rope.

You undid them all at once.
I see now the splendor of the student,
and that of the teacher's art.

Love and this body sit inside your presence,
one demolished, the other drunk.

We smile. We weep,
tree limbs turning sere, then light green.

Any power that comes through us is you.
Any wish. What does a rock know of April?

It is better to ask the flowery grass,
the jasmine, and the redbud branch.

I PASS BY THE DOOR

My face and hair age and gray with being apart
from the one who whispers in my ear, *Do not listen.*
To my eyes, *Do not look.*

With our grief-shoes tied by happy hands,
we keep reaching for big rocks to keep us from sinking.

I pass by the door where the source of my loving is,
and I see how it is: face wild, shirt torn,
no sense of right or left. *How can I help?*

Then begins a moaning
for the one already there in the room.

JOSEPH

Joseph has come, the handsome one of this age,
a victory banner floating over spring flowers.

Those of you whose work it is to wake the dead,
get up. This is a work day.

The lion that hunts lions charges into a meadow.
Yesterday and the day before are gone.

The coin of *now* slaps down in your hand,
with the streets and buildings of this city all saying,
The prince is coming! A drumbeat starts.

What we hear about the friend is true. The beauty
of that peacefulness makes the whole world restless.

Spread your robe out to catch
what sifts down from the ninth level.

You strange exiled bird with clipped wings,
now you have four full-feathered pinions.

You heart closed up in a chest, open.
The friend is entering you.

You feet, it is time to dance.
Do not talk about the old man. He is young again.

And do not mention the past. Do you understand?
The beloved is *here*.

You mumble, But what excuse can I give the king?
When the king is making excuses to you.

You say, How can I escape his hand?
When *that hand* is trying to help you.

You saw fire, and light came.
You expected blood. Wine is being poured.

Do not run from your tremendous good fortune.
Be silent and do not try to add up what has been given.

An uncountable grace has come to you.

NO DISCUSSION

West or East, there has been no lover like me.
My sky bends back like a bow at full draw for centuries.

I am the lucky one who wakes for a lover's touch.
With bitter medicine, I taste sweet juice.
If you resent the cure, you stay sick.

Apprentice bows to master in silence,
no impudent banter, no discussion.
Underwater, divers hold their breath.

BURNT KABOB

Last year, I admired wines.
This, I am wandering inside the red world.

Last year, I gazed at the fire.
This, I am burnt kabob.

Thirst drove me down to the water
where I drank the moon's reflection.

Now I am a lion
staring up totally lost in love with the thing itself.

Do not ask questions about longing.
Look in my face.

Soul-drunk, body-ruined,
these two sit helpless in a wrecked wagon.
Neither knows how to fix it.

And my heart, I would say
it was a donkey sunk in a mud hole,
struggling and miring deeper.

But listen to me.
For one moment, quit being sad.
Hear blessings dropping their blossoms around you. God.

OUR TURN

The ground is turning green.
The king's drum begins. Light arrives. Get up.

Commentaries on the heart have come in seven volumes.
A love-messenger runs with his head down
like an ink pen giving a dark sweetness to the page.

The pure spirits gather again, the ones we thought were dead.
Planets go anywhere they want.
Venus sways drunkenly over to the North Star.
The moon holds on to Leo.

I hope everything is all right.

The host who has no self has come.

Now it is our turn to look into those eyes.

A child is still a child even after he has learned the alphabet.
Joy reaches into the mountains.
Solomon holds out a morning cup, Welcome.
Sit down in this dazzling pavilion.
Be silent, and let the poet sing the delight that never ends.

LOVE'S NIGHTCAP

Yesterday you put a crown on my head
that, no matter how one strikes it, will not fall off,
love's nightcap, with your handstitching around the brow.

Even if my head is not in it,
because it is your gift to me.
My head becomes a pearl
lifted from the jewel box.

Prove it. Here is a heavy mace.
See if I am more bone and marrow than soul.

Inside this skull-nut there is almond essence
to sweeten lip and throat and put light in the eyes.

So no more complaining.
Jesus did not ask, Where is my donkey?
There was just one less donkey in the herd.

The strength of a rider does not come from his lean mount,
but from his love.

Do not say *Ah, ah,* when you are hurt. Say *Allah.*

Joseph did not talk about his time down in the well,
but rather of sitting on the throne in Egypt.

ANSWERS FROM THE ELEMENTS

A whole afternoon field inside me from one stem of reed.
The messenger comes running toward me, irritated.
Why be so hard to find?

Last night I asked the moon about the moon,
my one question for the visible world. *Where is God?*

The moon says, I am dust stirred up when he passed by.
The sun says, My face is bright from just now seeing him.
Water, I slide on my head and face like a snake
from a spell he said.
Fire, His lightning, I want to be that restless.
Wind, Why so light? I would burn if I had a choice.
Earth, quiet and thoughtful? Inside me,
I have a garden and an underground spring.

The world hurts my head with its answers,
wine filling my hand, not my glass.
If I could wake completely, I would say without speaking
why I am ashamed of using words.

SAY YES QUICKLY

Forget your life. Say *God is great.* Get up.
You think you know what time it is. It is time to pray.
You have carved so many little figurines, too many.
Do not knock on any random door like a beggar.
Reach your long hand out to another door,
beyond where you go on the street, the street

where everyone says, *How are you?*
And no one says, *How aren't you?*

Tomorrow you will see
what you have broken and torn tonight thrashing in the dark.
Inside you there is an artist you don't know about.
He is not interested in how things look different in moonlight.

If you are here unfaithfully with us,
you are causing terrible damage.
If you have opened your loving to God's love,
you are helping people you do not know
and have never seen.

Is what I say true? Say yes quickly,
if you know, if you have known it
from before the beginning of the universe.

BASRA DATES

Without you there is no joy in either world.
No fire, no wonder.

I often listen at the center of my chest,
and I hear much conversation there,
but I have seen no lips move.

You scatter compassion over me for no reason,
apple of eyesight.
No likeness of you has ever appeared in Persia or Arabia.

Be lavish with the wine not made from juice,
poured into glasses finer than Aleppo crystal.

Help me walk out of my selfhood, my tired existence.

You are the sun and the moon, sustenance,
father and mother, my only lineage,
eternity manifested, refuge unnameable.

Brother, leave your learning and culture.
Civilization lives inside this being drawn.

Shams, the best dates come from Basra,
but I would have known the taste of your soul
had I never been in the Basra of your presence.

RAGGEDNESS

I was dead, then alive,
weeping, then laughing.

The power of love came into me,
and I became fierce like a lion,
then tender like the evening star.

He said, You are not mad enough.
You do not belong in this house.

I went wild and had to be tied up.
He said, Still not wild enough to stay with us.

I broke through another layer into joyfulness.
He said, It is not enough. I died.

He said, You are a clever little man,
full of fantasy and doubting.

I plucked out my feathers and became a fool.
He said, Now you are the candle for this assembly.

But I am no candle. Look. I am scattered smoke.

He said, You are the sheikh, the guide.
But I am not a teacher. I have no power.

He said, You already have wings.
I cannot give you wings.

But I wanted his wings.
I felt like some flightless chicken.

Then new events said to me, *Do not move.*
A sublime generosity is coming toward you.

And old love said, *Stay with me.*
I said, I will.

You are the fountain of the sun's light.
I am a willow shadow on the ground.
You make my raggedness silky.

The soul at dawn is like darkened water
that slowly begins to say, Thank you. Thank you.

Then at sunset, Venus gradually changes
into the moon and then into the whole nightsky.

This comes of smiling back at your smile.
The chess master says nothing,
other than moving the silent chess piece.

That I am part of the ploys of this game
makes me amazingly happy.

A GREAT WAGON

When I see your face, the stones start spinning.
You appear. All studying wanders.
I lose my place.

Water turns pearly.
Fire dies down and does not destroy.

In your presence I do not want
what I thought I wanted,
those three little hanging lamps.

Inside your face the ancient manuscripts
seem like rusty mirrors.

You breathe. New shapes appear,
and the music of a desire
as widespread as spring
begins to move like a great wagon.

Drive slowly.
Some of us walking alongside are lame.

SEE WHERE IT COMES FROM

Word is, you are no longer looking for us.
Word is, your music,
which has always told the story of our friendship,
does not even hint of that now.

Did you hear me say how quick your temper is,
or that you are the world's sweetness
that sometimes turns sour?

Is that why you are distant?
Test this poem.
See where it comes from in me.

THE OVEN'S QUESTION

I am black cumin seeds thrown in the fire of your beauty.
I live inside this fire. It is my home,
this arrow being drawn back in a bow made of flame.

When a lover burns, he becomes the beloved.
Whoever enters this becomes a soul.

Your sword has opened my chest.
Sparks jump over one who has already burned completely up.

The pain of love is fire.
Make my dry wood ache to catch.

Some souls are like jasmine growing inside flame.
Others are roses thriving there.
Only Abraham speaks the language fire speaks.
He comes like smoke riding up out of a fire,
the reins of flame-turning-to-smoke in his hands.

I have heard him in the early morning
telling me to leap out of the world's fire into *his* fire.

Now the oven of my heart keeps asking,
How long do I have to talk with flame-language
about burning and being burned? How long?

15.
Ramana Maharshi

Ramana Maharshi (1879–1950) condensed the soul's longing to the question, "Who am I?" and the further refinement, "Who is asking that?" He was after the witness at the core, the I within the I of the most interior region, that place where we all meet and rest, the eye behind the mind that watches the other senses. The witness. Ramana suggests that we live in a continuous inquiry, a state of always looking into the wonder of identity. Ramana lived much of his life in a small cave in the mountain Arunachala, in south India, doing just that. He loved that mountain so deeply that it became a symbol of the inner Self that gave him such freedom and energetic delight. He claimed that *knowing who you are* is the easiest thing there is, the most natural and the most obvious. There is a stillness inside the heart. Discover the Self and live there. Ramana was asked once if one could have more than one spiritual master. He replied, "Who is a master? He is the Self after all. According to the stages of the development of the mind, the Self manifests as the Master externally. The most famous saint Avadhuta said that he had more than twenty-four Masters. The Master is one from whom one learns anything. The Guru may sometimes be inanimate also. God, Guru, and Self are identical." This quote is from *Talks with Sri Ramana Maharshi*, first published in 1955. It is available on Amazon. I highly recommend it to anyone who feels the truth of Ramana. Friends have given me a large picture of Arunachala. I have it above the chair where I meditate. I am not very successful in quieting the mind, but I have moments. The image of Ramana's mountain helps. Walking may be a better way for me than sitting with my eyes closed.

Perhaps I should have put more Westerners in here as names for the Mystery: Thoreau, Meister Eckhart, St. Francis, Dostoyevsky. And H. W. L. Poonja must be mentioned as the hilarious continuation of Ramana's insight. He has a wonderful *satsang* talk about emptiness. It is the best I know of. Or try to find a recording of his talks and listen to his laughing. Learn from that. In his talking with me, Osho made a pun that applies here. He said, "The word *Rumi* is beautiful, not in Persian, but in English. A *room*, when it is emptied of furniture, is more *roomy*." That *spaciousness* of deep being is what I feel around the quatrains, and also around the whole of his writing. It was the way it felt to enter his world in 1976, and the way it still feels, like a sky and a freedom within that.

WOULD YOU BOW?

If the friend rose inside you, would you bow?
Would you wonder where that one came from and how?

If you say, *I will bow,* that is important.
If you answer, *But can I be sure?*
it will keep the meeting from happening,
as busy people rush there and back here murmuring,
Now I know; no, I don't know now.

Have you seen a camel with its eyes covered
turn and walk one way, then turn and walk another?

Be silent and revolve with no will.
Do not raise your hand to ask anything.

Holy one, sitting in the body's well like Joseph,
a rope is there in front of you. Lift your hand to that.

A blind man has bought you for eighteen counterfeit coins.
Empty metal cups bang together,
and the full moon slides out of hiding.

Make one sound, please.
You are the precious hyacinth that the sickle will spare,
not the wheat plant Adam ate.

I remind you with these poems
to dress in the flower of God's qualities,
not your torn robe of self-accusation.

I AM NOT THIS

I am not this. Your beauty closes my eyes,
and I am falling into that.

You cut the umbilical with this love
that has been with me since birth.

My mother saw your mountain reflected in my face,
you that lift coverings, you that bring death.

We agreed on this before creation.
I have been so hidden.

Ask my body who I am. It says, *Solid ground*.
Ask my soul. *Dizzy as the wind*. Neither.
I stand here facing Shams Tabriz.

I MET ONE TRAVELING

In the evening between sleep and awakening,
I met one traveling.

He was the light of consciousness.
His body was soul.
His pure wisdom was apparent in his beautiful face.

He praises me for a while, then scolds:
You sit on the seven-sky throne, in prison.

The sign of Gemini has set a table for you,
yet you stick your head down a drainhole again.

Essence is not nourished with food and sleep.
Do no one any harm in this time-field of short crops,
where what you sow comes up very quickly.

You try to accomplish things, to win, to reach goals.
This is not the true situation.
Put the whole world in ambition's stomach,
it will never be enough.

Assume you get everything you want.
Assume you have it now.
What's the point? The next moment you die.

Friend, the youth you have lived is ending.
You sleep a drunken dreamless sleep
with no sense what morning you could wake inside.

THE ONLY OBLIGATION

Today a new madness is trying to set us free,
tearing open our sacks.

Some nameless Bedouin has bought Joseph again
for eighteen coins.

A narcissus sprouts through the ground.
Our souls, having pastured all night on jasmine,
leap up for the dawn.

The world is new,
and you have been chosen to say this poem,
because you are the one with the love-bites on you.

Your love has brought us to this silence,
where the only obligation
is to walk slowly through a meadow and look.

STRUCK TENT

I am the tent you set up, then strike.
Quill pen you sharpen, then bear down on and split.

Flagstaff with the emblem upside down,
particle in window light, galaxy.

I am all skin, yet soul as well.
Without you, I am a fake.
With, as real as the cool spring ground warming.

You say, I keep my distance
to see what dance you will do out in the air,
little dustgrain.

Why would the sun speak to one bit?
Friend, you destroy and you restore.

Do what must be done to this love
that has no fear and no sense of being safe.

EMPTY BOAT

Some huge work goes on growing.
How could one person's words matter?

Where you walk heads pop up from the ground.
What is one seed head compared to you?

On my death day I will know the answer.
I have cleared this house,
so that your work can, when it comes, fill every room.

I slide like an empty boat pulled over the water.

INFIDEL FISH

The ocean way is this fish way
of the water-souls of fish who die becoming the sea.
Fish do not wait patiently for water.

In this world full of shape there you are with no form.

You have made a universe from a drop of my blood.
Now I am confused. I cannot tell world from drop,
my mouth and this wine glass, one lip.

I am *Nohbdy*, the fool shepherd.
Where is my flock? What shepherd?

When I talk of you, there are no words.
Where could I put you,
who will not fit in the secret world, or this?

All I know of spirit is this love.

And do not call me a believer.
Infidel is better.

WHEN YOUR SECRET IS SPOKEN

This is your moment,
a drumbeat of faithfulness.

Red flowers open.
Grapes are being crushed into wine.
Soul and rational clarity sit down together at your table.
All desire wants is a taste of you.

The two realities are two small villages in your world.
Everyone longs for your presence.
As we start to step up, your ladder arrives.

You say, I am more compassionate
than your mother or your father.
I will make medicine out of your pain.
From your smoke I create new constellations.

I tell you everything,
and yet I do not say it all,
because, my friend, it is better
when your secret is spoken by you.

BABY PIGEON

A baby pigeon stands on the edge of a nest all day.
Then he hears a whistle, *Come to me.*
How could he not fly toward that?

Wings tear through the body's robe
when a letter arrives that says,

You have flapped and fluttered against limits long enough.
You have been a bird without wings
in a house without doors or windows.

Compassion builds a door.
Restlessness cuts a key.

Ask. Step off into air like a baby pigeon.
Strut proudly into sunlight, not looking back.

Take sips of this pure wine being poured.
Do not mind that you have been given an unwashed cup.

AN EGYPT THAT DOES NOT EXIST

I want to say words that flame as I say them,
but I keep quiet and do not try
to make both worlds fit in one mouthful.

I keep secret in myself
an Egypt that does not exist.
Is that good or bad? I do not know.

For years, I gave away sexual love with my eyes.
Now I don't. I am not in any one place.
I do not have a name for what I give away.
Whatever Shams gave, that you can have from me.

BE MELTING SNOW

Totally conscious, and apropos of nothing, you come to me.
Is someone here? I ask.
The moon. The full moon is in your house.

My friends and I go running out into the street.
I'm in here, comes a voice from the house,
but we aren't listening.

We are looking up at the sky.
My pet nightingale sobs like a drunk in the garden.
Ringdoves scatter with small cries, *Where. Where.*

It is midnight. The whole neighborhood
is up and out in the street
thinking, *The cat-burglar has come back.*
The actual thief is there too, saying out loud,
Yes. *The cat-burglar is somewhere in this crowd.*
No one pays attention.

Lo I am with you always means when you look for God,
God is in the look of your eyes,
in the thought of looking, nearer to you than your self,
or things that have happened to you.
There is no need to go outside.
Be melting snow.
Wash yourself of yourself.

A white flower grows in the quietness.
Let your tongue become that flower.

WHY AM I SO BLESSED?

You keep coming out of my chest into visibility,
singing songs, telling tangled stories.

With one breath a universe whirls into being.
You wash the world.
You tighten the string around my finger.

But why am I so blessed,
with a Joseph and a Job on every side,
whose houses have been broken into
and their sweet-smelling linens stolen?

Now you lead a procession into the cemetery
as though it is a garden.

You shout, *Rise and dance,*
and they do, the ancient dead, the newly dead,
so happy to be out in the air again,
the graveyard looks like a marketplace on holiday.

I am not saying these things to appear visionary and spiritual.
I have seen this happen in ways I cannot express.

Always test a high-sounding remark.
If someone claims, *I have left all that,*
see if his shirt is torn in the back.

Tell the word-men to quit talking
and listen to the grief a lover feels.

Be relentless in your looking,
because you are the one you seek.

WANDERING WILDERNESS

We have come to that knee of seacoast
no ocean can reach.

Tie together all human intellects.
They will not stretch to here.

The sky bares its neck so beautifully, but gets no kiss.
Only a taste. This is the food that everyone wants,
wandering the wilderness.

Please give us your manna and quail.

We are here with the beloved again.
This air, a shout. These meadowsounds,
an astonishing myth.

We have come into the presence of the one
who was never apart from us.

When the water bag is filling,
you know that the water-carrier is here.

The bag leans lovingly against your shoulder.
Without you I have no knowledge,
no way to touch anyone.

When someone chews sugarcane,
he is wanting this sweetness.

Inside this globe the soul roars like thunder.
Now silence, my strict tutor.

I will not try to talk about Shams.
Language cannot touch that presence.

COME BACK, MY FRIEND

What was in that candle's light
that opened and consumed me so quickly?

Come back, my friend.
The form of our love is not a created form.

Nothing can help me but that beauty.
There was a dawn I remember
when my soul heard something from your soul.

I drank water from your spring
and felt the current take me.

I AM MORE THE WAY YOU ARE

The one who loses patience with us
is the one who stays and protects.

You are the iris and the rose
and the fall that ruins flowers.

Sing the spring and admit that you are also thorn.
Everything that exists is talking and not talking at once.
Everything looks at and with and through you.

The nightingale bestows a definite desire.
There is the ocean and there is a bridge.
There are these two or three numbered days.

I am none of those.
I am more the way you are,
flowers opening and the soul in silence,
but something in *you* will not let *me* keep quiet.

I try to hide like a clever quarry,
but you hunt the hunter and the prey.
You purify by staying apart.

The fragrance of everyone's laughter
is your work and your gift to us,
as well as the weeping.

A CLOSED JAR

You wreck my mind with your foolishness.
I am the closed jar you ferment inside.

Beginning and end, outer and essential,
you are king and prince, doorkeeper, nightwatch,
bad manners, good, pleasure, discomfort.

You are tender, green, and fresh,
fascinating like an earring of intelligence.

Remote and close as kin.
Past and future, you are the friend who turns malicious.

You hurt and soothe like poison dissolved in sherbet.
An ecstatic, God-surrendered bunch is bumbling along the road.
You ambush and rob them.
The caravan then becomes a shape for your beauty.

Some days I argue and make noise.
Other days, more absorbed in you, I stay quiet.

ALMOST IN SIGHT

We cannot help being thirsty,
moving toward the voice of water.

Milk-drinkers draw close to the mother.
Muslims, Christians, Jews, Buddhists, Hindus,
shamans, everyone hears the intelligent sound
and moves, with thirst, to meet it.

Clean your ears.
Do not listen for something you have heard before.

Invisible camel bells, slight footfalls in sand.
Almost in sight.
The first word they call out
will be the last word of our last poem.

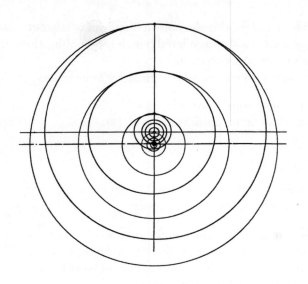

16.
Dissolving the Concept
of "God"

A Navajo prayer song says, "I walk in beauty." I have always felt the truth of that. We live within something like a presence, a beauty. Rumi sometimes calls it the "rose." Sometimes "absence" or "nothing." Simply to be is an act of praise. We are part of what is carrying us along. However we experience and participate in that is religion. The word "God" has become almost unusable for me. Whatever the sacred is, it is a flowing. Evolving qualities in consciousness. Music, changing light. That does not mean that what the word "God" tries to point to— the mystical layers, the mysterious source, the depths of love inside consciousness, inner-outer synchronicities, the ocean of energy and intelligence that animates everything—are not real. They are, it is, the great reality. But the word and the concept are so freighted with doctrine and violence for me, that I mostly leave them alone, though not always.

I do not necessarily recommend this as a way for others. I have to admit that I do like to hear others give it a try, the attempt to describe the mystery we inhabit, that inhabits us. Carl Jung says, "The Self (God) is a circle whose center is everywhere, whose circumference is nowhere." Heraclitus says, "The soul is undiscovered, though explored forever to a depth beyond report." And Bawa Muhaiyaddeen (who certainly does not shrink from using the word) says, "God has no form. God is a treasure without form or self-image, a treasure that can give peace and tranquility to human life. Just as there exists a point on the tongue that perceives taste and a point of light within the eye that can see, God exists as a point in the wisdom of life, a point within faith, a power. God is a power, and that power can be seen within you." Many would call that point, that power that comes through the human form especially, grace.

A QUESTION

We fall in love constantly
as we admire and closely watch our own faces.

There is a question about who is happier,
the onlookers or the soul?

Does the wine glass ever get tipsy?
There is wine, the soul, the heart, and this assortment of friends.
Where does the work take place?

Love is the religion, yet we are the blasphemy too,
belief and unbelief singing the same song.

You cannot grow knowledgeable enough to understand this,
and you cannot remain ignorant enough to understand this.

THE TASTE OF MORNING

Time's knife slides from the sheath,
as a fish from where it swims.

Being closer and closer is the desire of the body.
Do not wish for union.

There is a closeness beyond that.
Why would God want a second God?

Fall in love in such a way
that it frees you from any connecting.

Love is the soul's light, the taste of morning,
no *me*, no *we*, no claim of *being*.

These words are the smoke the fire gives off
as it absolves its defects,
as eyes in silence, tears, face.
Love cannot be said.

YOU ARE AS YOU ARE

Yesterday, you made a promise.
Today, you broke it. Yesterday, Bestami's dance.
Today, dregs thrown out.

In pieces, and at the same time,
a perfect glass filled with sunlight.

Give up on figuring the appearances,
the dressing in green like a Sufi.

You do not resemble anyone.
You are not the bride or the groom.

You do not fit in a house with a family.
You have left the closed-in corner where you lived.

Domestic animals get ridden to work.
Not you. You are as you are,
an indescribable message coming on the air.

Every word you say is medicine.
But not yet: Stay quiet and still.

THORN WITNESS

Apparent shapes and meanings change.
Creature hunts down creature.
Bales get unloaded and weighed to determine price.

None of this pertains to the unseen fire
we call the beloved. That presence has no form
and cannot be understood or measured.

Take your hands away from your face.
If a wall of dust moves across the plain,
there is usually an army advancing under it.

When you look for the friend,
the friend is looking for you.

Carried by a strong current, you and the others with you
seem to be making decisions, but you are not.

I weave coarse wool. I decide to talk less.
But my actions cause nothing.

A thorn grows next to the rose as its witness.
I am that thorn for whom simply to *be*
is an act of praise. Near the rose, no shame.

THE SELF WE SHARE

Thirst is angry at water. Hunger, bitter with bread.
The cave wants nothing to do with the sun.

This is dumb, the self-defeating way we have been.
A gold mine is calling us into its temple.
Instead, we bend and keep picking up rocks from the ground.

Every *thing* has a shine like gold,
but we should turn to the source.
The origin is what we truly are.

I add a little vinegar to the honey I give.
The bite of scolding makes the ecstasy more familiar.

But look, fish, you are already in the ocean.
Just swimming there makes you friends with glory.

What are these grudges about? You are Benjamin.
Joseph has put a gold cup in your grain sack
and accused you of being a thief.

Now he draws you aside and says,
You are my brother. I am a prayer. You are the amen.

We move in eternal regions,
yet we worry about property here.

This is the prayer of each: You are the source of my life.
You separate essence from mud. You honor my soul.

You bring rivers from the mountain springs.
You brighten my eyes. The wine you offer
takes me out of my self into the self we share.
Doing that is religion.

STRANDED SOMEWHERE

If you are the body,
that one is the soul of the universe.

If you are soul,
that one is the soul within all souls.

Wherever you go, whatever you are,
listen for the voice that asks, Who will be sacrificed tonight?

Jump up and volunteer.
Accept this cup that is offered every second.

Love has written the thousand subtleties of this on my face.
Read. If you are bored and contemptuous,
love is a walk in a meadow.

If you are stranded somewhere and exhausted,
love is an Arabian horse.

The ocean feeds itself to its fish.
If you are an ocean fish,
why bother with bread the ground grows?

These jars of grief and trouble we call bodies,
throw stones and break them.

My cage is this longing for Shams.
Be my worst enemy. Shatter it.

LET THE SOUP SIMMER

As the air of April holds a rosebush,
I draw you to myself.

But why mention roses?
You are the whole, the soul,
the spirit, the speaker, and what follows *Say*,
the quarry and the bowstring pulled to the ear.

The lion turns to the deer,
Why are you running in my wake?

There are thousands of levels
from what lives in the soil to humanity,
but I have brought you along from town to town.
I will not leave you somewhere on the side of the road.

Let the soup simmer with the lid on.
Be quiet.

There is a lion cub hidden in the deer body.

You are the polo ball.
With my mallet I make you run.
Then I track you.

LIKE A FIG

Who turns bitterness to love?
Who changes the poisonous snake around your neck to pearls?

The kind king who makes a demon a sweetheart,
who changes funeral to feast,
and blindness from birth to world-beholding sight.

Who pulls the thorn from your palm
and puts a pillow of roses under your head.

For one, he kindles fire.
For another, the flames blossom
to eglantine around the head.

The same that lights the stars
helps those who cannot help anyone anymore.

What used to be thought of as sin
scatters off like December leaves
and disappears, completely forgiven.

Amen says *who-is-it*, the joy of inside and out.
Like a fig this presence is all tasty.

A rapture that is physical strength in the hand and foot,
and reality for the soul.

I send my love out now to ride the sunlight
and take this account of Shams
to those waiting faithfully in Tabriz.

WINTER OR SUMMER

The great river that turns the bend of the sky is here.
The mallet that when it strikes the ball
becomes ball, sky, and ground is here.
Noah, who built the ark with his carpenter's discernment,
is here with us now.

He hands you a bite to eat.
You become a healer.

Do you love winter or summer more?
You may have whichever you like,
winter for you, summer for me.

Rose and thorn are equal here.
One contracts into itself with a wound.
One opens out and luxuriates.

One jumps in water that turns to fire.
One walks into fire, and it is sweet basil.

Doubt becomes proof.
A fallen angel, who did not see the human glory,
gets born as a person, and vice versa.

Khidr distributes living water.
Animals rise from the dead.

Philosophers call this the *primal cause*.
Now this blesses those philosophers with kindness.
The whole of existence is a mirror whose essence you are.

Breathe lightly, or it will cloud.
Belief and disbelief do not matter.

Be ignorant here.
Knowing and imagining are always after something,
like a blind man going door to door,
and *not* asking for salve to heal his own eyes.

These words would love to change your body to soul.
Fish do not worry where the shore begins.
Someone not in the water, not a fish, considers those boundaries.

Walk the lover's road with truth and humility.
Those two will take your hand and sit you down by Shams.

WHEREABOUTS UNKNOWN

Every moment is a taste of that beauty in our mouths,
another stashed in a pocket.

Impossible to say what: no cypress so handsome,
no sunlight, a lonely hiddenness.

Other pleasure gathers a crowd,
starts a fight, lots of noise there.

But soul beauty stays quiet.
Shams and his amazing whereabouts unknown
inside my heart.

DRAWN BY SOUP

I try to imagine the most sumptuous meal.
Bugra Khan, general of the armies east of here,
has an autumn night banquet celebrating himself.

The archangel Gabriel arrives as Abraham's guest,
fatted calf roasting.

Then the truly perfect setting, unimaginary,
your voice at dawn and the fragrance of soup.

I follow the simmering that pulls me
into a light-filled kitchen.

I ask the cook for a taste. This is not for human beings.
Please. You strike my head with a skimming spoon.
Mind drops away. *True hospitality*.

THE LAST OF YOUR WINE

I am sober now. Hand me my turban.
Fill the skin jug, or give it back empty, whichever.

A toast, innkeeper.
Half a cup for you, half for us.

No. Wait. Give us a full container.
You who lure men and women into this longing,
break down my door tonight. Steal what I claim to own.

The ocean could be fresh and clear
if you would spill two drops into its water.

The moon and the evening star would dip down like birds,
if you threw the last of your wine into the air.

I AM NOT

I am not the centuries-ago Muhammad.
I listen inside this day like a fresh-fired Phoenix,
not some pigeon looking for seed.

There is a king for whom other kings are stable boys.
Some sip Hallaj's wine.
I drink his truth by the jar, by the barrel.

Qibla for the soul, Kaaba for the heart.
I am the constant sky,
not a Friday mosque's ceiling dome.

Clean mirror, no rust.
I am the burning core of Mt. Sinai,
not a mind full of hatred.

I taste a wine not pressed from grapes.
The one everyone calls to
when they are in sudden mortal danger,
I am That.

Gabriel could sit here beside me,
if he became God.

THIS LOVE WHICH IS MADE OF OUR LOVE FOR EMPTINESS

Praise to the emptiness that blanks out existence.
Existence: This place made of our love for that emptiness.
Yet somehow comes emptiness, this existence goes.
Praise to that happening, over and over.

For years I pulled my own existence out of emptiness.
Then one swoop, one swing of the arm,
that work is over.

Free of who I was, free of presence,
free of dangerous fear, hope, free of mountainous wanting.
The here-and-now mountain is a tiny piece of a piece of straw
blown off into emptiness.

These words I am saying so much begin to lose meaning.
Existence, emptiness, mountain, straw.
Words and what they try to say,
swept out the window, down the slant of the roof.

THE WHOLE PLACE GOES UP

Today with spring here finally
we ought to be living outdoors with our friends.
Let's go to those strangers in the field
and dance around them like bees from flower to flower
building in the beehive air our true hexagonal homes.

Someone comes in from outside saying,
Do not play music just for yourselves.
Now we are tearing up the house like a drum,
collapsing walls with our pounding.
We hear a voice from the sky
calling the lovers and the odd, lost people.
We scatter lives. We break what holds us,
each one a blacksmith heating iron
and walking to the anvil. We blow on the inner fire.
With each striking we change.

The whole place goes up, all stability gone to smoke.
Sometimes high, sometimes low,
we begin anywhere. We have no method.
We are the bat swung by powerful arms.
Balls keep rolling from us, thousands of them underfoot.

Now we are still. Silence also is wisdom,
a flame hiding in cotton wool.

FLOOD RESIDUE

The taste of today is not that of yesterday.
A pot boils over.

A watchman calls down the ladder,
Did you hear the commotion last night
from the seventh level?

Saturn turns to Venus
and tells her to play the strings more gently.
Taurus milk runs red. Leo slinks from the sky.

Strange signs, because of a word that comes from the soul
to help us escape speaking and concepts.

I answer the nightwatchman,
You will have to assign meanings
for these ominous events.

I have been set free from the hunt,
the catching and being caught,
to rest in these dregs of flood residue, pure and empty.

SPOKEN THINGS

Bird catcher, you hide the snare well
with your fabric and smoke.

You lay out an ingenious feather-design
of all the birds you have caught before.

You have even trained birds to be lookouts,
but I hear what is concealed in their song.

The birds you want are thirsty,
so you open the wine vat and let the fragrance draw us.

This is the wine the Magi brought as a gift
and the wine musk that led them.

There are certain night-wanderers you especially want,
but not the drunkards,
and not those who just carry the cup to others.

This is how it is to come near you.
A wave of light builds in the black pupil of the eye.
The old become young.

The opening lines of the Qur'an open still more.
Inside every human chest there is a hand,
but it has nothing to write with.

Love moves farther in,
where language turns to fresh cream on the tongue.

Every accident, and the essence of every being,
is a bud, a blanket tucked into a cradle, a closed mouth.

All these buds will blossom,
and in that moment you will know what your grief was,
and how the seed you planted
has been miraculously, and naturally, growing.

Now silence.
Let soul speak inside spoken things.

SLEEP

Those who do not feel this love pulling them like a river,
those who do not drink dawn like a cup of springwater
or take in sunset like supper,
those who do not want to change,

let them sleep.

This love is beyond the study of theology,
that old trickery and hypocrisy.

If you want to improve your mind that way,
sleep on.

I have given up on my brain.
I have torn the cloth to shreds and thrown it away.

If you are not completely naked,
wrap your beautiful robe of words around you,
and sleep.

THIS NIGHT OF TALKING

I wish I knew what you wanted.
You block the road and will not give me rest.

You pull my lead-rope one way, then another.
You act cold, my darling. Do you hear what I say?

Will this night of talking ever end?
Why am I still embarrassed and timid about you?

You are thousands. You are one.
Quiet, but most articulate.

Your name is spring. Your name is wine.
Your name is the nausea that comes from wine.

You are my doubting
and the lightpoints in my eyes.

You are every image,
and yet I am homesick for you.

Can I get there?
Where the deer pounces on the lion?
Where the one I am after is after me?

This drum and these words keep pounding.
Let them both smash through their coverings into silence.

YOUR PRESENCE

When I press my hand to my chest,
it is your chest.

And now you are scratching my head.

Sometimes you put me in the herd with your other camels.
Sometimes you put me in the front of the troops as commander.

Sometimes you wet me with your mouth
like you do your seal-ring just before you plant your power.

Sometimes you round me into a simple door knocker.

You take blood and make sperm.
You take sperm and create an animal.
You use the animal to evolve intelligence.
Life keeps leading to more life.

You drive me away gently as a flute song does
a dove from the eaves.
With the same song you call me back.

You push me out on many journeys,
then you anchor me with no motion at all.

I am water.
I am the thorn that catches someone's clothing.

I do not care about marvelous sights.
I only want to be in your presence.

There is nothing to believe.
Only when I quit believing in myself did I come into this beauty.

I saw your blade and burned my shield.
I flew on six hundred pairs of wings like Gabriel.
But now that I am here, what do I need wings for?

Day and night I guarded the pearl of my soul.
Now in this ocean of pearling currents
I have lost track of which was mine.

There is no way to describe you.
Say the end of this so strongly
that I will ride up over my own commotion.

AT THAT MEETING

I may be clapping my hands,
but I do not belong to a crowd of clappers.
I am neither this nor that.

I am not a part of a group that loves flute music,
or one that loves gambling,
or one that loves drinking wine.

Those who live in time, descended from Adam,
made of earth and water, I am not part of that.

Do not listen to what I say, as though these words
came from an inside and are going to an outside.

Your faces are very beautiful,
but they are wooden cages.

You had better run from me.
My words are fire.

I have nothing to do with being famous,
or making grand judgments,
or feeling full of shame.

I borrow nothing.
I do not want anything from anybody.

I flow through all human beings.
Love is my only companion.

When union happens,
my speech goes inward toward Shams.

At that meeting,
all the secrets of language will no longer be secret.

A WALK YOU CAN TAKE

If you want a deep inwardness,
there is a walk you can take with a friend.

Your five senses do not understand what he says,
but look in his eyes: a bird is soaring there,
mounting beyond and beyond.

The sun that rises every day in the east
is a speck in that friend's intelligence,
a ray slipping into the courtyard garden
where a hundred different flowers grow.

Quiet now. Another sun has risen.
The Shams-sun floods with light
the most inner privacy of that friend.

HEADLESS CAMELS

There is a bird that flies inside a lover's heart
carrying bones to the great Qaf Mountain bird.
I see flocks going there and caravans of headless camels.
Lovers will not ride on anything that has its head attached.
And there is never a trace of jealousy near.

When lover-bones come to the kitchen,
a hundred elegant soups begin bubbling
particle music for the death-night wedding.

As a lover's body is lowered into the ground,
a thousand skylights open.
As a saffron stalk dries up, hedges of roses bloom.

Two or three more subtle points like these
may come before my dying mouth closes.

17.
Playing

A friend (Allaudin Mathieu, a.k.a. Sheikh Allegro) and I once lengthened the list of the names of God: Green Beans, Mozart, Van Morrison, the Brooks Range, Namer of Cheeses, Schwinn, Andante. The playing went on, to find a temporary resting point when we began substituting the word "lunch" for the word "love" in popular songs: "All You Need Is Lunch," "Lunch, Lunch Me Do," "But Will You Lunch Me Tomorrow?" "Lunch Is in the Air."

Presence plays through form, hiding and revealing itself, then fleeing, as the sky does in a lake. The Tennessee River was the watersky I worshiped in as a child, sparks igniting to flame. In the *Masnavi* Rumi asks, "What is it to praise?" He answers, "Make yourself particles." I take this to mean, "Become the pure play of dust motes in sunlight." There is a music in the flow of creative intuition. It is a loosening of springwater, an opening of roses. Ego and effort are about tightening around something you feel is yours, a concentration. Becoming particles is the reverse motion, moving outward into absence, molecular, galactic, elusive, expanding. Big Nothing walks in.

What if it is true that someone as powerfully alive as Shams Tabriz was, has now become a depth of awareness that rises every morning in the east? Red sky. "And even if the corpse washer binds my jaw shut, you will still hear this song coming out of my dead silence." "I praise stray dogs on the street." Plotinus sees all *motion* as forms of play: the plants growing, the birds that are guiding us toward contemplation, enlightenment. One of the images Rumi finds for the interaction of personality and soul is that of a small dog (the personality) trying to get an adult human (the soul) to play with it, to take a walk at the very least. Percy is the personality, the poet Mary Oliver, the soul, though she might say just the opposite. Her Percy poems are the delight of all outdoors.

PLAYING AND BEING PLAYED

There are no words to explain, no tongue,
how when that player touches the strings,
it is me playing and being played,

how existence turns around this music,
how stories grow from the trunk,
how cup and mouth swallow each other with the wine,
how a garnet stone from nowhere is puzzled by these miners,
how even if you look for us, hair's breath by hair's breadth,
you will not find anything. We are inside the hair.
How last night a spear struck, how the lion drips red,
how someone pulls at my robe of tattered patches.

It's all I have. Where are your clothes?

How Shams Tabriz lives outside time,
how what happens to me happens there.

INSIDE THE ROSE

That camel there with its calf running behind it,
Sutur and Koshek, we are like them,
mothered and nursed by where and who we are from,
following our fates where they lead,
until we hear a drum begin, grace entering our lives,
a prayer of gratitude.

We feel the call of God, and the journey changes.
A dry field of stones turns soft and moist as cheese.
The mountain feels level under us.

Love becomes agile and quick,
and suddenly we are there.

This traveling is not done with the body.
God's secret takes form in *your loving*.

But there are those in bodies who are pure soul.
It can happen. These messengers
invite us to walk with them. They say,
You may feel happy enough where you are,
but we can't do without you any longer. Please.

So we walk along inside the rose,
being pulled like the creeks and rivers are,
out from the town onto the plain.

My guide, my soul, your only sadness
is when I am not walking with you.

In deep silence, with *some* exertion to stay in your company,
I could save you a lot of trouble.

AS THE SKY DOES IN WATER

For the grace of the presence, be grateful.
Touch the cloth of the robe,
but do not pull it toward you,
or like an arrow it will leave the bow.

Images. Presence plays with form,
fleeing and hiding as the sky does in water,
now one place, now nowhere.

Imagination cannot contain the absolute.
These poems are elusive, because the presence is.

I love the rose that is not a rose,
but the second I try to speak it,
any name for God becomes *so-and-so,* and vanishes.

What you thought to draw lifts off the paper,
as what you love slips from your heart.

SEEDS AND RAIN

The mystery of action: We are seed.
You are rain. A dear stain,
our seed coverings decay. You mix with what is inside.
A toast to the new rises. A divine tool blade falls,
the keen edge of this moment.

The soul slides through these eyes,
as Shams Tabriz covers Shams Tabriz.

ONE THING I DID WRONG

The bird in the cage of my chest flutters excitedly.
My mad camel pulls at its tether.
A lion looks out through my eyes and sees quarry.
The river rises. Along the bank new grasses appear.
A dawn wind blows through the rose garden.

Love left, because of one thing I did wrong.
Now it returns.

Compassion curves back here,
and lightheartedness.

A blind man throws away his cane.
A baby begins to eat from the plate.
A falcon lifts toward the king's drum.
Now silence unweaves the shroud of words we have woven.

HOMETOWN STREETS

Sleep dissolves your mind,
but how do the insane sleep?

What do the love-crazed know
of night-and-day differences?

God-lovers, mostly in another world,
read another book with another eye.

Try changing to a bird or a fish.
Be lost on some road inside the beloved.

You will not know what a *matzoob* feels
until you are one of them.

Shams sets these new lights adrift
through our hometown streets, the universe.

PICTURES OF THE SOUL

My soul, there is an image of you
on each side of the six-sided mirror cube
that we call the universe,
but mirrors can only reveal according to their capacity.

They cannot picture the stages of the soul's growing.
The sun asks the inner sun, How can I see you?
When you set, I rise, comes the answer.

Intellect wants to restrain the soul
like a camel with its feet tied,
and love longs to hold the soul's seven levels,
but neither intention is possible.

Sometimes in a harvest circle
a single piece of grain in the cloud of chaff and stems
seems to have legs and wings.

That is the size and effect of mind in the region of soul.
In the ocean once you saw what the soul is.
Since then awe has flooded you.

When the soul asks questions,
the pleasure of gold earrings comes to everyone's ears.

Personality is a small dog trying to get the soul to play.
I hear you call, and I am out walking the road
without legs or feet.

What could we do that resembles what you do?
Days, nights? We are shade under your tree.

Adam left the spirit world because you are here.
Love is an ocean storm moving for your touch.

To have your words in this, I must stop speaking.

BORDER STATIONS

We make heads into feet, we enter and cross the river.
We sic armies into a fight, then jump out of the world.

We sit on love's horse and fly. We break through form,
human definitions scattered behind us on the road.

The first stage, a blood swamp, our red feet slogging,
then the border station where Majnun and Layla live.

Horses nervous. Then the self with its legendary wealth.
That left, we are walking a beach
crunching pearls with every step.

Now the soul is flying straight like a moth to the candleflame
of Shams Tabriz. We were always heading there.

NO MORE THE *PRESENCE*

No more meanings.
My pleasure now is with the inner sun, the inner moon.

No longer two worlds signaling each other.
Shapes do not come to mind.

This giving up has nothing to do with exhaustion.
I walk from one garden to another,
waves against my boat, ocean flames refining,
as fresh as flowers and fish calligraphy.

Let us see what they are writing.
Green itself begs me dive in this that Shams has given.

GIVENS

The drums beating now inside us,
we will hear them tomorrow too.

We have such fear of what comes next,
fear of death.

These loves are like pieces of cotton.
Throw them in the fire.

Death will be a meeting like that flaring up,
a presence you have always wanted to be with.
This body and this universe keep us from freedom.

Those of you decorating your cells so beautifully,
do you think they will not be torn down?

Fire-change and the demolishing of prisons
are givens here.
Trust that they will come to you.

I KEEP USING TWO PRONOUNS

The universe swings again into your orbit.
Am I looking for you, or you for me?

The question is all wrong.
As long as I keep using two pronouns,
I am this inbetween, two-headed thing with no name.

Some of the water in my stream flows quickly by.
Some stays frozen in an ice ledge against the bank.

Sun says to stone, Let me shine inside you
and change your stoniness to a jewel.

The sun of infinite love comes into your love,
and you are given more and more humble work.
Then you are given mastery.

The sun says to an unripe grape, There is a kitchen inside you,
where you can make vinegar, or if I help, sweet juice.

The king says to the falcon, I cover your eyes with a hood,
so that you will break with your kind and see only my face.
The falcon replies, Only you.

The rose says to the garden, I display these robes,
so that you will let the other flowers go
and be a one-rose garden.

Imagine a man who sells a donkey in order to be with Jesus.
Now imagine him selling Jesus to get a donkey.
This does happen.

Jesus can transform a drunkard into gold.
If the drunk is already golden, he can be changed to pure
  diamond.
If already that, then the circling planets,
Jupiter, Venus, the moon.

Never think that you are worthless.
God has already bought you for an enormous amount.
Gifts keep arriving.

Dates from a withered branch.
Wisdom, the same that came to Jesus in the cradle.

My face now makes the world's bathhouse hot.
Do not look at the wet paintings on the wall.
Look here.

There is a light in us that has nothing to do with night and day.
There are grapes that never saw a vineyard.
These gifts are yours now, if you can see.

We Are All Returning.

says the text. Enjoy Shams.
Or if not that, at least listen
to what honest people tell you.

YOUR OLD AUNT AND UNCLE

My mother was destiny. My father, grace.
I am the prince of synchronicity and serendipity.

If I meet a wolf, he turns into a kind friend.
If I am lowered into a well, it becomes a garden.

A stony miser comes to me and starts giving his wealth away.
Do not offer me money.
I have a teacher whose fragrance brings statues to life.

If his face appears,
your old aunt will leave your uncle and never return.
I ask, Will you finish this story
and give the explanation?
You say, Yes.

THIS PRAISING SOUND

There is a tradition that God can be seen in the color red.
In the lights that come from red hair.

They draw you, don't they?
The unknowable spirit has eyebrows and eyes and skin.

Muhammad in a living form.
He looked at people!

Hundreds of doors swung open.
His form went away,
and now this praising sound floods the world.

WHEN COMPLETELY NAKED

If my words are not saying what you would say,
slap my face.
Discipline me as a loving mother does
a babbling child caught up in nonsense.

A thirsty man runs into the sea,
and the sea holds a sword to his throat.

A lily looks at a bank of roses,
wilts, and says nothing.

I am a tambourine.
Do not put me aside until the fast-dancing starts.
Play me some all along.
Help me with these little sounds.

Joseph is most beautiful when he is completely naked,
but his shirt gives you an idea,
as the body lets you glimpse the glitter
on the water of the soul.

Even if the corpse washer binds my jaw shut,
you will still hear this song
coming out of my dead silence.

FRIENDS WITH SUNLIGHT

Play no music but the soul's,
that friend who sometimes takes a form like Joseph,
a handsomeness that tears coverings,
beauty that says secrets and gets bewildered.

As dogs lap blood, we drink life.
This is how we are with love's melody,
a taste of springwater, birdsound near.

Wherever Jesus walks in time and space,
there is a robe. This is it.

The sun was born from the friend,
not out of an east-west convergence.

We move as particles.
That motion is all we need do.

Shams became our friend,
so we are friends with sunlight.

I'M NOT SAYING THIS RIGHT

You bind me, and I tear away in a rage to open out
into air, a round brightness, a candlepoint,
all reason, all love.

This confusing joy, your doing,
this hangover, your tender thorn.

You turn to look, I turn.
I'm not saying this right.

I am a jailed crazy who ties up spirit women.
I am Solomon.

What goes comes back. Come back.
We never left each other.

A disbeliever hides disbelief,
but I will say his secret.

More and more awake, getting up at night
spinning and falling with love for Shams.

THE STEAMBATH

Steam fills the bath, and frozen figures on the wall
open their eyes, wet and round,
Narcissus eyes that see enormous distances.
And new ears that love the details of any story.
The figures dance like friends diving into red wine,
coming up and diving again.

Steam spills into the courtyard. It is the sound of resurrection.
They move from one corner laughing across to the other corner.
No one notices how steam opens the rose of each mind,
fills each beggar's cup solid with coins. Hold out a basket.
It fills up so well that emptiness becomes what you want.

The judge and the accused forget the sentencing.
Someone stands up to speak,
and the wood of the table becomes holy.
The tavern in that second is actually made of wine.
The dead drink it in. Then the steam evaporates.
The figures sink back into the wall, eyes blank, ears just lines.

Now it is happening again, outside.
The garden fills with bird and leaf sounds.
We stand in the wake of this chattering and grow airy.
How can anyone say what happens, even if each of us
dips a pen a hundred million times into ink?

18.
Shams Tabriz: The Friend

Now all distinctions run together. There is a being who is your whole life, who does not exist, a tenderness, a ruin, rain, one with wonderful friends. Avalanche. There is a sun within you that nurtures the fruit trees of your invisible being. Shams is the name of that sun. Shams Tabriz, your face, is what every religion tries to remember. Rumi's son Sultan Velad describes what it felt like to be with Shams: "When he spoke the Qur'an and the sayings of Muhammad, he sowed new love in my soul. He revealed secrets. He made me fly without wings and reach the ocean with no boundaries, where I found peace and, like a bird freed from a trap, felt safe from all dangers" (*Veladnama*).

Here is a story from Shams's *Maqalat*. A great caravan arrives at a place where there is no habitation and no water. There is a deep well, but no bucket or rope. To test for freshwater, the caravaners tie a kettle to a rope of their own and let it down. It strikes something, and they pull, but the kettle breaks away. They send down another and lose it too. After that they lower a thirsty volunteer from the caravan, then another, and another, but they also disappear. A wise man says he will go down. He is nearly to the bottom, when a terrible dark creature appears.

"I can never escape from you," says the man to the monster, "but I hope at least to stay aware, so I can see what is happening to me."

"Don't tell me long stories," says the monster. "You are my prisoner. You will never leave unless you answer one question."

"Ask it."

"Where is the best place?"

The wise man reflects to himself, "I am totally helpless here. If I say Baghdad or some other beautiful place, it may be that I will insult his hometown by not mentioning it." He replies, "The best place for someone to live is where he feels at home. If that is a hole in the middle of the earth, then that is his home. That is the best place."

"Well said. You are a rare human being," says the monster. "Because of your blessing, I will set the others in your care free and give you authority over the earth. I will take no more prisoners, and I will release the waters of this well."

Shams in his wild wisdom advises us to bless the monster in his home, where he lives. I like what you have done with the place.

THE FRIEND

> There is a being who is drunk without wine,
> full without food, and buried in a ruin,
> someone not made of earth, air, fire, or water,
> a rain out of the clear blue,
> hundreds of nightskies and suns,
> one who is given wisdom directly,
> not from books, one beyond any religion,
> or right and wrong, one with wonderful friends,
> one who does not exist,
> a hidden glory like Shams.
> There is no need to look anywhere for this one,
> who is your whole life.

AN INVISIBLE BEE

Look how desire has changed in you,
how light and colorless it is,
with the world growing new marvels
because of your changing.

Your soul has become an invisible bee.
We don't see it working,
but there's the full honeycomb.

Your body's height, six feet or so,
but your soul rises through nine levels of sky.

A barrel corked with earth and a raw wooden spile
keeps the oldest vineyard's wine inside.

When I see you, it is not so much your physical form,
but the company of two riders,
your pure-fire devotion and your love
for the one who teaches you.
Then the sun and moon on foot behind those.

A GRAINY TASTE

Without a net, I catch a falcon and release it to the sky,
hunting God.

This wine I drink today was never held in a clay jar.
I love this world,
even as I hear the great wind of leaving it rising,

for there is a grainy taste I prefer
to every idea of heaven: human friendship.

THE MIRROR BETWEEN US

The mirror between us is breath-mist when I speak.
Your face in water. I reach. The work grows muddy.

Even *friend* and *beloved* are wrong words for this.
Even *ahhhhhh* retreats back into my mouth.

The same if the moon's behind cloud or being released.
A pure silent look is better.

THE PLEIADES

In absence aloes wood burns fragrant.
The love we feel is smoke from that.

Existence gets painted with nonexistence, its source,
the fire behind a screen.

Smoke born of this fire hides the fire.
Pass through the smoke.

Soul is a moving river; body, the riverbed.
Soul can break the circle of fate and habit.

Take hold the hand of absence,
and let it draw you through the Pleiades,
giving up on wet and dry, hot and cold.

You become the confidante of Shams Tabriz.
You see clearly the glory of nothing
and stand, inexplicably, there.

PARINDA, THE ONE WHO FLIES AWAY

The one my soul is searching for is not here.
Where has he gone?

The one like a lit candle,
like a seat with roses growing around it.

Our eyes look for that one first,
but I do not see him today.

Say his name. If anyone here
has kissed his hand, give us your blessing.

I do not know whether to be more grateful
for the existence of his face,
or for what is inside that.

There is no one like him in the world.
But if there is no form for that now,
how is it everything turns with the motion of his love?

Say all the possible nicknames for Shams Tabriz.
Do not hide anything from someone
who only wants to be in his presence.

THE ONE WHO LEFT

Bring back the one who left.
Lure him with music,
or any irresistible pretext.

If he says, I will be there in a little while,
that is part of his beguiling,
his art that can tie strands of water into knots
and make weavings of the wind.

Do not accept those. Bring his presence.
Sit down within that,
and live inside what is beyond physical beauty,
beyond the sun's extravagance,
or the handsomeness of human beings.

Yemen has the most exquisite rubies,
but the one I want to see coming through the door
is the one who lives *here*.

AVALANCHE

Poet, rake the strings. Strike fire.
Staying quiet is not for now. Be generous.

A baby must cry before the mother nurses.
Make a noise, poet.
Want the deep friendship, *outloud*.

Dilate this love.
Mention the name of the one who started this.

What am I saying?
Shams is Jesus walking a mountain road.

I am a slow, bewildered avalanche
moving along somehow trying to follow him.

YOUR TURN AT DICE

As the sun sinks below the edge,
the senses close.

As the sun is with shadows,
as the heart takes form in a body, then rules it,
as man is born of woman,

so there is a secret inside your loving,
a horseman cloaked in a dustcloud
that he himself has raised.

This is not a chess problem
to concentrate on and solve.

Trust, as when it is your turn at dice.
Throw the elements here down.
Read what has been given you.

There is a sun warmth inside,
nurturing the fruit of your being.
Shams is the name of that.

BACK TO BEING

The ocean can do without fish.
My soul, let me tell you a secret.

It is rare to meet a fish like the ocean.
Seawater is the nursing mother,
fish the crying babies.

But sometimes the ocean comes looking
for a particular fish to hear what it wants.

The ocean will not act before it knows.
The fish is an emperor then, the ocean, its minister.

How long will I keep talking in riddles?
Shams is the master that turns the earth fragrant.
When plants feel him near, they open out.

I would not have a soul,
if after tasting the taste of Shams,
I could go back to being who I was.

YOUR FACE

You may be planning departure,
as a human soul leaves the world
taking almost all its sweetness with it.

You saddle your horse. You must be going.
Remember you have friends here
as faithful as grass and sky.

Have I failed you? Possibly you are angry.
But remember our nights of conversation,
the well work, yellow roses by the ocean,
the longing, the archangel Gabriel
saying, *So be it.* Shams Tabriz, your face
is what every religion tries to remember.

THE SWEET BLADE OF YOUR ANGER

What is the use of going to see a mountain cliff
if your face is not there?

Why hear the secret of secrets
if you are not mentioned?

If Adam and Eve and their family knew nothing of you,
whom should I ask?

What if I get prosperity and honors
and all the satisfactions anyone could want,
and never meet you?

What use is understanding
if I do not see the blade of your anger
with honey curling around it?

What use is water, wedding gifts, Joseph's soul,
sparks igniting, hair?

The hundreds of lies composing one truth?
The two worlds calling each other?

I praise stray dogs on the street,
lions wandering wilderness, and Shams Tabriz.
It does not matter what I say.

SOUL, HEART, AND BODY ONE MORNING

There is a morning when presence comes over your soul.
You sing like a rooster in your earth-colored shape.

Your heart hears and, no longer frantic, begins to dance.
At that moment, soul reaches total emptiness.

Your heart becomes Mary, miraculously pregnant,
and your body, like a two-day-old Jesus, says wisdom words.

Now the heart, which is the source of your loving,
turns to universal light, and the body
picks up the tempo in the elegance of its motion.

Where Shams Tabriz walks the footprints become
notations of music and holes you fall through into space.

WHAT I SAY MAKES ME DRUNK

The beloved grumbles at me, *Come on. Come on.*
But which way do I go to that one?

Torches at the door. Who's there? *I am.*
The one asking from inside and the one
walking up to the door, who steals the doorknob.

Oil and water together, how can I be whole?
I am like this hair, all strands and hiding places.

Yet out in the open too like the moon.
I look around the house for the one who stole my clothing,
with the garment thief's head laughing
through the open window.

I try every possible way out,
when I have been free of this cage now,
since . . . ah . . . eternity. What I say makes me drunk.

Nightingale, iris, parrot, jasmine, I speak those languages,
along with the idiom of my longing for Shams Tabriz.

ANY CHANCE MEETING

In every gathering, in any chance meeting on the street,
there is a shine, an elegance rising up.

Today I recognized that that jewel-like beauty is the presence,
our loving confusion,
the glow in which watery clay gets brighter than fire,
the one we call *the friend.*

I begged, Is there a way into you, a ladder?
Your head is the ladder. Bring it down under your feet.

The mind, this globe of awareness, is a starry universe
that when you push off from it with your foot,

a thousand new roads come clear,
as you yourself do at dawn, sailing through the light.

SITTING TOGETHER

We sit in this courtyard,
two forms, shadow outlines with one soul.

Birdsound, leaf moving, early evening star,
fragrant damp, and a sweet sickle curve of moon.

You and I in a round, unselved idling
in the garden-beauty detail.

The raucous parrots laugh,
and we laugh inside their laughter,
the two of us on a bench in Konya,
yet amazingly in Khorasan and Iraq as well.

Friends abiding this form,
yet also in another, outside of time, you and I.

I THROW IT ALL AWAY

You play with the great globe of union,
you that see everyone so clearly,
and cannot be seen.

Even universal intelligence gets blurry
when it thinks you might leave.

You came here alone,
but you create hundreds of new worlds.

Spring is a peacock flirting with revelation.
The rose gardens flame. Ocean enters the boat.

I throw it all away,
except this love for Shams.

A KING DRESSED AS A SERVANT

A sweet voice calls out, The caravan from Egypt is here.
A hundred camels with what amazing treasure.

Midnight, a candle and someone quietly waking me,
Your friend has come.

I spring out of my body, put a ladder to the roof,
and climb up to see if it is true.

Suddenly, there is a world within this world.
An ocean inside the waterjar.

A king sitting with me wearing the uniform of a servant.
A garden in the chest of the gardener.

I see how love has *thoughts*,
and that these thoughts are circling
in conversation with majesty.

Let me keep opening this moment like a dead body reviving.

Shams Tabriz saw the placeless one,
and from that he made a place.

THE SPIRIT-LION IN A HUMAN BEING

You are the soul of the soul of the soul, the door.
Open us into existence.

When separation makes us angry,
you strike its neck with a sword.

When union becomes vague, you nourish it.
You feed everything for nothing.

Ancient civilizations begin to flourish again.
The March sun warms the world like singing,
like tambourine and harp.

When branches are covered in buds,
who is sober enough to take a message to the king?
No one. All right.

Do you remember how a gnat once got drunk
and walked into the ear of a tyrant,
then into his brain, and killed him?

If grape-wine can do that to a gnat,
what will the wine of infinity do to you and me?

A cave dog watched over the sleepers.
If a dog can become a shepherd,
what can the spirit-lion in a human being become?

Sparks from a fire lift into the sky and turn to stars.
Shams is now a depth of awareness
that rises every morning in the east.

SUN AND SKY

Sit with lovers and choose their state.
Do not stay long with those who are not living in the heart.

There is one who shines inside the face,
whose hair grows with the world,
whose eyes recognize you,
whose body is all honey and milk,
who holds absolute beauty in an embrace,
full morning without a dawn,
essence without attributes,
living without grief,
twilight with no dark streaks in it.

How can this be?
Can the sun borrow light from the sky?
Can a rose smell like jasmine?

Be a fish in this ocean, speechless.
I will whisper the answer in your ear.
Do not tell anyone.
In Tabriz, the one named Shams.

A MYSTIC AND A DRUNK

The universe turns on an axis.
Let my soul circle around a table like a beggar,
like a planet rolling in the vast,
totally helpless and free.

The knight and the castle move jaggedly across the chessboard,
but they are actually centered on the king. They circle.

If love is your center, a ring gets put on your finger.
Something inside the moth is made of fire.

A mystic touches the annihilating tip of pure nothing.
A drunkard thinks peeing is absolution.
Lord, take these impurities from me.

The lord replies, First, understand the nature of impurity.
If your key is bent, the lock will not open.

I fall silent.
King Shams has come.
Always when I close, he opens.

A CAVE WHERE SHAMS TABRIZ IS RESTING

Every day this separation, this December hoping for spring,
city after city refusing me, because of a prince I serve.

My house and shop are torn down,
because of the tulips I grow.

I suffer the cold arrogance of strangers
because of a mountain with a ruby mine inside,
the quarry that cannot be caught.
Still I keep spreading traps.

You say, Will you endure this failure
and homelessness without relief?

Yes. Because my chest
is a cave where Shams Tabriz is resting.

A LANTERN

You so subtle you can slip into my soul,
how would it be if you, for a time, were living visibly here?

So hidden you are hidden from hidden things,
you enter me and my hiddenness shines like a lantern.

You Solomon, who understands bird-language and speaks it,
what will you say now through my mouth?

King, whose bow no one can draw,
use me for an arrow.

Shams is the way I know God.

A GIFT FOR SHAMS

There is a passion in me
that does not long for anything
from another human being.

I was given something else.
A cap to wear in both worlds.
It fell off. No matter.

One morning I went to a place beyond dawn,
a source of sweetness that flows and is never less.

I have been shown a beauty
that would confuse both worlds,
but I will not cause that uproar.

I am nothing but a head,
set on the ground as a gift for Shams.

THIS INK

I am wary of virtue and knowledge,
of crowns and the alphabet work we do.

I carouse above the Little Dipper,
that some call the Minor Bear.

Enlivening water takes *my* shape
and spills itself before Muhammad.

All desiring flows inside this ink
as it moistens and enters the page
when I write *Shams Tabriz*.

CONVERSATION AT NIGHT

Do not go to sleep one night.
What you most want will come to you then.
Warmed by a sun inside, you will see wonders.

Tonight do not put your head down.
Be tough, and strength will come.

That which adoration adores appears at night.
Those asleep may miss it.
One night Moses stayed awake and asked,
and saw a light in a tree.

Then he walked at night for ten years,
until finally he saw the whole tree illuminated.

Muhammad rode his horse through the nightsky.
The day is for work. The night for love.
Do not let someone bewitch you.
Some people sleep at night, but not lovers.
They sit in the dark and talk to God,
who told David, Those who sleep all night every night
and claim to be connected to us, they lie.

Lovers cannot sleep
when they feel the privacy of the beloved around them.

Someone who is thirsty may sleep for a little while,
but he will dream of water, a full jar beside a creek,
or the spirit water you get from another person.

All night, listen to the conversation. Stay up.
This moment is all there is.
Death will take it away soon enough.

You will be gone,
and this earth will be left without a sweetheart,
nothing but weeds growing inside thorns.

I am through.
Read the rest of this poem in the dark tonight.
Do I have a head, and feet?

Shams, so loved by Tabrizians, I close my lips.
I wait for you to come and open them.

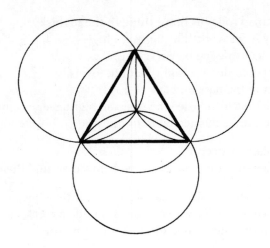

19.
Tenderness Toward Existence

Galway Kinnell says that all good writing has a certain quality in common, a tenderness toward existence. We will never finish noticing what is going on. We have a great love for what we cannot quite say, but Galway takes us closer, burning with the olive wood. The dear time of our talking. Rumi tells of opening a rosewater shop, but keeping the garden a secret. Let's not do that, he says. When the river floods in spring, it is time to toss the ducklings in. Here is a short poem of Galway's that I love for its remarkable line of poetry consisting of three *is*'s in a row with *what* on either side.

PRAYER

Whatever happens. Whatever
What is is is what
I want. Only that. But that.

A GENERAL INTRODUCTORY LECTURE

A nightingale flies nearer the roses. A girl blushes.
Pomegranates ripen. Hallaj will be executed.

A man walks a mountain path, solitary and full of prayer.
Trust grows for nine months, then a new being appears.
Narcissus on the edge, creekwater washing tree roots.

God is giving a general introductory lecture.
We hear and read it everywhere,
in the field, through the branches.
We will never finish studying.

Neither of us has a penny,
yet we are walking the jeweler's bazaar,
seriously considering making a purchase.

Or shall I say this with other metaphors?
A barn crowded with souls.
Quietness served around a table.
Two people talk along a road that is paved with words.

AN ARMOR OF ROSES

Take January's advice. Stack wood.
Weather inevitably turns cold,
and you make fires to stay healthy.
Study the grand metaphor of this yearly work.

Wood is a symbol for *absence*.
Fire for your love of God.

We burn form to warm the soul.
Soul loves winter for that,
and accepts reluctantly the comfort of spring,
with its elegant, proliferating gifts.

All part of the plan: fire becoming ash,
becoming garden soil, becoming mint, willow, and tulip.

Love looks like fire. Feed yourself into it.
Be the fireplace and the wood.

Bravo, for this metallurgy
that makes a needle from an iron ingot.

Calm fire now. For the moth, a window.
For you, an armor of roses.

Pharaoh dissolves like yogurt in water.
Moses comes to the top like oil.

Fine Arabians carry royalty.
Nags, the sacks of dried dung.

Language is an annoying clatter in the mill of meaning.
A silent river turns the millstone.

The word-grains get noisily dumped in the tray,
pulverized under the stone as gossip.

Let this poem be thus ground.
Let me go back to the love-fire
that refines the pure gold of my friend, Shamsuddin.

BOTH WORLDS

There is God's wine, and this other.
Do not mix them.

There are naked pilgrims who wear only sunlight.
Do not give them clothes.

There are lovers content with hoping.
I am not one of them.

Give a cup of pure fire to your closest friend,
healing salve to the wounded.

To Shams Tabriz, offer up both worlds.

AUTUMN ROSE ELEGY

You have gone to the secret world.
Which way is it? You broke the cage and flew.

You heard the drum that calls you home.
You left this humiliating shelf,
this disorienting desert where we are given wrong directions.

What use now a crown?
You have become the sun.

No need for a belt.
You have slipped out of your waist.

I have heard that near the end
you were eyes looking at soul.

No looking now. You live inside the soul.
You are the strange autumn rose
that led the winter wind in by withering.

You are rain soaking everywhere from cloud to ground.
No bother of talking.
Flowing silence and sweet sleep inside the friend.

THIS HIGH MEADOW

I break out laughing. I frown. I yell and scream.
Sometimes if one jokes and giggles, one causes war.

So I hide how tickled I am.
Tears well up in my eyes.

My body is a large city.
Much grieving in one sector.
I live in another part. Lakewater.
Something on fire over here.

I am sour when you are sour,
sweet when you are sweet.

You are my face and back.
Only through you can I know
this back-scratching pleasure.

Now, people the likes of you and I come clapping,
inventing dances, climbing into this high meadow.

I am a spoiled parrot who eats only candy.
I have no interest in bitter food.

Some have been given harsh knowledge. Not I.
Some are lame and jerking along.
I am smooth and glidingly quick.

Their road is full of washed-out places and long inclines.
Mine is royally level, effortless.

The huge Jerusalem mosque stands inside me,
and women full of light.

Laughter leaps out.
It is the nature of the rose to laugh.
It cannot help but laugh.

Lilies and roses open inside me. I hear voices.
Patience says, Good news. Union happens.
Gratitude says, I have made some fortunate investments.

Reason says, I feel sick.
Spirit, I have a sacred pearl.
The pearl itself says, I am near the wall's foundation.

Ignorance: I have nothing.
Knowledge: I own the whole bazaar.

Abstinence: I begin to understand.
Poverty says, I have no hat and no need for a hat.

When Shams comes back from Tabriz,
all this will be explained by his presence.

GRANTED

What happens in the world,
what business of that is yours?

Two existences have merged in a single temple,
but where is your smiling image?

Granted, there are terrible famines
with no bread dipped in wine anywhere.

You control what is manifest and what is hidden.
Where is your warehouse of grain?

Granted, thorn, scorpion, and snake exist.
But where is your rose-petal bed,
your joy that is a deep rest.

Granted, human generosity has dried up,
but you could still give us a pension and a silk robe.

Granted, the sun and moon go down daily into hell,
but not your light and your fire.

Granted, the jeweler has nothing to sell.
He stands by his empty stall.
You could rain down pearls, if you chose.

Granted, there is no mouth, or any language,
but where is your surging impulse?

Come with me while the wine shop is still open.
We are dizzy with meeting each other.

Friend inside my chest and inside my hand,
find your coat and your turban,
if you have not gone completely senile.

Whores have stolen your hat and carried off your clothes.
Who will take care of you now?

A stranger blocks us.
You could be the arresting officer in this matter,
the judge, and the gallows, if that were your inclination.

Word-scatterer, hush this conversation.
Say instead silence to those who never talk.

ABRAHAM AND ISAAC

The beloved arrives.
My roof and door become living tissue.
Stay tonight.

I have business in the city.
If you leave, I will not survive.
Give me one night.

Many people are in my care.
Their blood is my ascending planet.
I must follow that.

Taste my blood, I beg.
A rare offer. Do you know how it is for those with me?
To die seventy times and seventy times be born again.

The prophet Isaac is dust by the door.
Die. I will bring you back.

Do not flutter in my hand.
Do not wince at the knife blade.

Laugh as you are pulled from the garden
and plunged into powdered sugar.

You are Isaac. I am Abraham.
How could I hurt you? Love is a father.

The beloved leaves like a gust of wind.
Do not hurry, I call. Go slowly.

This is as slow as I can move.
No one has ever seen me when I hurry.

Be quiet now. The gray sky-horse is lame.
Flame reaches to the thicket.
Quieter. Save some for another day.

I ASK ONE MORE THING

Today pour the full cup.
Slap the wheel already spinning so frantically.

This wine is invisible, yes, but the effect is not.

I ask one more thing
from the love that has given us
this dear time talking together.

Lift the veil from the face of the king.
Why open a rosewater shop and keep the garden secret?

You have set the river flowing.
Now toss the ducklings in.

We are the first double-leaf sprout,
two inches out of the ground.
We need rain, or we may not grow more than this.

Cynics on all sides say,
You look for what does not exist,
and saying that, they steal laughter from the fool,
and music from the lute player.

I want these words to stop.
Calm the chattering mind, my soul.
No more camel's milk.
I want silent water to drink
and the majesty of a clear waking.

FORTH

You that pour the pourers day and night,
so that in sleep we keep tasting,
no head, no turban, the soul's heart sliced to bits,
Egyptian women out of hand, waterbag full of wind,
this is how love catches up and wants to be our friend,
as we hold each other,
and the good secret inside slides forth continuous.

FOURTEEN QUESTIONS

What if I broke off a whole branch of roses?
What if I lost myself in the friend?

How would it be to have no faith?
What if I picked a pickpocket's pocket?

Does it mean anything
when a single basket is lost in Baghdad,
when one wheat grain is missing from the barn?

How long will this illusion last?
What remains when a lover sits quietly
with the beloved *for one second?*

Will it involve you at all if I say some unsayable things?
Will my heart feel relieved doing that?

Something has passed between lover and beloved.
Are you part of these goings-on?

What does the soul feel when Jesus heals the body?
This is the night when life decrees can change.

If the moon came to visit me,
would that affect other people?

Shams Tabriz, if I gave workers a holiday,
and if I turned the marketplace upside down,
would that be a kind of image for how you love the world?

REFUGE

I see the lamp, the face, the eye,
an altar where the soul bows, a gladness and a refuge.

My loving says, Here. I can leave my personality here.
My reason agrees, How can I object
when a rose makes the bent backs stand up like cypresses?

Such surrender changes everything.
Turks understand Armenian. Body abandons bodiness.
Soul goes to the center. Rubies appear in the begging bowl.

But do not brag when this happens.
Be secluded and silent. Stay in the delight
and be brought the cup that will come.

No artfulness. Practice quiet and this new joy.

WHAT HAPPENS TO SEEDS INSIDE THEIR PRISONS

Gardener, listen to the grieving trees,
these tongueless ones with dying screech-marks on them.

There is a reason why the raven perches in the rose bower.
Where are the roses now?
Where is the jasmine? And the beautiful parrots?

There is no answer to his mocking.
The black-robed trees stand in silent groups.

Finally, the lordly heron, the village teacher, comes out.
Be patient three months more.
The lantern will be lit again.
Your denial and your doubt will turn to joy.

Stamp on the grave and call to the watchman,
Is it dawn yet?

The sweet-working sun will come back.
Remember the perfumes of March, the laughing,
the roads that look decorated for a holiday.

What happens to seeds inside their prisons
will happen to us in our houses.

The garden will bring out gifts it has hidden for years.
Presents, presence.

Now the crane folds his wings over the palace, saying,
Your need is your kingdom.

The nightingale enters, playing the lute, the dove cooing.
Other birds come with their songs.

This resurrection, this spring, is here now inside me.
Language cannot say it. Silence is lord.

Birds are landing all around us like arrows
with messages from placelessness tied to their legs.

A LINE OF CLOUDS

The moon has come back out, *the other moon,*
that was never above us, or seen in dreams,
the moon that brings fire and pours wine,
the host that cooks us to tenderness.

Our eyes look at the prepared sight and say,
Well done. Bravo.

Then we remember the ocean
and leap out of our personalities into that.
Try to find us.

The sun goes down,
with a line of clouds running to catch up.

THE IMAGE OF YOUR BODY

You have made it out of the city.
That image of your body, trembling with traffic
and fear, slips behind.
Your face arrives in the redbud trees and the tulips.

You are still restless.
Climb up the ladder to the roof.
You are by yourself a lot.
Become the one that when you walk in,
luck shifts to the one who needs it.
If you have not been fed, be bread.

INFINITESIMAL DUST

What is the light in the center of the darkness inside your soul?
A royal radiance or a fantasy
the way the full moon sometimes comes up in daylight?

But this is the sun itself,
Shams and a truth prior to the soul.

Human beings cannot endure such clarity.
We make statues, apply paint,
and use words with hidden allusions.

When the eye that has seen Shams
turns to look somewhere else,
what does it see?

In the love-ocean clothes are an embarrassment.
Do not look to be famous here,
and do not expect payment.

An east wind bringing infinitesimal dust from Tabriz
is the most I expect.

THE ELEGANCE OF THE ERMINE

Midnight, and a messenger comes from a prayer niche,
someone as quiet as moonlight,
yet with a torch that burns away our sleeping.

A king knocks on the doorkeeper's door and, laughing,
leads everyone out to a table.

Our lips tremble at the cup,
with the same trembling as a drop of mercury.

The gentleness of the host is the same
as that which made the elegance of the ermine.

The dry and wet of a love affair,
those tears are identical to the taking in
and giving away of a waterwheel's turning.

The keys that open all gates are strapped to love's chest.
When a bird is completely broken and still,
it gets removed from the snare.

This list of rude likenesses does not come near saying
what happens in our lives.

NIGHT AND CANDLE

Yesterday at dawn my friend said,
How long will this unconsciousness go on?

You fill yourself with the sharp pain of love
rather than its fulfillment.

I said, But I cannot get to you.
You are the whole dark night,
and I am a single candle.

My life is upsidedown because of you.

The friend replied, I am your deepest being.
Quit talking about wanting me.

I said, Then what is this restlessness?

The friend, Does a drop stay still in the ocean?

Move with the entirety
and with the tiniest particular.

Be the moisture in an oyster
that helps to form one pearl.

THIS OUT OF CONTROL

Of these two thousand I and We people,
which am I?

Do not try and keep me from asking.
Listen, when I am this out of control,
but do not put anything breakable in my way.

There is an original inside me.
What is here is a mirror for that, for you.

If you are joyful, I am.
If you grieve, or if you are bitter, or graceful,
I take on those qualities.

Like the shadow of a cypress tree in a meadow.
Like the shadow of a rose, I live close to the rose.

If I separated myself from you,
I would turn entirely thorn.

Every second, I drink another cup of my own blood-wine.
Every instant, I break an empty cup against your door.
I reach out, wanting you to tear me open.

Saladin's generosity lights a candle in my chest.
Who am I then? His empty begging bowl.

WANDERING AND COMING BACK

I have gone to many cities,
but I have never found anyone like you.
Coming back, a strange joy fills me.

What can I say about this wandering with unlucky travelers?
I was dead. Now I live.
Is it that I have seen your face and heard your voice?
Allow the evidence to show.
Give me something.

Say, I have a gift for you, Joseph,
this bright-polished face.

STAY IN A LISTENING POSTURE

What is wrong with this handsome face?
Does it mirror your heart's purity?

Before you crawl in a sack,
ask the sack owner what is in it.

Make him talk, then catch the fragrance.
Has he taken in roses and tulips and jasmine?

When he speaks of scripture,
do you feel the presence of David,
Noah, Jesus, and Moses, each with a distinct essence.

When he does evening prayer,
do you feel Muhammad coming near,
that cleansing desert nightwind?

If you want to know who someone is,
what is flowing through or not flowing,
stay in a listening posture.

Close your eyes inside your companion's shadow.
But always remember, you have your own source.
Never leave that. Explore the inner foundation stone by stone.

Look at this three-stringed instrument,
and that piece of amber there,
and whatever is beside the amber, a drum.

The outer is only decor.
Do not become a scholar of straw.

Do not be the farmer who throws seed *up*
and tries to harvest a storm.

20.
As-Sabur, The Patient

I used to think I had too much patience, but it was stubbornness instead, and a fear of speaking. A morning wind in the leaves is making the branches move. What binds and releases us is different in every individual case. Discipline is needed, required to live inside presence with patience. In the actual sun, feeling the nearness of Shams Tabriz. There is a fierce courtesy to be learned, as grapes hurry inwardly toward their own sweetness. They ripen, holding a taste of light. Wait, and trust the waiting.

DISCIPLINES

Do not expect to be always happy on this way.
You have been caught by a lion, my dear.

The friend dumps plaster on your head.
Think of it as expensive perfume.

Inside you there is a monster
that must be tied up and whipped.

Watch the man beating a rug.
He is not mad at it.
He wants to loosen the layers of dirt.

Ego accumulations are not loosened with one swat.
Continual work is necessary, disciplines.

In dreams, and even awake,
you will hear the beloved screaming at you.

A carpenter saws and chisels a piece of wood,
because he knows how he wants to use it.

Curing a hide, the tanner
rubs in acid and all manner of filth.
This makes a beautiful soft leather.

What does the half-finished hide know?
Every hard thing that happens works on you like that.

Hurry, Shams. Come back like the sun comes back
every day with new and powerful secrets.

CONTINUOUSLY

Listening to the prophet David play psalms and music,
a strange excitement came, presence *and* patience.

Egyptian granaries full of grain *and* Joseph's handsomeness.
Actual sun *and* nearness.

Sky, undecided; earth, silent.
In this precarious unknowing we live,
love does not want to say the name of *Hu*.

You stay concealed. A falcon lights.
How far away? Mt. Sinai under Moses.

The indications are that you are the one who appears,
not again, but continuously.

FIERCE COURTESY

The connection to the friend is secret
and very fragile. The image of that friendship

is in how you love, the grace and delicacy,
the subtle talking together in full prostration

outside of time. When you are there,
remember the fierce courtesy of the one with you.

WHAT HAVE YOU BEEN DRINKING?

I am drifting off to sleep.
You wake me up wanting new musical words,
new language-like flute notes.

My hands and feet are dormant.
You pull my ear.
Tell the story again from the beginning.

Dark strands of evening cover the earth.
You beg for poems about the night's hair,
how sweetness rises in the canebrake.

I finish one poem. You want another, another.
Imagine this. You are dead tired, ready for sleep.

Your assistant comes wanting to hear about *ambergris*.
What would you do?
What have you been drinking
that you want so many ecstatic poems?

These are not real questions. I am joking.
In your presence call me any name, *Kaymaz, Sencer*.
It is all the same, particle underfoot, floating dust mote.

LOOK AT A FOUNTAIN

Those with no energy have gone.
You that remain, do you know
who you are? How many?

Can you look at a fountain and become water?
Can you recognize the great self
and so enjoy your individual selves?

Do you run from joy?
Perhaps the lion should not flee the fox.
Let your loving and your soul
burn up in this candle. Let new life come.

The friend is at the door.
You are the lock his key fits.

You are a piece of candy,
the choice words of a poem,
the friend and the swallow
of silence here at the end.

SICK OF SCRIPTURE

My head turns around my feet,
one of which is fixed to the ground like a compass,
the other mad with the wandering moon
and the slow-burning of Mars.

Bored, ashamed, floating in a gold sky,
in deep ecstasy, all secrets told.

The son of a lion is out looking for heart-blood to drink.
You think I am sick, so you read the first sura,
but scripture is what I am sick of.

When Hallaj spoke his truth,
they crucified him for his words.
If Hallaj were here, he would point them to me.

Unlike this teacher here who will not bow,
I do not wash corpses or carve markings on stone.

The universe itself recognizes Shams Tabriz,
but not you.
I am tired of being around such blindness.

TWO HUMAN-SIZED WEDDING CANDLES

A message comes like honey to your heart.
Seven friends and a dog have slept three hundred and nine days
with God's wind turning them to rest on one side,
then the other.

There is another way of sleeping I pray we avoid,
the kind that is running after joy with its grief shadow behind it,
or the other, persistently trailing grief,
meeting chance elation at the corner.

Help us to give up back-and-forth, matter-illusion alternating
with the mind's calibration of what is good and bad,
wet and dry. Anything alligator swallows becomes alligator.

Two human-sized wedding candles walk toward fire.
A piece of paper covered with numbers and curving color streaks
drops in water, blurs, and flows away.

WE PRESCRIBE A FRIEND

We are wisdom and healing,
roasted meat and the star Canopus.
We are ground and the spilled wine sinking in.

When illness comes, we cure it.
For sadness, we prescribe a friend.
For death, a friend.

Run to meet us on the road.
We stay modest, and we bless.

We look like this, but this is a tree,
and we are morning wind in the leaves
that makes the branches move.

Silence turning now into this, now that.

WRETCHED, BUT LAUGHING

In this river the soul is a waterwheel
that no matter how it is facing,
water pours through, turning, returning to the river.

Even if you put your side or your back to the river,
water still comes through.

A shadow cannot ignore the sun
that all day creates and moves it.

The soul lives like a drop of mercury
in the palm of a palsied man.

Or say the soul is a moon,
that every thirty nights has two so empty, in union,
that it disappears.

The other twenty-eight nights
it endures stages of separation, wretched, but laughing.

Laughter is the way of lovers.
They live and die tickled, and always fresh-faced,
knowing the return that is coming.

Do not question this.
The answers and your questions in response
will cause your eyes to see wrongly.

Live the laughing silence.

I AM INSIDE YOUR THIRST

Do not run away.
Run inward,
as unripe grapes hurry toward their own sweetness.

Do not try to bite through this rope.
You are the bow. This is the bowstring.

You kick your hindlegs up,
thinking you are permanently through with work.
I have just put you out to pasture for the day.

I am deep inside your thirst and your hunger.
There is no escaping me.

That other wanting, that other rationality,
those are donkey's milk, or worse.
Do not drink them.

There is no security, except for what you feel among lovers.
Crawl in with those.

Remember the ababil birds, who picked up little stones
and dropped them from a great height onto invading elephants.

The love in your chest is like an ababil bird,
searching the ground, listening, then flying higher and higher.

The rose opens.
A cauldron begins to boil.

The sun heats up,
but you must wait a long time. Wait.

Shams put a taste of light inside patience.
The bat flies back to his cave.

THE BOTTLE IS CORKED

The rock splits open as wings beat air, wanting.
The campfire gives in to rain,
but I cannot go to sleep, or be patient.

Part of me wants to eat the stones
and hold you back when you are leaving,
until your good laughter turns bitter and wrong.

I worry that I won't have someone to talk to,
and breathe with. Don't you understand
that I am some kind of food for you?
I am a place where you can work.

The bottle is corked and sitting on the table.
Someone comes in and sees me without you,
and puts his hand on my head like I am a child.
This is so difficult.

YOUR FIRST EYES

A lover has four streams inside,
of water, wine, honey, and milk.

Find those in yourself and pay no attention
what so-and-so says about such-and-such.

The rose does not care
if someone calls it a thorn, or a jasmine.

Ordinary eyes categorize human beings.
That one is a Zoroastrian. This one, Muslim.

Walk instead with the other vision given you,
your first eyes.
Do not squint, and do not stare blankly like a vulture.

Those who love fire fall in the fire.
A fly slips from the edge into the whey.

If you are in love with the infinite,
why grieve over the ground washing away in the rain?

Bow to the essence in a human being.
A desert drinks war-blood,
but if it knew this secret, springs would rise, rose gardens.

Do not be content with judging people good and bad.
Grow out of that. The great blessing is
that Shams has poured a strength into the ground
that lets us wait and trust the waiting.

YOU NEVER LEFT

The lord of beauty enters the soul
as a man walks into an orchard in spring.

Come into me that way again.
Light the lamp in the eye of Joseph.
Cure Jacob's sadness.

Though you never left,
come and sit down here and ask,
Why are you so confused?

Like a fresh idea in an artist's mind,
you fashion things before they come into being.

You sweep the floor
like the man who keeps the doorway.

When you brush a form clean,
it becomes what it truly is.

You guard your silence perfectly
like a waterbag that does not leak.

You live where Shams lives
because your heart-donkey
was strong enough to take you there.

WHO IS THE FRIEND?

Circulate the cup.
Take me out of who I am and what I have done,
my name and my shame.

You who pour the wine, keep after me.
Trick me. When I have none of your joy,
I worry about everything. Lay your traps.

I should fast.
Someone who fasts visits the friend at night.

But more often I come in the front door,
and you fly through the roof.
Be more patient.

Muslims, what is there to do?
I am burning up and yet unsatisfied.

There is no cure
but the taste of what the saints pass around.

The story of lovers has no end,
so we will be happy with this, just this, *Goodbye*.

And the answer to Mutanabbi's riddle is,
Someone whom no wine consoles.

MORNING TALK

Holiday over, people go back to work,
the clever ones to the bazaar, hunting new sources of capital.

Lovers move back inside presence,
which is their bazaar and their art.

They are bored with other kinds of making and trading,
those lovers who appear to be insane,
in a broken line, glazed and stumbling.

Now they open their wings and lift,
turning in circles over the high plain,
their way of worshiping the sun.

Inside you they grow more alive,
as those living outside you get sad and compulsive.
Soul becomes itself when it dies on a gallows like Hallaj.

Sometimes lovers take vows of silence.
Then a clear morning comes, and they talk all through it.
Listening to Shams is a fine way of deepening into soul.

THE GROUND CRIES OUT

I feel like the ground,
astonished at what the atmosphere has brought to it.
What I know is growing inside me.
Rain makes every molecule pregnant with a mystery.
We groan with women in labor.
The ground cries out, *I am truth* and *Glory is here,*
breaks open, and a camel is born out of it.
A branch falls from a tree, and there is a snake.

Muhammad said: A faithful believer is a good camel,
always looking to its Master, who takes perfect care.
He brands the flank. He sets out hay.
He binds the knees with reasonable rules,
and now he loosens all bindings and lets his camel dance,
tearing the bridle and ripping the blankets.

The field itself sprouts new forms,
while the camel dances over them,
imaginary plants no one has thought of,
but all these new seeds, no matter how they try,
do not reveal the other sun.

Still the effort is joy,
one by one to keep uncovering pearls in oyster shells.

21.
Ar-Rahman, The Kind

The current Dalai Lama says, "Kindness is my religion." There are no separating distances. Kitchen smoke drifts up into clouds, cumin seeds browning. I am inside all of this as a continuous question about soul. In this new health we become servants to one another, a mother's hand held out for her hurt child. We drink in this place with our breathing, and the nightbirds start singing. How else should we get ready for death? Just to be held by the ocean is the best luck we could have, in this tenderness of buoyancy.

AS LAKEWATER RISES INTO MIST

The singer sings about love,
until the friend appears in the doorway.

Kitchen smoke drifts up into clouds
and becomes a thousand-year-old wine.

I am here, not reckoning the credit accumulated
or future speculation. I am the vineyard
and the barrel where the grapes are crushed.

The entire operation, whose transaction pours
this glass of wine, this moment, this poem.

A man stumbles by with baggage,
papers from the house, regret and wishing,
not knowing which to tend to. Neither.

After you see the face, concerns change,
as lakewater rises into mist.

A SMILE AND A GENTLENESS

There is a smile and a gentleness inside.
When I learned the name and address of that,
I went to where you sell perfume.
I begged you not to trouble me so with longing.

Come out and play. Flirt more naturally.
Teach me how to kiss.
On the ground a spread blanket,
flame that's caught and burning well,
cumin seeds browning.
I am inside all this with my soul.

NEW BLOSSOMS

Sit near someone who has had the experience.
Sit under a tree with *new* blossoms.

Walking the section of the market where chemists sell essences,
you will receive conflicting advice.

Go toward kindness. If you are not sure
where that is, you will be drawn in by fakes.

They will take your money and sit you down
on their doorstep saying, *I'll be right back.*
But they have another door they leave by.

Do not dip your cup in a pot
just because it has reached the simmering point.

Not every reed is sugarcane.
Not every *under* has an *over*.

Not every eye can see.
Or it may be that you cannot thread the needle
because it already has thread in it.

Your loving alertness is a lantern.
Keep it protected from wind that makes it crazy.

Instead of that airy commotion
live in the water that gently cools as it flows.
Be a helpful friend,
and you will become a green tree
with always new fruit,
with always deeper journeys into love.

THE TALKING

I have come here to lay my head at your feet,
to ask forgiveness,
to sit in the rose chair and burn my thorns.

Whatever I thought to do,
when I am here with you, is nothing.

I come to weep.
There is no escape from grief.

Outwardly, I am silent.
Inwardly, you know how I am screaming.

Make my face yours.
I will shorten this poem.
Read the rest inside me.

Poor silent lover,
you have no one to talk to?

But your thoughts keep surging through
like an army of firebrands.

Alone, every person stays quiet.
No one talks to a closed door.

But you are convinced
that you have lost your best companion.

Maybe you are already in the pure world,
beyond this scroungy wanting
and the metabolizing of nature. No doubt.

GREEN WRIT

From behind a thin cloth
a blaze of straw pretends to be the moon.

There are those who destroy soul growth
by using sacred symbols in their talk.

When you fall in love with clothing,
it is like you ride a donkey
into deep mud and sit there.

Even a dog sniffs greasy bread before eating.
Have you ever seen lions fighting over a piece of bread?
Why are you drawn to a beautiful corpse?

You are a continuous question about soul.
When the answer comes in, the question changes,
the way a kindness in grape juice turns it to wine,
the way you were born into this life.

Fire lightens and rises.
You bow when you hear truth.
Fall thieves the garden barren.

Then a spring justice knocks on the door.
You read the green writ removing all restraint.

SALADIN'S LEAVING

You decide to leave and once more darken into iron.
You bring to this place rose and lily and eglantine.
Let no one ever say you work for the adversary.

You brighten where you are.
You hold us together.

Now you lay on your side
in the laughing love-play we have had.

You honor this dance with gold-scattering sleeves, Saladin.
Like the moon you turn a grain-field silver.

FEET BECOMING HEAD

The sun came up differently today.
Souls move in the changing light.

Jupiter, the moon, the good luck house we inhabit,
the friend, all one presence today,
this grand health where we are servants to each other.

One who pours wine and makes toasts
arrives at the banquet just as it is over.

It is the perfect beginning for ending,
as feet become head in this new way.

BOTH WINGS BROKEN

Love draws a dagger and pulls me close.
Lock and key. Bird with both wings broken.

The love religion is all that is written here.
Who else would say this?

You open me wide open, or you tie me tighter.
The ball waits on the field to be hit again.

You push me into fire like Abraham.
You pull me out like Muhammad.

Which do you like better? you ask.
All the same, if it is your hand, troubles or peace.

Friends become enemies, faithless faithful.
Some knots tighten, some loosen.

Unruly tangle of caution and rebellion,
ropes and uncombed hair, no one can tell.

Then comes the sure attention
of a mother's hand for her hurt child.

BLESSING THE MARRIAGE

This marriage be wine with halvah,
honey dissolving in milk.

This marriage be the leaves and fruit of a date tree.
This marriage be women laughing together for days on end.

This marriage, a sign for us to study.
This marriage, beauty.

This marriage, a moon in a light blue sky.
This marriage, this silence fully mixed with spirit.

WAKE AND WALK OUT

If I flinched at every grief, I would be an intelligent idiot.
If I were not the sun, I would ebb and flow with sadness.

If you were not my guide, I would wander lost in Sinai.
If there were no light,
I would keep opening and closing the door.

If there were no rose garden,
where would the morning breezes go?
If love did not want music and laughter and poetry,
what would I say?

If you were not medicine, I would look sick and skinny.
If there were no leafy limbs in the air,
there would be no wet roots.

If no gifts were given, I would grow arrogant and cruel.
If there were no way into God,
I would not have lain in the grave of this body so long.

If there were no way from right to left,
I could not be swaying with the grasses.

If there were no grace and no kindness,
conversation would be useless, and nothing we do would matter.

Listen to the new stories that begin every day.
If light were not beginning again in the east,
I would not now wake and walk out inside this dawn.

AUCTION

As elephants remember India perfectly,
as mind dissolves, as song begins, as the glass fills,

wind rising, a roomful of conversation,
a sanctuary of prostration,

a bird lights on my hand in this day born of friends,
this ocean covering everything, all roads opening,

a person changing to kindness,
no one reasonable, religious jargon forgotten,

and Saladin there raising his hand
to bid on the bedraggled boy Joseph.

SCATTERBRAIN SWEETNESS

There is a glory that breathes life back into a corpse
and brings strangers together as friends.

Call that one back who fills the held-out robe
of a thornbush with flowers, who clears muddied minds,
who gives a two-day-old infant wisdom
beyond anyone's learning. *What baby?* you ask.

There is a fountain, a passion circulating.
I am not saying this well because I am too much
in the scatterbrain sweetness. Listen anyway.

It must be said. There are eyes that see into eternity.
A presence beyond the power and magic of shamans.

Let that in. Sink to the floor, full prostration.

ONE WHO CAN QUIT SEEING HIMSELF

I look for one simple and open enough to see the friend,
not an intelligence weighing several perspectives.

I want an empty shell to hold this pearl,
not a stone who pretends to have a secret center,
when the surface goes all the way through.

I want one who can quit seeing himself, fill with God,
and instead of being irritated by interruption
and daily resentments, feel those as kindness.

TALKING IN THE NIGHT

In the middle of the night I cry out,
Who lives in this love I have?

You say, I do, but I am not here alone.
Who are these other images with me?

I say, They are reflections of you,
just as the beautiful inhabitants of Chigil in Turkestan
resemble each other.

You say, But who is this other living being?

That is my wounded soul.

Then I brought that soul before you as a prisoner.

This one is dangerous, I say.
Do not let him off easy.

You wink and give me one end of a delicate thread.

Pull it tight, but do not break it.

I reach my hand to touch you.
You strike it down.

Why are you so harsh with me?

For good reason.
But certainly not to keep you away.
Whoever enters this place saying, Here I am
must be stopped.

This is not a pen for sheep.
There are no separating distances here.
This is love's sanctuary.

Saladin is how the soul looks.
Rub your eyes, and look again with love at love.

MAYBE THEY ARE SHY

Now the nightbirds will be singing
of the way we love each other.
Why should they sing about flowers
when they have seen us in the garden?

Maybe they are shy.
They cannot look at the face,
so they describe the feet.

If they keep dividing love into pieces,
they will disappear altogether.
We must be gentle and explain it to them.

Think of a mountain so huge
the Caucasus Range is a tiny speck.
Normal mountains run toward her when she calls.
They listen in their cave-ears and echo back.
They turn upsidedown when they get close,
they are so excited.

No more words.
In the name of this place we drink in with our breathing,
stay quiet like a flower, so the nightbirds will start singing.

FOLDED INTO THE RIVER

Your face is the light in here
that makes my arms full of gentleness.
The beginning of a monthlong holiday,
the disc of the full moon, the shade of your hair,
these draw me in.
I dive into the deep pool of a mountain river,
folded into union,
as the split-second when the bat meets the ball
and there is one cry between us.

DISSOLVER OF SUGAR

Dissolver of sugar, dissolve me,
if this is the time.
Do it gently with a touch of a hand, or a look.
Every morning I wait at dawn.
That is when it has happened before.
Or do it suddenly like an execution.
How else can I get ready for death?

You breathe without a body like a spark.
You grieve, and I begin to feel lighter.
You keep me away with your arm,
but the keeping away is pulling me in.

HOW FINITE MINDS MOST WANT TO BE

You are the living marrow. The rest is hay,
and dead grass does not nourish a human being.

When you are not here,
this desire we feel has no traveling companion.

When the sun is gone, the soul's clarity fades.
There is nothing but idiocy and mistakes.
We are half dead, inanimate, exhausted.

The way finite minds most want to be
is an ocean with a soul dissolved and swimming in it.
No one can describe that.
These words do not touch *you*.

Metaphors mentioning the moon
have no effect on the moon.

My soul, you are a master, a Moses, a Jesus.
Why do I stay blind in your presence?
You are Joseph at the bottom of his well.
Constantly working, but you do not get paid,
because what you do seems trivial, like play.

Now silence.
Unless these words fill with nourishment from the unseen,
they will stay empty,
and why should I serve my friends bowls with no food in them?

BUOYANCY

Love has taken away my practices
and filled me with poetry.

I tried to keep quietly repeating
No strength but yours, but I couldn't.

I had to clap and sing.
I used to be respectable and chaste and stable,
but who can stand in this strong wind
and remember those things?

A mountain keeps an echo deep inside itself.
That is how I hold your voice.

I am scrap wood thrown in your fire,
quickly reduced to smoke and ash.

I saw you and became that empty.
This emptiness, more beautiful than existence,
it obliterates existence, and yet when it comes,
existence thrives and creates more existence.

The sky is blue.
The world is a blind man sitting beside the road.

But whoever sees your emptiness
sees beyond blue and beyond the blind man.

A great soul hides like Muhammad or Jesus
moving through a crowd in a city where no one knows him.

To praise is to praise
how one surrenders to the emptiness.

To praise the sun is to praise your own eyes.
Praise, the ocean. What we say, a little ship.

So the sea journey goes on,
and no one knows where.

Just to be held by the ocean
is the best luck we could have.
It is a total waking up.

Why should we grieve that we have been sleeping?
It does not matter how long we have been unconscious.

We are groggy, but let the guilt go.
Feel the motions of tenderness around you.
the buoyancy.

BLACK TULIP

If someone claims to know my friend,
bring him or her close and let me look in the eyes.
I can recognize presence there.

You were so kind to us last night
that I felt your hand scratching behind my ears until dawn.
You are a clever pickpocket, but I have stolen more from you.

Now I hear there is an even better thief.
I leave the profession. Things are missing.

Birds fly with wings. I fly without.
I break my cup against a stone.
I tear my shirt and dig for roots. I rain.

A black tulip mocks *my* strangeness.
The one who teaches me is spring.
That show will open soon.
Outside, I grieve. Inside, pure laughter.

RAMADAN SILENCE

When the Ramadan banner flies, soul restrains nature,
so it can taste its own food.

The strength of horses and the intensity of fire,
these are the powers of sacrifice.
Fasting, we honor the guest.

Clouds of courage give rain,
because it was in this month that the Qur'an rained down,
light through an opening.

Grab the rope.
Be lifted out of the body's pit.

Announce to Egypt, Joseph of Canaan has come.
Jesus dismounts the donkey,
and the sacramental table descends.

Wash your hands. Wash your face.
Do not eat or speak as you normally do.
Other food and other words will come in the silence.

22.
Al-Mutakabbir, The Majesty

There is a quality of kingliness that does not *do* anything, but simply *is:*

> *When the king goes hunting, the forest smiles.*
> *Now the king has become the place, and all the players,*
> *prey, bystanders, bow, arrow, hand and release.*

A sovereign inclusiveness who, when silent, becomes eloquent. When the king stops weaving, the pattern improves. The quality is an intuitive grandeur expressed in great works of art—*King Lear,* Bach's Suite for the Cello in D minor, Qian Xuan's thirteenth-century insect screen, *Early Autumn,* Machu Picchu. Majesty is that abundantly generous place in consciousness that one can sometimes speak from. Storytelling gets more vivid, and luck shifts to the one who needs it. In that moment, that region, Rumi says, you *might* meet Shams Tabriz.

God knows what orchard you will be walking then.

THIS DAY'S GREAT WOODEN BOWL

Still dizzy from last night's wine?
Wait a while. Do not reach yet for this we serve.

You cannot really be on the ocean
with scenes of familiar creeks
and your loved home-river in your eyes.
Wait, if you are still caught in memory.

As those with business ideas
were driven from the temple courtyard,
so bitter, self-important people need to be excluded
from the mix being stirred in this day's great wooden bowl.

In the room with the Chinese princess, popular songs fade.
Do not boil the hard unripened grapes,
and do not sell vinegar. This moment is the perfect grape
you crush to make your life-wine interesting.

You might, in such a moment,
meet someone as I met Shams.
God knows what orchard you will be walking then.

BIRDS NESTING NEAR THE COAST

Soul, if you want to learn secrets,
your heart must forget about shame and dignity.

You are God's lover,
yet you worry what people are saying.

The rope the early Christians wore
to show who they were, throw it away.

Inside, you are sweet beyond telling,
and the cathedral there, so deeply tall.

Evening now, more your desire
than a woman's hair. And not knowledge.
Walk with those innocent of that.

Faces inside fire. Birds nesting near the coast,
earning their beauty, servants to the ocean.

There is a sun within every person,
the *you* we call companion.

THE BRIGHT CORE OF FAILURE

Sometimes you enter the heart.
Sometimes you are born from the soul.
Sometimes you weep a song of separation.
All the same glory.

You live in beautiful forms,
and you are the energy that breaks images.
All light, neither this nor that.

Human beings go places on foot.
Angels, with wings.

Even if they find nothing but ruins and failure,
you are the bright core of that.

When angels and humans are free of wings and feet,
they will understand that you are that lack, pure absence.

You are in my eyes
like a taste of wine that blocks my understanding.
That ignorance glorifies.

You talk and feel in the talking: kingdom, finances, fire,
smoke, the senses, incense, all are your favorites.

A ship, Noah, blessings, luck,
troubles that pull us unknowingly toward treasure.

Look. He is being dragged away from his friends.
No one will see him anymore.
This is your story.

I ask you, Should I talk to this one?
Is he being drawn to me?
Silence. That too.

What is desire? What *is* it?
Do not laugh, my soul.

Show me the way through this desiring.
All the world loves you,
but you are nowhere to be found,
hidden and completely obvious.

You are the soul.
You boil me down in a saucepan,
then ask why I am spilling out.

This writing, the record of being torn apart in your fire,
like aloes wood, becomes most itself when burning up.

Enough *talk about* burning.
Everything, even the end of this poem,
is a taste of your glory.

OUTDOORS AND THE PASSION OF THE GRASS

From now on the nightingales
will sing of us sitting here outdoors,
where wind lifts the hair of the willow
and starts her dancing.

God knows what they say to each other then.

The plane tree holds out its broad hands
in praise of the meadow,
understanding just a little of the passion of the grass.

I ask the rose, Where did you get such skin?
She laughs. How could she answer?
She is drunk, but not enough to say secrets,
not so dissolute as I am.

Wander with drunks if you want to know
what they have been hiding.

They will open the purse-mouth
and spend the lavishness.

There is a wine fermenting in the breast of a mystic,
and a voice there inviting you to a banquet.

A human breast can give milk, but also wine,
and also there is a flowing there that tells stories.

Listen, as you take in the milk,
and then the wine, and then the stories.

Lay down your cap and your cloak.
Start talking from the majesty itself.

And now be quiet. Very few will hear.

Most copper does not change to gold
for any philosopher's stone.

Bring your words to Shams.
Let sunlight mix with language and be the world.

THE PATTERN IMPROVES

When love itself comes to kiss you,
do not hold back.

When the king goes hunting, the forest smiles.
Now the king has become the place, and all the players,
prey, bystanders, bow, arrow, hand and release.

How does that feel?
Last night's dream enters these open eyes.

When we die and turn to dust,
each particle will be whole.

You hear a mote whirl taking form?
My music. Love, calm and patient.

The friend has waded down into existence,
gotten stuck, and will not be seen again outside of this.

We sometimes make spiderwebs of smoke and saliva,
fragile thought-packets.

Leave thinking to the one who gave intelligence.
In silence there is eloquence.

Stop weaving,
and watch how the pattern improves.

THIS IS ENOUGH

Sugar merchants, I have news.
Joseph has arrived from Egypt with the essence of sweetness.

A fruit cobbler that can save your soul. Spirit wine.
And if there is something else you want, that came too.

Khidr through an open window.
Aphrodite singing ghazals.
A sky with gold streaks across.

A stick that finds water in a stone.
Jesus sitting quietly near the animals, night so peaceful.

This is enough was always true.
We just have not seen it.

The hoopoe already wears a tufted crown.
Each ant is given its elegant belt at birth.

This love we feel pours through us like giveaway song.
The source of *now* is *here*.

REMEMBER EGYPT

You who worry with travel plans,
read again the place in the Qur'an
where Moses is taking the Jewish nation out of slavery.

You so frantic to have more money,
recall what they abandoned to wander in the wilderness.

You who feel hurt by some neglect,
remember the pavilions and houses they left behind.

You that lead the community through difficulties,
read about the abundant fountains
they walked away from to have freedom.

You who dress in clothes that appear to have elegant meaning,
you with so much charm,
remember how your face will decay to dirt.

You with lots of property, read again,
They left their gardens and the quietly running streams.

You who smile at funerals going by,
you that love language, measure the wind in stanzas,
and recall the exodus, the wandering forty-year sacrifice.
Remember Egypt.

LOVE DERVISHES

It takes the courage of inner majesty to stand in this doorway,
where there is no celebrating good fortune,
where talk of luck is embarrassing.

However your robe of patches fits is right.
If you are God's light, keep moving east to west as you have
   been.
Do not pretend something other than the truth.

Measuring devices do not work in this room
where the love dervishes meet.

No tradition grows here, and no soup simmers.
We sit in pure absence without expectation.

SAY I AM YOU

I am dust particles in sunlight.
I am the round sun.

To the bits of dust I say, *Stay*.
To the sun, *Keep moving*.

I am morning mist,
and the breathing of evening.

I am wind in the top of a grove,
and surf on the cliff.

Mast, rudder, helmsman, and keel,
I am also the coral reef they founder on.

I am a tree with a trained parrot in its branches.
Silence, thought, and voice.

The musical air coming through a flute,
a spark off a stone, a flickering in metal.

Both candle and the moth crazy around it.
Rose and nightingale lost in the fragrance.

I am all orders of being, the circling galaxy,
the evolutionary intelligence, the lift and the falling away.

What is and what is not.
You who know Jelaluddin,

You the one in all, say who I am.
Say I am you.

INWARD SKY

You are the soul, the universe,
and what animates the universe.

I live and work inside you.
I speak with what was found in the ruins of a former self.

Concealed in your garden, I have become a ladder,
propped against and leading up into the sky-dome.

Why cry for what is closer than voice?
I ask to hear the wisdom that uncovers the soul.

These four come with their answers.

Fire: You have a saucepan to cook what is raw.
Wear it like a saddle on your back.

Water: You have a spring inside.
Soak the earth.

Jupiter in its good-luck aspect: Show your talent.
Do something outside time and space.

Jupiter in its bad mood: Be consumed with jealousy.
What else is there?

Prophets come and go for one reason,
to say:

Human beings, you have a great value inside your form, a seed.
Be led by the rose inside the rose.

Doubt is part of existence.
There is no proof of the soul.

So I ask in this talking with soul, this prayer, this kindness:

When the soul leaves my body, where will these poems be?

Answer: It was like that in the beginning, before you were born,
so what are you worrying about?

Love, finish this *ghazal*, please.
You know which words will last.

Shams, say the meaning of the names,
the inward sky that you are.

AS RIPENESS COMES

What souls desire arrives.
We are standing up to our necks in the sacred pool.
Majesty is here.

The grains of the earth
take in something they do not understand.

Where did this come from?
It comes from where your longing comes.

From which direction?
As ripeness comes to fruit.

This answer lights a candle
in the chest of anyone who hears.

Most people only look for the way when they hurt.
Pain is a fine path to the unknowable.

But today is different.
Today the quality we call *splendor*
puts on human clothes, walks through the door,
closes it behind, and sits down with us
in this companionship.

LIMB-SHADOWS

You have polished the mirror that now you shine within.
Any direction I look I see your engraving.

The sun asks the inward sun, When will I see you?
At sunset.

But why does reason keep me from drowning in your love?
What use is this being rational inside majesty?

As many earrings as are in the world,
that is how many answers you give that question.

You give the questions too.
Any piece of broken pot handed me from you is gold.

Every second the call comes.
Who considers meanness within such generosity?

During the day we slip in and out of your tree
like limb-shadows.
At night we wait for dawn.

Adam rushed to be punished
because punishment was a kind of reconnection.

There is an ocean inside surging with praise for you,
but I close my eyes, hoping you will talk.

A SPRINGLIKE NIGHT IN MID-DECEMBER

Candle, wine, and friends,
on a springlike night in mid-December.

This love I have for you makes everywhere I look blaze up.
The tip of every feather burns.

A deep sweetness comes through sugarcane,
into the cut reed,
and now it is in the empty notes of the flute.

Beheaded lovers do not complain.
They live hidden underground like people in lava cities.

There is no worse torture than knowing *intellectually*
about love and the way.

Those Egyptian women, when they saw Joseph,
they were not *judging* his handsomeness.
They were lost in it,
cutting their hands as they cut their food.

Muhammad was completely empty
when he rose that night through a hundred thousand years.

Let wind blow through us.
Let Shams cover our shadows like snow.

FRESHNESS

When it's cold and raining,
you are more beautiful,
and the snow brings me
even closer to your lips.

The inner secret,
that which was never born,
you are that freshness,
and I am with you now.

I cannot explain
the goings and the comings.

You enter suddenly,
and I am nowhere again,
inside the majesty.

THE BURNING OCEAN

Where are those who died serving God
on the plain of Karbala?

Where are those who know how to open the gate?
There is no rational answer to this.

A prison full of debtors has been let out.
Where has everyone gone? Where are you?

You are in the ocean,
of which this world is just foam thrown up on shore.

Something huge inside me surges,
and the *foam* of this poetry takes *form*.

Let foam form be.
Dive into the burning ocean,
as that source of light, Shams, comes up in the east.

ENTIRELY JEWELS

Notice how each particle moves.
Notice how everyone has just arrived from a journey.
Notice how each wants a different food.
Notice how the stars vanish as the sun comes up,
how all streams stream toward the ocean.

Look at the chefs preparing special plates for everyone,
according to what they need.
Look at this cup that can contain the ocean.
Look at those who see the face.
Look through Shams's eyes
into the water that is entirely jewels.

A NEW KIND OF WAKING

Is there anything better than selling figs to the fig seller?
That is how this is.

Making a profit is not why we are here,
nor pleasure, nor joy.

When someone is a goldsmith,
wherever he goes, he asks for the goldsmith.

Clouds build with what we share.
Wheat stays wheat right through the threshing.

How just do you feel when you load a lame donkey?
The earth has tasted from this cup.
That is why it turns green.

Let the lean and wounded be revived in this garden.
How would the soul feel in the beloved's river?
Fish washed free and clean of fear.

You drive us away, but we return like pet pigeons.
Ten nights becoming dawn flow into us as a new kind of waking.

Shahabuddin Osmond joins the circle.
I will say this poem again,
so that he can play.
There is no end to anything round.

ANGRY AT THE ROAD, AT GOD

A black sky hates the moon. I am that dark nothing.
I hate those in power.
I am invited in from the road to the house,
but I invent some excuse. Now I am angry at the road.

I do not need love. Let something break me.
I do not want to hear anyone's trouble.
I have had my chance for wealth and position.
I do not want those.

I am iron resisting the most enormous magnet there is.
Another pulls straw to it. That makes me angry.

We are molecules spinning here, four, five, six of us.
What does that mean, *five, six?* I am angry at God.

You do not understand, being out of the water.
You resemble the sun? I hate likenesses.

23.
As-Sami, The Hearing

Sufis have experimented for at least a thousand years with what they call *sema*, deep listening. All day and night there are changing musical modes. Give your life to this listening. It is the knack of how spirit breathes into us. We are learning a new sense, earsight. Every moment has a music. A four-year-old girl, with snarls in her hair, says of the choppy sea: "The waves aren't listening to each other, and they are not taking turns." Absence is the ocean we swim. The grave is a wormhole into this. And it may be, in the next stage of existence, that we move into beyond death, that language plays no part at all. Enjoy it while you can.

TAMBOURINE FEET

When you are not with me, I sometimes resemble
a fish put live in the skillet,
writhing its little cooking time left,
or the empty eyes of graffiti faces,
or a house with no one home.

Other times my love for your soul
spreads out over the city like music.
Quadrant to quadrant the jeweled tambourine feet move,
palace to ghetto, from cultured artist to craftsman to slave.
All begin to hum and sing *this*.

A WORLD DENSE WITH GREETING

The soul comes every day at dawn.
Good to see you again, my friend.
The peace of God be with you.

No matter where you are or what you are doing,
talking, silent, asleep, soul comes and greets you
like that. Your soul sees your purity.

Body sees your pretensions and deceit.
You are a rose that heals woundedness.
Hello again, call out the thorns.

I go to the village chief. I say,
God be with you. He gives me a glass of wine.
Hold this carefully. Keep it safe.

The peace of God, I tell him.
But did you know that I am crazy.
I like to sit in the fire with Abraham.

Then I turn and thank God. *Salaam Aleichem.*
I walk out. The world is dense with greeting.

I respond in kind, then back into the cave
with my beloved. Subtle artwork appears
everywhere. *It is so fine to be with you.*

David from the throne agrees to be thrown down.
Hallaj nods *namaste* from the cross.

One who is longing for your praise
waves without expecting anything.

Someone deeply in need signals helplessly.
The king puts up an appropriate banner.
The sick mouth *Hey*. I undress
and walk toward whatever is next.

Every string on the instrument sings *salaam*
to every other. Death brings good health.

I let words loose like mountain runoff,
read Sura 62, which warns of finding images
for what has no likeness, and leave the job
I imagined for myself with one thought:

God bless. Adios, do svidanye, toodle-oo,
au revoir, ciao, aloha, teshekkur ederim.

May your well run deep.

EVEN BETTER

With three strings play the mode of *Rehavi* . . .

Sing us into union, no more ambivalence.

If you don't have *zir* or *bem*, the high and low strings on the lute,
even better.

Now grief comes over with a *Neva* song.
Sing our lack of songs.

You go away on the *Irak* mode . . .
Draw near stroking *Ispahan* . . .
Wild with *Zingule* . . . finishing the matter,
but still we are nervous and dull.

This music is and is not.

A stretch of *Rast* . . . reaches into *Hicaz* . . .
Huseyni into *Uzzak* . . .
on to the pure joy of *Buselik* . . . *Maye* . . .

We ask for *Dugah* . . . You give *Cargah* . . .

Candle, sunlight over countryside.
I call you a changing beauty
that sings and blesses this place with every mode.

MUSIC IS MY *ZIKR*

As the hoopoe loves to hear Solomon's whistle,
I want the reed flute and the harp
the rebab and the drum,
burning in the mode of *Ispahan* . . . then *Hicaz*.

Take a chord from *Irak* . . . with some *Uzzak* . . . to *Rast* . . .

The wail of *Buselik* . . . Now slip into *Huseyni* . . .

Maye . . . The vast and tiny melodies singing me to sleep.

Rehavi . . . to wake with *Zingele* . . .

Music is my *zikr*. These names are all I know.
Let the mind's other concerns go.

This love is more subtle.
As wind through a field stirs wildflower scent,
by music-light fresh beauties appear.
This is all I want.

LISTENING

What is the deep listening?
Sema is a greeting from the secret ones
inside the heart, a letter.

The branches of your intelligence
grow new leaves in the wind of this listening.

The body reaches a peace.
Rooster sound comes,
reminding you of your love for dawn.

The reed flute and the singer's lips.
The knack of how spirit breathes into us
becomes as simple and ordinary as eating and drinking.

The dead rise with the pleasure of this listening.
If someone cannot hear a trumpet melody,
sprinkle dirt on his head and declare him dead.

Listen and feel the beauty of your separation,
the unsayable absence.

There is a moon inside every human being.
Learn to be companions with it.
Give more of your life to this listening.

As brightness is to time, so you are
to the one who talks to the deep ear in your chest.

I should sell my tongue and buy a thousand ears
when that one steps near and begins to speak.

EARSIGHT

Do you want the sweetness of food
or the sweetness of the one who put sweetness in food?

There are amazing things in the ocean,
and there is the one who *is* the ocean.

Think of a carpenter's alert comprehension
as he builds a house.
Now think of the one who creates consciousness.

It takes skill to extract oil from a nut.
Now consider how sight lives in the eye.

There is a night full of the wildness of wanting.
Then dawn comes. You take my hand in yours.
There are those who doubt that this can happen.

They pour powdered gold into barley bins.
They follow donkeys to the barn.

Enough words.
Friend, you can make the ear *see*.
Speak the rest of this poem in that language.

ASLEEP AND LISTENING

Day before yesterday,
fire whispered to the fragrant smoke,

Aloes wood loves me,
because I know how to untie it
and let it loose.

This burning must occur,
or nothing will happen.

Sperm cell disappears into egg.
Then a new beauty appears.

Bread and broth must dissolve in the stomach
before energy comes.
Raw ore gets refined into coins.

It is necessary for you to experience nonbeing.
Love takes you toward that.

Asleep beside the splashing water,
let it say secrets into you.

Be a sleep and a pure listening
at the same time.

INSIDE SHAMS'S UNIVERSE

Inside a lover's heart there is another world,
and yet another inside the friend of this community of lovers,
an ear that interprets mystery,
a vein of silver in the ground, another sky.

Intellect and compassion are ladders we climb,
and there are other ladders.
As we walk in the night, the voice that talks of forgiveness.

Inside Shams's universe candlelight itself
becomes a moth to die in his flame.

WE NO LONGER SEE THE ONE WHO TEACHES US

Musicians, play this moment's music as grace
for those who block our road, grace for bandits.

Musician, you learned this from a true bandit.
I hear the teacher's accent in the student's art.

Musician, turn your face to absence,
because existence is deceitful and afraid.

The soul knows it is not from here.
It feels bound in a body, yet it knows the pleasure of absence.

Absence is the ocean we swim. Existence, a fishhook.
Anyone caught loses the joy of freedom.

Being nailed to the four elements is a crucifixion.
If you keep running after your wishes and desires,
that is your crucifixion, be sure of it.

There is a fire in patience that burns what of you is born
to ash. Strike the flint of Sura 100, *Honor the one
who loses breath*. And, *Fire rises where they walk*.

These are brave souls, musician igniting musician.
What is the point of a chess-game world,
where a pawn cuts off a king?

I walk awkwardly, but the smoke goes straight up.
Sometimes a pawn makes it to the other side
and redeems a queen.

The knight says, *Your plodding is one or two moves for us*.
Judgment Day is closer than that for everyone, one step away.

The chess king says, *Without me this motion and figuring
mean nothing. The bishop might as well be a mosquito*.

Winning and losing are the same. There is checkmate in both.
We no longer see the one who teaches us.
You might say we have been checkmated. What happens now?

MUSIC LOOSENS DEAFNESS

You that pour, people do not see the beauty anymore
of this joy we call wine. The clear saying of wisdom
cannot now be easily heard by the soul.

And sign language will not help.
We need the sword of Shams to free us.

We have wanted material things more
than the deep connection of this circle, bread more than wine.

You have heard how Moses was with God on Sinai.
That closeness is far away now.

Look at the overcast sky. It is not the splendor of feeling near.
We have been lazy. We should either disband altogether,
or not stay apart so long.

Let music loosen our deafness to spirit.
Play and let play.

NOT A FOOD SACK, A REED FLUTE

You that add soul to my soul, who hear my night grief,
timely, unlikely fire in every grain of my being,
mountain sound harmonizing with my song,
magnet for form, you have none.

With your joy I live my entire life in a small valley.
Without you, every natural pleasure,
of tasting, of being outdoors,
becomes a heavy hobble tied to my feet.
I untie it and see that it is immediately there again.

Tonight is a night
when grace gives me a love book to read.

I empty out whatever blocks a clear note.
Not a food sack, I am a reed flute.
There is no cure for this soul but you, Averroës.

NEW LIGHT ON THE GROUND

Another year, another spring.
The fragrance of love arrives.

So dancy, this new light on the ground,
and in the tree.

The one who heals us
lets whatever hurts the soul
dissolve to a listening intelligence,
where what we most deeply want, union with eternity,
grows up around and inside us now.

MORE OF WHAT WE SAY

A door springs open; the roof flies off.
I say, Tonight you are my provocative guest.

You say, *But I have business elsewhere.*
I must leave now.

Just one night.

You say, *All human beings are in my care.*

I say, Then kill me.

You say, *The prophet Isaac*
should have been sacrificed in this doorway.
Do not tremble as I bring the knife close.

Death chooses you,
then pushes you into the sugar bowl.

You leave like the wind.
I say, Leave more slowly.

You say, *This is the laziest pace I have.*

I say, But walk along like a lame horse of overcast sky.
Let my flame catch in your thicket.

If I say more of what we say,
I will not be here.

A FROG DEEP IN THE PRESENCE

Since you have left, death draws us in.
A fish quivers on rough sand until its soul leaves.

For those of us still living,
the grave feels like an escape hole back to the ocean.

This is no small thing,
the pulling of a part into the whole.

Muhammad used to weep for his native land.
To children who do not know where they are from,
Istanbul and Yemen are similar. They want their nurses.

As animals love the ground,
a star goes out to graze in the nightsky pasture.

When I close my mouth, this poetry stops,
but a frog deep in the presence
cannot keep his mouth closed.
He breathes, and the sound comes.

In the same way a mystic cannot hide his breathing light-burst.

I reach this point, and the pen breaks,
as Sinai once split open for the generosity.

A WELL-BAKED LOAF

Forget the world, and so command the world.

Be a lamp, or a lifeboat, or a ladder.
Help someone's soul heal.
Walk out of your house like a shepherd.

Stay in the spirit fire. Let it cook you.
Be a well-baked loaf and lord of the table.
Come and be served to your brothers.

You have been a source of pain.
Now you will be the delight.

You have been an unsafe house.
Now you will be the one who sees into the invisible.

I said this and a voice came to my ear,
If you become this, you will be *that*.

Then silence, and now more silence.
A mouth is not for talking.
A mouth is for tasting this sweetness.

SING LOUD

Advice does not help lovers.
They are not the kind of mountain stream
that you can build a dam across.

An intellectual does not know what the drunk is feeling.
Do not try to figure what those lost inside love will do next.

Someone in charge would give up all his power,
if he caught one whiff of the wine musk
from the room where the lovers are doing who knows what.

One of them tries to dig a hole through a mountain.
One flees from academic honors.
One laughs at famous mustaches.

Life freezes if it does not get a taste of this almond cake.

The stars come up spinning every night,
bewildered in love.
They would grow tired with that revolving if they weren't.

They would say, *How long do we have to do this?*

God picks up the reed-flute world and blows.
Each note is a need coming through one of us,
a passion, a longing pain.

Remember the lips where the breath originated,
and let your note be clear.

Do not try to end it.
Be your note.

I will show you how that is enough.
Go up on the roof at night in this city of the soul.

Let everyone climb on their roofs
and sing their notes. Sing loud.

THE JOY OF THE SUN

You that love lovers,
this is your home. Welcome.

In the midst of making form,
love made this form that melts form,
with love for the door,
and soul, the vestibule.

Watch the dustgrains
moving in the light near the window.

Their dance is our dance.

We rarely hear the inward music,
but we are all dancing to it nevertheless,
directed by Shams,
the pure joy of the sun,
our music master.

EYES THAT LOVE SUNSET

Here comes July, who likes to hear the stories travelers tell,
those that journey in full prostration,
not the self-important pilgrims.

Listen to one who moves as he or she is led to,
with no complaining, who lives in the great heart,

like Damascus on the Syrian plain.

Harvest comes with August.
Then Ramadan silence and fasting,
with eyes that love sunset.

Tell someone in the middle of health and success,
This will change to a bout with malaria.

No one but Khidr knows who will prosper and who will not.
Remember Muhammad's boot with the snake inside?

It is good to be quiet. Say less.
Those obsessed with gaining recognition
do nothing but talk the entire day.

24.
Al-Basir, The Seeing

There is a deep knowing that gets embodied in sight:

Shams Tabriz is the act of seeing,
the one who looks, and the sun itself.
There is no way to understand such a presence.

It is vast and minute at the same time, this presence that sees through a lover's eyes:

Close these eyes to open the other.
Let the center brighten your sight.

This is a clear indication of the need for meditation in a lover's life. I once asked my teacher, Bawa Muhaiyaddeen, if what I saw in his eyes would ever come up inside me, behind my eyes, and look out through me. He said that if you want something hard enough, you will get it. He also made a pun. It will happen when "the *eye* (I) becomes a *we*."

I SEE THE FACE

I see the face that was my home.
My loving says, *I will let go of everything for that.*

My soul begins to keep rhythm,
as if music were playing.

My reason says, *What do you call this cypress-energy
that straightens what was bent double?*

All things change in this presence.
Armenians and Turks no longer know which is which.

Soul keeps unfolding inward.
The body leaves the body.

A wealth you cannot imagine flows through you.

Do not consider what strangers say.
Be secluded in your secret heart-house,
that bowl of silence.

Talking, no matter how humble-seeming,
is really a kind of bragging.
Let silence be the art we practice.

ASHES, WANDERERS

In this battle we do not hold a shield in front of us.
When we turn in *sema,*
we do not hear the flute or the tambourine.

Underneath these feet we become *nazar,*
the guide's glance, ashes, wanderers.

As the moon diminishes every day, and then it is gone,
to come back changed.

Send for the planet Venus to play here.
Flute, drums, and strings are not enough.

No. Who but these musicians
could stand the heat that melts the sun?

WOODEN WALKINGSTICK

Friend, you are Moses.
I am his wooden walkingstick.

Sometimes that simple use.
Other times, a dragon earth-energy.

You decide.
There is no time or place in the air you inhabit.
Days you give me, I give back to you.
I have seen your unseeable beauty
and taken report without words to my heart,
which became all eye with the news.
Long life to eyes,
says my heart now over and over.

Hundreds of candles search the turning sky.
No bread in the basket, no money, no home.
Family, work in shambles,
with your light shining on the ruins.

Crushed in grief's mortar,
let me be medicine for other eyes.

What is the soul? Half a leaf.
What is the heart? A flower opening.

I am not the one speaking here.
Even so, I will stop.
Anything anyone says is your voice.

WHAT I SEE IN YOUR EYES

Out of myself, but wanting to go beyond that,
wanting what I see in your eyes,

not power, but to kiss the ground
with the dawn breeze for company,
wearing white pilgrim cloth.

I have a certain knowing.
Now I want sight.

AS FISH DRINK THE OCEAN

This world eats men and women.
We become ground,
and yet God sends us here to eat the whole universe.

Earth tries to work a sorcery on us, saying,
Tomorrow, tomorrow,
but we outwit that spell by enjoying this now.

Say we were born from invisible beings
that gather in the middle of the night.
Say that is why we love the night so.

We love, and taste the wine of being human,
as fish drink the ocean.
Do you think that alters the sea?

Sea and see: How one values the beloved
depends on the state of the lover.

What are *you* worth?
Which candle draws you to die in its light?

Shams of Tabriz is the act of seeing,
the one who *looks*, and the sun itself.
There is no way to understand such a presence.

TOO VAST FOR PARTNERSHIP

Will it be better for us when we dissolve into the ground,
or worse? Let's learn now what will happen.

This is lovers' work, to break through and become the earth,
to die before we die.

Do not think of somehow pairing up with God.
That claim is a righteous self-indulgence.

You know it by the smell.
Smoke coming off dried dung is different
from that coming from burning aloes wood.

The presence that one second is soil, then water, fire,
smoke, warp, woof, a friend, a shame, modesty,
is too vast and intimate for partnership.

Observers watch as presence takes thousands of forms.
But inside your eyes,
the presence does not brighten or dim.
It just lives there.

A saint or a prophet, one like Muhammad,
can see the trees of heaven, the fruit hanging so close
he could reach and pick one for his friend.

But it is not time for that.
They melt and flow away from sight.

YOU ARE NOT YOUR EYES

Those who have reached their arms into emptiness
are no longer concerned with lies or truth, with mind or soul,
or which side of the bed they rose from.

If you are still struggling to understand,
you are not there.

You offer your soul to one who says,
Take it to the other side.

You are on neither side,
yet those who love you see you on one side or the other.

You say *Illa*, Only God,
then your hungry eyes see that you are in Nothing, *La*.

You are an artist who paints with existence and non.
Shams could help you see who you are.

But remember. *You are not your eyes.*

THE BREAST MY HEART NURSES

You are the breast my heart nurses now,
God's shadow, sun that casts no shadow.

You stir the particles of this universe,
giving love to lovers, laughter and dance steps.

You burn thought to ash. You turn where you wish.
Soul saw a bit of light in an eye and went there.

Toothless geezers sing love songs. Mind loses track.
Beyond existence, beyond absence, Shams Tabriz,
the mountain of gentleness we are hidden in,
watches through a cleft.

COOKED HEADS

I have been given a glass
that has the fountain of the sun inside,
a friend to both worlds,
like the fragrance of amber inside the fragrance of musk.

My soul-parrot gets excited with sweetness.
Wingbeats, a door opening in the sun.

You have seen the market where they sell cooked heads.
That is what this is,
a way of seeing beyond inner and outer.

A donkey wanders the sign of Taurus.
Heroes do not stay lined up in ranks for very long.

I set out for Tabriz,
even though my boat is anchored here.

CUISINE AND SEX

You risk your life to feed desires,
yet you give your soul only short grazing spans,
and those grudgingly.

You borrow ten and repay fourteen.
Most of your decisions can be traced back
to cuisine and sex.

The fuel basket goes from one stoke hole to the next.
Six friends hoist your handsomeness
and carry it to the cemetery.

Food changes going from table to latrine.
You live between deaths
thinking that's right enough.

Close these eyes to open the other.
Let the center brighten your sight.

THE FLOWER'S EYE

Find me near the flower's eye
that takes in provocation and begins to grow.

Love a baby that struggles and fights,
stops nursing, and runs out through the door,
escaping as fire jumps to the next burn.

BREAKING LOOSE

I have broken out again,
escaped from the tricky, wiry shamans of ecstasy.

Running night and day to escape night and day.
Why fear grief, when death walks so close beside?
Do not fear the general,
when you are good friends with the prince.

For forty years, I made plans and worried about them.
Now sixty-two, I have moved beyond being reasonable.

By definition, human beings do not see or hear.
Break loose from definition.

Skin outside, seeds inside, a fig lives caught between,
and like that fig, I wriggle free.

Hesitation, deadly. Hurrying, worse.
Escape both delay and haste.

Fed first with blood in the womb,
then milk from the breast,
my clever teeth came in, and I escaped even those.

Off balance, I grope for bread, a loaf or two,
until God gives the next food, and I am gone.

No more garlicky detail, no more meanings,
only clean-breathed, silent escaping.

NO WAY TO COMPARE

Intricate sound, not words.
I catch what I cannot quite make out.
Fire burning down along the roots,
as well as in the branches. The whole tree gone.

Stories about the Green Man Khidr,
and stories Khidr himself told.
We thought they were lost.
The oldest love in new shapes.

For the sun, we say, and the sun comes up.
Lam Yakon. We begin reading Sura 112.
There is no way to compare God to anything.
But look.

SOMEONE DIGGING IN THE GROUND

An eye is meant to see things.
The soul is here for its own joy.
A head has one use: For loving a true love.
Legs: To run after.

Love is for vanishing into the sky.
The mind, for learning what men have done and tried to do.
Mysteries are not to be solved.
The eye goes blind when it only wants to see *why*.

A lover is always accused of something.
But when he finds his love,
whatever was lost in the looking
comes back completely changed.

On the way to Mecca, many dangers:
Thieves, the blowing sand, only camel's milk to drink.

Still, each pilgrim kisses the black stone there
with pure longing, feeling in the surface
the taste of the lips he wants.

This talk is like stamping new coins.
They pile up,
while the real work is being done outside
by someone digging in the ground.

LET'S GO HOME

Late and starting to rain, it is time to go home.
We have wandered long enough in empty buildings.
I know it is tempting to stay and meet those new people.
I know it is even more sensible

to spend the night here with them,
but I want to be home.

We have seen enough beautiful places
with signs on them saying, *This Is God's House.*
That is seeing grain like the ants do,
without the work of harvesting.
Let's leave grazing to cows
and go where we know what everyone really intends,
where we can walk around without clothes on.

AN EMPTY GARLIC

You miss the garden,
because you want a small fig from a random tree.
You do not meet the beautiful woman.
You are joking with an old crone.
It makes me want to cry how she detains you,
stinking-mouthed, with a hundred talons,
putting her head over the roof edge to call down,
tasteless fig, fold over fold, empty
as dry-rotten garlic.

She has you tight by the belt,
even though there is no flower and no milk in her body.

Death will open your eyes to what her face is.
Leather spine of a black lizard.
No more advice.

Let yourself be silently drawn
by the stronger pull of what you really love.

INSIDE SIGHT

You are the king's son.
Why do you close yourself up?
Become a lover.

Do not aspire to be a general
or a minister of state.

One is a boredom for you,
the other a disgrace.

You have been a picture on a bathhouse wall long enough.
No one recognizes you here, do they?

God's lion disguised as a human being.
I saw that and put down the book I was studying,
Hariri's *Maqamat*.

There is no early and late for us.
The only way to measure a lover
is by the grandeur of the beloved.

Judge a moth by the beauty of its candle.

Shams is invisible because he is inside sight.
He is the intelligent essence
of what is everywhere at once, seeing.

NO ROOM FOR FORM

On the night when you cross the street
from your shop and your house to the cemetery,
you will hear me hailing you from inside the open grave,
and you will realize how we have always been together.

I am the clear consciousness-core of your being,
the same in ecstasy as in self-hating fatigue.

That night, when you escape the fear of snakebite
and all irritation with the ants,
you will hear my familiar voice,
see the candle being lit, smell the incense,
the surprise meal fixed
by the lover inside all your other lovers.

This heart-tumult is my signal to you
igniting in the tomb.

So don't fuss with the shroud
and the graveyard road dust.

Those get ripped open and washed away
in the music of our finally meeting.

And don't look for me in a human shape.

I am inside your looking.
No room for form with love this strong.

Beat the drum and let the poets speak.
This is a day of purification
for those who are already mature
and initiated into what love is.

No need to wait until we die.
There is more to want here than money
and being famous and bites of roasted meat.

Now, what shall we call this new sort of gazing-house
that has opened in our town
where people sit quietly and pour out their glancing
like light, like answering?

25.
Al-Wadud, The Loving

All of the qualities signified by the names of God infuse and inform the others, but this one, love, is especially pervasive. Love is the whole. It is more than human, more than imagination, more than relationship. It leads into nonexistence, absence. A flowering, a rose underfoot, roses under all our feet, the absurdity no image can contain. Candleflame become moth. The pearl diver does not know how to swim. Pearls are brought to him where he sits on the beach. The sun is completely generous with its light. The parts and the whole are equals.

MORE IS REQUIRED

You have disappeared into the way?
Leave even that behind.

Sit with the essence inside love.
In that Chinese mirror you will see hundreds
of sword blades. Do not be afraid to use them.

You have given up everything.
You must live in absence. More is required.

Mix an eye medicine with the ground.
Sweep the memory pictures clean.

Swing down and cut.
A voice comes in the broken place.

Pull the tree-wing up by its roots.
Love wants an arm and a leg.

WHAT IS THE HEART?

What is the heart?
It is not human and it is not imaginary.
I call it you.

Stately bird, who one moment combines with this world,
and the next, passes through the boundary to the unseen.

The soul cannot find you,
because you are the soul's wings, how it moves.

Eyes cannot see you.
You are the source of sight.

You are the one thing that repentance will not repent,
nor news report.

Spring comes. One seed refuses to germinate
and start being a tree. One poor piece of wood
blackens but will not catch fire.

The alchemist wonders at a bit of copper
that resists turning to gold.

Who am I that I am with you
and still myself?

When the sun comes up,
the complicated nightmind of the constellations fades.

Snow-forms do not last through July.

The heart quality embodied by our master, Shams Tabriz,
will always dissolve the old quarrel between those
who believe in the dignity of a human being's decisions
and those who claim that those are all illusion.

SECRET PLACES

Lovers find secret places inside this violent world
where they make transactions with beauty.

Reason says, Nonsense.
I have walked and measured the walls here.
There are no places like that.

Love says, There are.

Reason sets up a market and begins doing business.
Love has more hidden work.

Hallaj steps away from the pulpit
and climbs the stairs of the gallows.

Lovers feel a truth inside themselves
that rational people keep denying.

It is reasonable to say, Surrender is just an idea
that keeps people from living their lives.

Love responds, No.
This thinking is what is dangerous.

Using language obscures what Shams came to give.
Every day the sun rises
out of low word-clouds into burning silence.

NO EXPECTATIONS

A spirit that lives in this world
and does not wear the shirt of love,
such an existence is a deep disgrace.

Be foolishly in love,
because love is all there is.

There is no way into presence,
except through a love exchange.

If someone asks, But what is love?
Answer, Dissolving the will.

True freedom comes to those who have escaped
the questions of freewill and fate.

Love is an emperor.
The two worlds play across him.
He barely notices their tumbling game.

Love and lover live in eternity.
Other desires are substitutes for that way of being.

How long do you lay embracing a corpse?
Love rather the soul, which cannot be held.

Anything born in spring dies in fall,
but love is not seasonal.

With wine pressed from grapes,
expect a hangover.

But this path has no expectations.
You are uneasy riding the body?
Dismount. Travel lighter.
Wings will be given.

Be clear like a mirror reflecting nothing.
Be clean of pictures
and the worry that comes with images.

Gaze into what is not ashamed
or afraid of any truth.

Contain all human faces in your own
without any judgment of them.

Be pure emptiness.
What is inside that? you ask.
Silence is all I can say.
Lovers have some secrets that they keep.

GONE FOR GOOD

I have stumbled over buried treasure again.
What I thought came first comes last.

How shall we celebrate?
Do not expect your heart to return.

When it is dissolved in love,
it is gone for good.

Fire-messengers come running.
All troubles begin here.

There is no sleep left in me,
nor any eyesight.

It is possible my head is a pumpkin,
full of red wine.

I sit at table tasting bread and milk.
It is myself I taste.

I dip a jar in the ocean.
Filled containers become seawater.

At the evening prayer time I go to see a friend,
who looks out of an upstairs window and comes down.

We grow quiet.
Our souls become one another and Shams Tabriz.

I ROCKED MY OWN CHEST

Yesterday I sent a message
as clear and steady as a star.

You that turn stones to gold,
change me.

I showed you the longing
and rocked my own chest
like an infant to hush it from crying.

Undo your breast.
Take me back to love's first place,
where we were in union.

How much longer do I have to wander apart?

I will be quiet now and patient,
waiting for you to turn and look.

MIDNIGHT AND SUNRISE

This midnight restlessness does not originate on earth.
No headache, no fever, no black bile, no dropsy,
but it seems epidemic, this love.

No advice helps, no cool restraint.
This intensity is invisible.
Have you seen this love? Or heard it?

There are no chants to chant. Keep silent.
No theatrical magic.

Shams Tabriz is the source
that can melt this diseased and frozen world,
as now his healing splendor rises.

WATCH A ONE-YEAR-OLD

Anger rises when you are proud of yourself.
Humble that. Use the contempt of others,
and your own self-regarding, to change,

like the cloud in folklore that became three snake shapes.
Or if you like the dog-barking lion wrath,
enjoy the hurt longer.

Watch a one-year-old, how he walks,
the slow wisdom there.

Sometimes a sweet taste makes you sour and mean.
Listen for the voice that says,
It was for you I created the universe.

Then kill and be killed in love.
You have been two dogs dozing long enough.

ROSES UNDERFOOT

The sound of *salaams* rising as waves diminish down in prayer,
hoping for some trace of the one whose trace does not appear.

If anyone asks you to say who you are,
say without hesitation, Soul within soul within soul.

There is a pearl diver who does not know how to swim.
No matter. Pearls are handed him on the beach.

We lovers laugh to hear, "This should be more that,
and that more this," coming from people
sitting in a wagon tilted in a ditch.

Going in search of the heart, I found a huge rose
under my feet, and roses under all our feet.

How to say this to someone who denies it?
The robe we wear is the sky's cloth.
Everything is soul and flowering.

WILDER THAN WE EVER

The one who pours is wilder than we ever become drinking,
wilder than wine, the one who fills to the brim
and leaves to live in absence with a toast,
Go home. There is nothing for you here.

A pearl in the shell does not touch the ocean.
Be a pearl without a shell, a mindful flooding,
candle turned moth, head become empty jar,
bird settling nest, love lived.

NOT HERE

There is courage involved if you want to become truth.
There is a broken-open place in a lover.

Where are those qualities of bravery and sharp compassion
in this group? What's the use of old and frozen thought?

I want a howling hurt. This is not a treasury
where gold is stored. This is for copper.

We alchemists look for talent that can heat up and change.
Lukewarm won't do. Half-hearted holding back,
well-enough getting by? *Not here.*

ONE SWAYING BEING

Love is not condescension, never that, nor books,
nor any marking on paper, nor what people say of each other.

Love is a tree with branches reaching into eternity,
and roots set deep in eternity, and no trunk.

Have you seen it? The mind cannot. Your desiring cannot.
The longing you feel for this love comes from inside you.

When you become the friend,
your longing will be as the man in the ocean
who holds to a piece of wood.

Eventually wood, man, and ocean
become one swaying being,
Shams Tabriz, the secret of God.

A TRACE

You that give new life to this planet,
you that transcend logic, come.

I am only an arrow.
Fill your bow with me and let fly.

Because of this love for you
my bowl has fallen from the roof.
Put down a ladder and collect the pieces, please.

People ask, But which roof is your roof?

I answer, Wherever the soul came from,
and wherever it goes at night, my roof is in that direction.
From wherever spring arrives to heal the ground,
from wherever searching rises in a human being.

The looking itself is a trace of what we are looking for,
but we have been more like the man who sat on his donkey
and asked the donkey where to go.

Be quiet now and wait.
It may be that the ocean one,
that we desire so to move into and become,
desires us out here on land a little longer
going our sundry roads to the shore.

NO OCCUPATION

I have no occupation other than this love.
I do not need to smell every rose and touch every thorn.
You are seeing through my eyes and tasting with my tongue.

Now that I have had this honey,
why should I sell vinegar?
Why should I *do* anything?
After breakfast at the king's table,
there is no appetite for lunch.

I do not complain, and I do not brag about ascetic practices.
I would explain this, but there are no words.
There is nothing to grieve about.

Those of you who have no trace of this madness,
tell me how you are.
I have forgotten how it is to say how I am.

Since Shams has shone on me, I have no interest
in describing the moon as it rises over the dormitory roof.

FRESH ROOTS

Be with those who help your being.
Do not sit with indifferent people,
whose breath comes cold out of their mouths.

Not these visible forms.
Your work is deeper.

A chunk of dirt thrown in the air breaks to pieces.
If you do not try to fly, and so break yourself apart,
you will be broken open by death,
when it is too late for all you could become.

Leaves get yellow.
The tree puts out fresh roots and makes new green.
Why are you so content with a love that turns you yellow?

A CONSTANT CONVERSATION

I am here by the gate.
Maybe you will throw open a door and call.
I am drenched with being here.

Things dissolve around me,
but I am still sitting here.

One clap in the emptiness of space.
New centuries begin. Laughter. A rose,
a wise loveliness, the sun
coming out brilliantly, on horseback.

All this day we will be close,
talking and joking, close to your face.

Whenever I say *your face*,
my soul jumps out of its skin.

Is there some other roof somewhere?
Any name other than yours?
Any glass of wine other than this you bring me so perfectly?

If I find my life, I will never let go,
holding and twisting the cloth of your coat,
as in that dream when I saw you.

By this gate kings are waiting with me.
Your eyes, I am lost remembering your eyes.
Look at us out here moaning with our shirts ripped open.

Anyone seeing your face and not obsessed with the sight
is cold as a rock in the ground.
What further curse could I put on him?

What is worse than having no word from you?
Do not waste your life with those who do not see you.
Stay with us, who are each running across the beach,
torn loose from friends, making friends with the sea.

One flood moves in its sleep.
One is confused out of its channel.
One says, All praise to God.
Another, No strength but yours.

You are sunlight come as wagonloads of presents
and free wine for the poor.
A rose looks up, the calyx rips open.
The lute player with quick hands sees your hands
and stops and closes her eyes.

Who is luckiest in this whole orchestra? The reed.
Its mouth touches your lips to learn music.
All reeds, sugarcane especially, think only of this chance.
They sway in the canebrakes,
free in the many ways they dance.

Without you, the instruments would die.
One sits close beside you. Another takes a long kiss.
The tambourine begs, Touch my skin, so I can be myself.

Let me feel you enter each limb bone by bone,
that what died last night can be whole today.

Why live some soberer way and feel you ebbing out?
I will not do it.

Either give me enough wine or leave me alone,
now that I know how it is
to be with you in a constant conversation.

LET THE LETTER READ YOU

Why stay so long where your words are scattered
and doing no good? I have sent a letter a day
for a hundred days. Either you do not read them,
or you have forgotten how to leave.

Let this letter read you. Come back.
No one understands who you are in that prison
for the stone-faced. You have escaped,
but you sit there like a falcon on the window ledge.
You are both water and stream,
but you think you need something to drink
like a lion or a deer.

How far is it back here?
How far is the light of the moon from the moon?
How far is the taste of candy from the lip?

Every second you give away light.
We accept. We like this market.

Your love is a sweet poison
that we eat from your hand
to dissolve and drain away the ego-life
now spraying this fountain from us.

START YOUR LIVES OVER

Last night the elephant wandered India again
and tore the darkness to shreds.
Let our daylight lives be like last night.

Let mystics constantly remember,
and the parts and the whole be happily equal.

In our hands, wine.
In our heads, wind.

Night contains the day.
The ocean breaks into waves.

The sky wears the gift we gave.
Whatever customs humanity had
become ways of compassion.

Nothing with shape and dimensions
can keep still when passion moves.

Start your lives over.
Everyone is totally forgiven, no matter what.

This is the surge that cannot be resisted,
a grace that is this time named Saladin,
an annihilating friendship, like the one with Joseph,
which the king of Egypt paid for with Egypt.

WHAT WOULD I BE?

Come near, you so like me.
My love feels held in until you ask, Do you hurt?

As I feel love rise, I fight with it.
You say, Bravo. The general takes command.

Last night this body was a stringed instrument
playing love songs.

There is a kind of accounting going on with you and me.
But all I want from this exchange is your peace.

I fly inside mystery.
You say, Try to keep up, my lame friend.

There is a grapevine hanging here.
Should I climb it?

When you stay away, I am miserable.
What would I be
if you wanted to be with me all the time?

Grief and unexpected joy live in a doorway
where there is no time or distance.

Aging changes to childhood.
My face is new again.
You say, My confused and silent friend.

SHUTTLES

With their shop in ruins, their clothing torn,
lovers run headlong for the ocean.

Nothing else will cure them, they think,
but they never get there.

Why can't they rejoice in what is already theirs?
All beauty is God's beauty.

They climb like secret troops to take some fortress
when they have no home of their own.
No sign in the pitchblack night.

Lovers claim to see only the face.
Where then are the back, the sides, the feet, and the rest?
What they search for is free of form.
It is rather the source of form.

Lovers will never transcend form, until they become that.

Listen to the great heart coming from within the body,
a lion's roar in the shape of a deer.

In this woven workmanship
our souls are shuttles thrown back and forth.

Prayer rugs point to the weaver's address.
The sky is a streetsweeper. This planet, his wife.

Now the lover is a guest in my house,
having traveled enough.

My greeting, *hey-ah*, becomes his breathing *huuuu*,
through with searching.

LIKE THIS

If anyone asks you
how the perfect satisfaction
of all our desiring will look,
lift your face and say,
Like this.

When someone mentions the gracefulness of the nightsky,
climb up on the roof and dance and say,
Like this?

If anyone wants to know what spirit is,
or what God's fragrance means,
Lean your head toward him or her.
Keep your face there close.
Like this.

When someone quotes the old poetic image
about clouds gradually uncovering the moon,
slowly loosen knot by knot
the strings of your robe.
Like this?

If anyone wonders how Jesus raised the dead,
do not try to explain the miracle.
Kiss me on the lips.
Like this. Like this.

When someone asks
what it means to *die for love*, point
here.

If someone asks how tall I am,
frown and measure with your fingers
the space between the creases on your forehead.
This tall.

The soul sometimes leaves the body, then returns.
When someone does not believe that,
walk back into my house.
Like this.

When lovers moan, they are telling our story.
Like this.

I am a sky where spirits live.
Stare into this deepening blue,
while the breeze says a secret.
Like this.

When someone asks what there is to do,
light the candle in his hand.
Like this.

How did Joseph's scent come to Jacob?
Huuuuuuu.

How did Jacob's sight return?
Huuuuuuuuu.

A little wind cleans the eyes.
Like this.

When Shams comes back from Tabriz,
he will put just his head
around the edge of the door to surprise us.
Like this.

LOW IN THE ROOTS

An intellectual is all the time showing off.
Lovers dissolve and become bewildered.

Intellectuals try not to drown,
while the whole purpose of love is drowning.

Intellectuals invent ways to rest,
then lie down in those beds.
Lovers feel ashamed of comforting ideas.

You have seen a glob of oil on water?
That is how a lover is with intellectuals,
there, but alone in a circle of himself.

Some intellectual tries to give sound advice to a lover.
All he hears back is, I love you. I love you.

Love is musk.
Do not deny it when you smell the scent.

Love is a tree.
Lovers, the shade under the long branches.

To the intellectual mind,
a child must grow up and learn to be an adult.

In the station of love,
you see old men getting younger and younger.

Shams chose to live low in the roots for you,
so now he soars in the air
of your sublimely articulating love.

LOST IN YOU

Why did I cross the road in front of your horse
and then cross again?

I am the ground beneath those hooves.
You say nothing,
yet I feel the grace of being lost in you
as color lives in a garden.

As David knows metallurgy
and the craft of welding chainmail,
I am inside the smooth linkage.

Your secret army infiltrates me.
Nothing remains to look for.

This wine is clear,
and this one clouded with sediment.
I drink both.

26.
Everything and Everyone Else

The whole in its multiplicity, and apart from the personal. The glorious mundane. A murmur of conversation floating on silence. We are dressed in friendship. This is the infinite present where everything happens, where we know the value of every moment. We keep time as we dance here in this music, not in spirit, where there is no time. We live inside each other. Things change overnight. Any ending is possible, as polisher melts into mirror. I have been drawn to the Sufis for their emphasis on the numinous as it transpires through beauty and harmony, and love. I find that when I am around them (and around Taoist and Zen masters too) the possessiveness of the ego loosens and I feel the joy flowing through the createdness. And that feels like the soul's truth.

HALLAJ

Hallaj said what he said and went to the origin
through the hole on the scaffold.

I cut a cap's worth of cloth from his robe,
and it swamped over me head to foot.

Years ago, I broke a bunch of roses from the top of his wall.
A thorn from that is still in my palm, working deeper.

From Hallaj, I learned how to hunt lions,
but I became something hungrier than a lion.

I was a frisky colt. He broke me
with a quiet hand on the side of my head.

A person comes to him naked. It's cold.
There is a fur coat floating in the river.

Jump in and get it, he says.
You dive in. You reach for the coat.
It reaches for you.

It is a live bear that has fallen in upstream,
drifting with the current.

How long does it take? Hallaj yells from the bank.
Don't wait, you answer.
This coat has decided to wear me home.

A little part of a story, a hint.
Do you need long sermons on Hallaj?

SPRING MURMUR

Young, loving, springlike, these qualities
come up in many combinations.

Watch the fields, the garden, the forest,
how they change in time.

Their prayer in winter, *No God but you.*
Their prayer in spring, the same, both asking for help.

Listen now to the murmur of their conversations.

Branch with fruit, I'm about to break!
That's funny, says the tulip.

Narcissus looks love at jasmine.
Iris jabbering, *Now don't be bitter.*

Violet kneels, pretending. Waterlily knows everything.
Hyacinth wags her head. Mint turns to stare
at grass running everywhere barefooted.

Bud hides. Willow drags a watery arm
in the mirror of the river.

Dove keeps the query going, *Where . . . where . . .*
have you been . . .where . . .

Partridge, *No where.*
Falcon, *What brought you here from there?*

Look around. These are just a fraction
of who might be wandering in.

See now: fig, pomegranate, October apple, orange.
And finally, grapes. They like to walk slow,
the first coming last, sweet and stringent,
like the mind that trusts and doubts.

Melon arrives in a house with no door,
as pumpkin, broken open, fills with rain.

We argue about food. We want what we want.

These gorgeous details fascinate
like a Chinese painting, soul being the artist.

That is what I used to call Shams,
the great Chinese screen painter.

FASTENED TO A POLE

I keep turning around this misfortune,
this troubled illusion I call myself,
when I could be turning around *you,*
the giver of blessings, origin and presence.

My chest is a grave that you have made into a rose garden.
What goes in the grave?
What fits in that two-by-two-by-seven?

Not soul. Soul cannot be contained in the sky.
I turn around God. I have become a mirror,
yet for these few days I turn around a piece of white wool.

If I were a rose in this spring,
I would change into a hundred rosebushes.

I turn around this frustrated body, tethered in a barn of words,
when I could be free in the infinite pasture.
Free, why do I keep turning as though fastened to a pole?

ANY SPRIG OF AN HERB

Learned theologians do not teach love.
Love is nothing but gladness and honor.

Ideas of right and wrong operate in us until we die.
Love does not have those limits.

When you see a scowling face,
it is not a lover's.

A beginner in this way
knows nothing of any beginning.

Do not try to be a shepherd.
Become the flock.

Someone says, This is just a metaphor.
But that is not so.

It is as clear and direct
as a blind man stubbing his foot against a stone jar.

The doorkeeper should be more careful,
says the blind man.

That pitcher is not in the doorway,
replies the doorkeeper.

The truth is, you do not know where you are.
A master of love is the only sign we need.

There is no better sign
than someone stumbling around among the waterpots
looking for signs.

Every particle of love,
any sprig of an herb, speaks of water.

Follow the tributaries.
Everything we say has water within it.

No need to explain this to a thirsty man.
He knows what to do.

CURRENCY

There is a tree and a fire that call to me,
My darling.

For forty years I wander wilderness,
tasting manna and quail.

A ship on the ocean is a marvelous thing.
But I have been sailing this boat of mine through dry desert.

Moses, my soul, my friend,
when you hold me, this body is a walkingstick.
You throw it down, it becomes a snake.

You are the boy Jesus,
and I am your clay bird.
Breathe on me. Let me fly out of sight.

I am the column you lean against
that moans when you leave.

What cover do you draw over me now?
In one moment I am a stone,
then iron, then pure fire.

Now a jangling scale flopping about with nothing on it.
Now poised in balance showing weight and purchase.

Feeding on a certain pasture,
I am the pasture.

They are tasting me,
wolf, sheep, and shepherd.

Matter is meant to move and change.
That currency reveals meaning.

Those who belong with me
know I am the value these forms are tokens of.

A PREPOSTEROUS GUESS

Friend, you change what I lost
to a surprise gift.

You open my mouth in desire
and hand me the key.

A strange preposterous guess
seems righter and righter.

I let other fictions go.
I am the contents of your seed bag.
Scatter me over the ground.

Let me be quiet
in the middle of the noise.

THE VALUE OF THIS MOMENT

Morning wind and the feel of your face close.
A fragrance from China
through western Turkestan to here.
Is there word of Shams?

I am dressed with friendship.
Your voice says in my chest
the value of this moment: Partridge cry
on the mountainside, a human eye,
what people say in praise of sunlight and the nightsky,
of Joseph's face and Jesus' healing breath,
a walking cypress shadow, a field in spring, firelight.

Shams is all these,
and a guide, the hand that never pulls away.

TWO LOVINGS

Soul comes wearing a shape,
with fragrance, with the new-green,
with a trembling hand, with generosity.
No. That implies a being apart.

Companion and confessor at once,
red and yellow, you join me in the gathering,
and you stay away. You come late.

You are the source of two lovings,
fire one day, ice another.

THE CREATION WORD

Three days now it has been like this.
I dip my pitcher in the fountain.
It fills with blood.

The rose garden is all desert thorns and stone.
I chant spells to lure the genii back into the bottle.
Nothing happens.

A beloved's frown destroys the lover.
Come back. Brighten my eye,
even if I do not deserve it.

My loving asks, What have I done?
A voice replies, Do not look to yourself.
The cause is beyond every here and now.
The life gift is given and then taken away.
It is not for us to know why, or how.

Grace comes with the creation word, *Be*.
That gate opens without hesitating.
Between the push of *buh* and the smooth launch of *ee*,
there is an infinite moment when everything happens.

AMAZED MOUTH

The soul: a wide listening sky
with hundreds of candles.

When anything is sold,
soul gets given in the cash.

People waiting at a door,
a ladder leaning on a roof,
someone climbing down.

The market square bright with understanding.
Listening opens its amazed mouth.

MASHALLAH

There is someone swaying by your side,
lips that say, *Mashallah. Mashallah.*

Wonderful, God inside attraction.
A spring no one knew of wells up on the valley floor.
Lights inside a tent lovers move toward.

The refuse of Damascus gets turned over in the sun.
Be like that yourself. Say *Mercy, mercy,*
to the one who guides your soul, who keeps time.
Move, make a mistake, look up. *Checkmate.*

COME HORSEBACK

Come horseback through the spiderwebs of twilight,
as fifteen evenings of full moon, as the sun on holiday.

The stars performing every small zodiac wish
wheel into the presence of these lovers
where you remember me, look around,
and draw the blade of your question,
Where is the one whose candle burns in the dawn?

Where is the handful of dirt
that somehow joins with the light of the Pleiades?

You keep resurrecting like St. George.
Again. Where is the friend who calls presence
out of absence and cuts the umbilical
by mentioning Shams Tabriz?

YHU

Flow inside me, source of the source of joy,
life essence, the wine of peace that moves in my hand,
then out, around . . . You know the rest.

Wound that opens in the ground, perfect shot,
wing-shadow, face of a strong worker, still delicate,
candle, a secret completely obvious.

You bring in the gift. You hand us each moment.
You are the value rivering along in any belonging,
lock of hair. You are the human center.

The ocean of meanings gets a puzzled look
when it sees this hilarious presence moving through.
Yhhhuuuuuuuuuu.

FORM *IS* ECSTATIC

There is a shimmering excitement in being sentient and shaped.
The caravan master sees his camels lost in it,
nose to tail, as he himself is, his friend,
and the stranger coming toward them.

A gardener watches the sky break into song,
cloud wobbly with what it is, bud and thorn the same.

Wind, water, wandering this essential state.
Fire, ground, gone. That is how it is with the outside.
Form *is* ecstatic.

Now imagine the inner. Soul, intelligence, the secret worlds.
And do not think the garden loses its ecstasy in winter.

It is quiet, but the roots are down there riotous.
If someone bumps you in the street, do not be angry.

Everyone careens about in this surprise. Respond in kind.
Let the knots untie, turbans be given away.

Someone drunk on this could drink a donkeyload a night.
Believer, unbeliever, cynic, lover,
all combine in the spirit-form we are.
But no one yet is awake like Shams.

GRACE GOT CONFUSED

One maddening drop, then another.
You pour wine like that for us now.

Remember when you poured full light,
all at once, a whole day?

You put your finger on your lips wanting quiet,
but those drops you drip keep talking.

It is not us. As you were killing Junnaiyd,
he said, More, more.

In each blood drop of his, a new Bestami.

The first that fell on ground grew Adam.
In the sky, Gabriel.

Those old days you poured according to merit.
Then grace got confused,
and you poured everybody some.

Bread does not deserve you,
yet you lived your life for bread.

You brought water and threw it at the water carrier.
What you showed Moses was not fire,
but a shape of consciousness.

Will that Friday ever come again
when you served your close friends *individually?*

Each moment a stranger and a friend meet. Shy.
Their bloods mix. Roses drop petals in autumn.

Offer your friendship to the prophets.
Do not think that they are ordinary people.

There is a huge difference in the quality of praying,
as between those you bless, and those you turn from.

THE MOON-SHAPED THRESHING FLOOR

I have heard enough *Dos—Dismount,*
when I am still looking for the road.
Enough *Gos—Let's go,*
before I have even set up my tent.

Could I be spared these *gos* and *dos?*
Will I get to the moon-shaped threshing floor before I die?
I feel blessed with wandering in the love sun,
but I do not see the road.
I know it is here somewhere,
but I do not see its justice or its peace.

I ask the wind for word.
I look in wells for the moon's image.
I am drying up like an August garden.

But I learn quickly like the same spot in spring,
in both states amazed at what happens
to just a piece of ground.

EVERY DETAIL SHOWS HOW THAT ONE IS IN LOVE

Daylight comes glowing from your green vault.
You measure and pour out a beaker of twilight bloodredness.

Gliding and whirling, many miles wide,
your ocean storms come into shore.

With all its trying and giving up,
the moon's cap falls off the back of its head
as it lifts to see you.

Every morning the birds reword their praising,
the songs they sing,
by musicians already with you inside the grass.

Spirit wants to see. Love wants a lover.
You set flowing four flowings through the orchard.
Pure streamwater, glowing honey, fresh milk, dark red wine.

You do not give me a chance.
Wine on top of wine, I have no head,
no way to describe this cup.

In a sky so restless and changing
the moon wears a silver belt.

Every detail, every feature of every thing,
shows how that one is in love.

We strain and ask, then grow tired of talking.
The reed flute crying with breath gets quiet.

As we open your door, please be there.
Be held by a gratefulness that wants you head to toe.

THERE IS NOTHING AHEAD

Lovers think they are looking for each other,
but there is only one search.

Wandering this world is wandering that,
both inside one transparent sky.
In here there is no dogma and no heresy.

The miracle of Jesus is himself,
not what he said or did about the future.

Forget the future.
I would worship someone who could do that.

On the way you may want to look back, or not,
but if you can say, There is nothing ahead,
there will be nothing there.

Stretch your arms,
and take hold the cloth of your clothes with both hands.
The cure for pain is in the pain.
Good and bad are mixed.
If you don't have both, you don't belong with us.

When one of us gets lost, is not here,
he must be inside us.
There is no place like that anywhere in the world.

THE NEW RULE

It is the old rule that drunks have to argue
and get into fights.
The lover is just as bad. He falls into a hole.
But down in that hole he finds something shining,
worth more than any amount of money or power.

Last night the moon came dropping its clothes in the street.
I took it as a sign to start singing,
falling *up* into the bowl of sky.
The bowl breaks. Everywhere is falling everywhere.
Nothing else to do.

Here is the new rule. Break the wine glass,
and fall toward the glassblower's breath.

UNMARKED BOXES

Don't grieve. Anything you lose
comes round in another form.

The child weaned from mother's milk
now drinks wine and honey mixed.

God's joy moves from unmarked box to unmarked box,
from cell to cell. As rainwater, down into flowerbed.
As roses, up from ground.

Now it looks like a plate of rice and fish,
now a cliff covered with vines,
now a horse being saddled.

It hides within these
until one day it cracks them open.

Part of the self leaves the body when we sleep
and changes shape. You might say, "Last night
I was a cypress tree, a small bed of tulips,
a field of grapevines." Then the phantasm goes away.
You are back in the room.
I do not want to make anyone fearful.
Hear what is behind what I say.

Ta-tum-tum, ta-tum, ta-ta-tum.
There is the light gold of wheat in the sun
and the gold of bread made from that wheat.
I have neither. I am only talking about them,

as a town in the desert looks up
at stars on a clear night.

SOMETIMES I FORGET COMPLETELY

Sometimes I forget completely
what companionship is. Unconscious and insane,
I spill sad energy everywhere.

My story gets told in various ways.
A romance, a dirty joke, a war, a vacancy.

Divide up my forgetfulness to any number.
It will go around.

These dark suggestions that I follow,
are they part of some plan?

Friends, be careful. Do not come near me
out of curiosity, or sympathy.

NO NEED TO ASK

The one who pours the wine pours again,
no need to ask.

Do you ask the moon to rise and give its light?

When ranks of soldiers dissolve, dismissed for a holiday,
when a lost hand reaches for the rescuing hand,
when a candle next to a mirrored sconce gets lit,

your presence enters my soul.

ALL RIVERS MOVING AT ONCE

Do not unstring the bow.
I am your four-feathered arrow that has not been used yet.

I am a strong knife-blade word,
not some *if* or *maybe,* dissolving in air.

I am sunlight slicing the dark.
Who made this night?
A forge deep in earth-mud.

What is the body?
Endurance.

What is love?
Gratitude.

What is hidden in our chests?
Laughter.

What else?
Compassion.

Let the beloved be a hat pulled down firmly on my head.
Or drawstrings pulled and tied tight around my chest.

How does love have hands and feet?
Love is the sprouting bed for hands and feet.

Your father and mother were playing love-games.
They came together, and you appeared.

Do not ask what love can make or do.
Look at the colors of the world.

The riverwater moving in all rivers at once.
The truth that lives in Shams's face.

DRUNK WITH THE WHOLE

There are wild, wondering Sufis called *qalandars,*
who are constantly tickled with life.

It is scandalous how they love and laugh at any small event.
People gossip at them,
and that makes them deft in their cunning,
but really a great God-wrestling goes on
inside these wandering warriors,
a flood of sunlight that is drunk with the whole thing.

Someone is putting a spell on me.
Another expects me to repent.
Another runs alongside without feet,
drunk with the whole thing.

Friends rush out in the rain to be soaked with the sky.
Eyesight is holding understanding,
with the moon's polite manner.

Tell the soldier about to go to war
how the cypress tree is turning green,
drunk with the whole thing.

Someone beyond questions of how and what for
sews patches on my robe.

Someone who watches the sea,
Mt. Sinai and friend, that one
comes whispering, Be drunk with the whole thing.

Tell the festival of sacrifice,
tell the Qur'an, tell the gate of heaven,
that there is a bunch out here singing
and drunk with the whole.

KISS OF SOLITUDE

I want a long kiss of solitude with the friend.
I have been unfaithful but I still want that beauty,
what we sometimes imagine as a husband-and-wife harmony.
though that has never happened even once.

Strangers meet and pass,
holding out a hand to bring *that one*
to the center of the dance.

Each is longing to hold you naked.
Absence deepens the soul.

THE FACE

So the frowning teacher came and left.
He is very consistent with that vinegar face.

But maybe he shows *that* to us
and smiles with others.

Such a beautiful teacher, but so sour,
the pure standard for tartness.

Consider how your face is a source of light.
If you enter a grieving room
with the friend in your eyes,
light will bloom there
according to the laws of sweet and sour.

Locked in a cell, you grow bitter and dark.
But out walking in morning sunlight with friends,
how does that taste?

There *are* exceptions.
Joseph caught the rose fragrance
down in his abandoned wellhole.

In this quietness now
I feel someone seated on my right
like a kindness that will never leave.

ONE BEING, AND SEPARATE BEINGS TOO

As everything changes overnight,
I praise the breaking of promises.
Whatever love wants, it gets,
not next year, *now!*

I swear by the one who never says *tomorrow*,
as the circle of the moon refuses to sell *installments* of light.
It gives all it has, whatever that is at the moment.

How do fables conclude, and who will explain them?
Every story is ours. That is who we are,
from beginning to no-matter-how it ends.

Should I use the pronoun *we?*
The friend walks by, and bricks in the wall feel conscious.
Infertile women give birth. Beauty embodies itself.

Those who know the taste of a meal
are those who sit at the table and eat.

Lover and friend are one being,
and separate beings too,
as the polisher melts in the mirror's face.

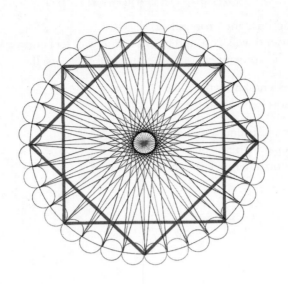

27.
The Name That Cannot Be Spoken or Written

We cannot *say* the beauty we inhabit, nor can we *believe* it. Inside everything that happens, there is a flow, a music where all the wantings mix. Who tuned this instrument, Rumi asks, where wind is one string and Shams's eyes another? As creekwater animates the landscape it moves through, so the absolute, the unknowable, appears as fall begins. Signs come, and the more subtle essence is present, but also absent. Solomon controls the wind of our speaking. Something opens and closes inside our heart. Silence, annihilation, absence. I go back where everything is nothing. What Shams Tabriz is now cannot be said. It is as though a star were growing on a low branch of an olive tree. There is a great spaciousness around where we are standing with David and Rabia and Jesus and Muhammad and Rinzai and Lao-tse. Everything drops away. Bawa Muhaiyaddeen once said, "God has no form, no shape, no color, no differences, no race, no religion, no country, no place, no name, neither beginning nor end. God is the grace that lives within all lives."

IN LOVE THAT LONG

I am here, this moment, inside the beauty,
the gift God has given, our love.

This gold and circular sign
means we are free of any duty.

Out of eternity I turn my face to you,
and into eternity. We have been in love that long.

HOOFBEATS

The sound of hoofbeats leaving a monastery where all
is timed and measured: you are that rider: someone
who does not care very much about things and results,
illness or loss: you are the soul inside the soul
that is always traveling.

Mind gathers bait. The personality carries a grudge.
You weave cloth like the moon leaving no trace on the road.

There is a learning community where the names of God
are talked about and memorized,
and there is another residence where meanings live.

You are on your way from here to there,
and don't claim you are not carrying gifts.

Your graceful manner gives color and fragrance,
as creekwater animates a landscape it moves through.

Hundreds of caravans sail into the sky.
You travel alone, by yourself, those caravans:
sun inside one dazzling mote, the emperor's serenity
on nightwatch as alert as his palace guard.

You enchant this visible place, so that we imagine
you are going somewhere, off to new country.

The absolute unknowable appears as spring,
and disappears in fall. Signs come,
not the essence signified.

How long will you be a shepherd single-filing us
in and out of the human barn? Will I ever
see you as you secretly are in silence?

READY FOR SILENCE

The devotional moon looks into the heart and is in the heart.
When the friend has a friend like you,
the universe cannot contain their pleasure.

Anyone warmed by sun feels courage coming in.
If grief arrives, you enjoy it.
Generosity. That is your hand in my pocket
giving your wealth away.

Yet you run from me like one raised in the wild.
Here comes this strange creature, me, in a hands-and-feet shape.
The formless tries to satisfy us with forms.

A transparent nakedness wearing pure light says,
Blessed are those wearing gold brocade.

You may not see him, but Moses is alive in this town,
and he still has his staff.

There is water and thirst, wherever and however water goes,
and the one who brings water.

The morning wind broke off a few branches in the garden.
No matter. When you feel love inside you,
you feel the invitation to be cooked by God.

It is that creation that the heart loves.
For three winter months the ground keeps quiet.
But each piece of earth knows what is inside waiting:
beans, sugarcane, cypress, wildflowers.

Then the spring sun comes talking plants out into the open.
Anyone who feels the point of prayer
bends down like the first letter of *pray*.

Anyone who walks with his back to the sun
is following his shadow.

Move into your own quietness.
This word-search poem has found you ready for silence.

EMPTY

Come out here where the roses have opened.
Let soul and world meet.

The sun has drawn a fine-tempered blade of light.
We may as well surrender.

Laugh at the ridiculous arrogance you see.
Weep for those separated from the friend.

The city seethes with rumor.
Some madman has escaped from prison.
Or is a revolution beginning? What day is it?

Is this when all we have done and been
will be publicly known?

With no thinking and no emotion,
with no ideas about the soul, and no language,
these drums are saying how empty we are.

MUSIC AND SILENCE

Lovers, union is here,
the meeting we have wanted,
the fire, the joy.

Let sadness and any fear of death
leave the room.

The sun's glory comes back.
Wind shakes our bells.

We are counters in your hand
passing easily through.

Music begins.
Your silence, deepen that.

Were you to put words with this,
we would not survive the song.

PIECES OF A BROKEN CUP

Give me again what you gave last night,
the huge cup. I threw it down,
and now it is dangerous to walk barefooted in here.
People are wounding their feet.

I am not talking about glass,
or wine fermented in a vat.

I am up and down at once, helpless and nowhere.

A fine hanging apple, in love with your stone,
the perfect throw that clips my stem.

Ask me who I am talking about.
Tell me who I am talking about.

Do not stand on the bank.
Jump in the river with me.

If you stay there, I will stay.
When you sit down to eat, I sit down.

I am the wandering drummer
who marches alone into the arena
with his drum wobbling crazily,
tied to the top of his lance.

You are happy to be leading me around.
We escape from existence together.

Why do we have to go back and be silent
like fish pulled up out of the water?

SOLOMON AND THE WIND OF SPEAKING

Solomon is here. Prepare the house.
No need to mention the soul
when the soul within soul is present.

I was wandering without love.
Then love entered.

I was a mountain.
I became straw for the king's horse.
No matter what the king's country, Turkey or Turkestan.

I am his servant, close as soul is to body,
but the body cannot see the soul as I behold the king.

Drop the load you have been carrying.
This is a lucky time, my friends.
Do not wait. Leap up,
and ask the hoopoe the way to Solomon's throne.
Say all your secrets and desires.

Your speech is a thousand distracting winds,
but Solomon gathers those
into a flock, a listening shape.

Solomon knows the language of birds,
and he controls the wind of speaking.

PEARL

What kind of pearl are you
that other birds love to fly in the air of?

There is nothing in this world
that is not a gift from you.

Every king wants to be checkmated by your rook.
I will not run away or flinch
from however you raise your arm to strike.

Just to be in your presence is the point of my life,
cooked and drowned, nothinged, nowhere.

Someone who has not dissolved
still loves places.

But you say, *Leave.*
There is no *place* for you.

Remember Nizami? You are my king,
but I will not survive your reign.

A SHIP GLIDING OVER NOTHING

Only union with you gives joy.
The rest is tearing down one building to put up another.

But do not break with forms.
Boats cannot move without water.

We are misquoted texts, made right when you say us.
We are sheep in a tightening wolf circle.

You come like a shepherd and ask, *How are you?*
I start crying.

This means something to anyone in a body,
but what means something to you?

You cannot be spoken, but you listen to all sound.
You cannot be written, yet you read everything.

You do not sleep, but you are the source of dream vision,
a ship gliding over nothing, deep silence,
praise for the one who told Moses on Sinai,
You shall not see me.

THERE YOU ARE

You are inside every kindness.
When a sick person feels better, you are that,
and the onset of disease too.

You are sudden, terrible screaming.

Some problems require we go for help.
When we knock on a stranger's door, you sent us.
Nobody answers. It's you.

When work feels necessary,
you are the way workers move in rhythm.

You are what is, the field, the players,
the ball, those watching.

Someone claims to have evidence that you do not exist.
You are the one who brings the evidence in,
and the evidence itself.

You are inside the soul's great fear,
every natural pleasure, every vicious cruelty.

You are in every difference and irritation.
Someone loves something. Someone else hates the same.
There you are.

Whatever eyes see, what anyone wants or not,
political power, injustice, material possessions,
those are your script, the handwriting we study.

Body, soul, shadow.
Whether reckless or careful, you are what we do.

It is absurd to ask your pardon.
You are inside repentance and sin.

The wonder of various jewels, agate, emerald.
How we are during a day, then at night,
you are those moods and qualities.

The pure compassion we feel for each other.

Every encampment has a tent where the leader is
and also the wide truth of your imperial tent overall.

THIS DISASTER

Why am I part of this disaster,
this mud hole for donkeys?

Is this the place where Jesus spoke? Surely not.
A table has been set,
but we have not been served sweet springwater yet.

Evidently we came here to be bound hand and foot.
I ask a flower, How is it you are so wise so young?

With the first morning wind and the first dew,
I lost my innocence.

I follow the one who showed me the way.
I extend one hand up,
and with the other I touch the ground.

A great branch leans down from the sky.
How long will I keep talking of *up* and *down?*

This is not my home. Silence, annihilation, absence.
I go back where everything is nothing.

ASTROLOGICAL BICKERINGS

The doctor leans close to the yellow ones in his garden,
A little water will turn you rose.

Red and saffron are things we control,
and yet earth beauty steals from us,
from our kindness and our grace.

Earth beauty withers and fails.
That is what happens to thieves in this community.
It is morning. Time to give back what you took.

Then night comes, and the stars begin talking.
Venus. This section of sky is mine.
The moon. But this over here is my territory.

Jupiter pulls out a unique coin and shows it to Saturn.
Mercury at the head of the table says, The whole sky
belongs to me since all signs begin here at the top.

We are beyond these astrological bickerings.
Jupiter begs for our help.
The sun rides his horse into the courtyard.
We wave him away. Come back tomorrow.

Whoever gets sacrificed rises again
as a ceremony and a holiday.

Shams Tabriz went through that change,
but what he is now cannot be said.

It is as though a remote star
grew on the low branch of an olive tree.

THE NOTHING OF ROSELIGHT

Death comes,
and what we thought we needed loses importance.

The living shiver, focused on a muscular dark hand,
rather than on the glowing cup it holds,
or the toast being proposed.

In that same way, love enters your life,
and the I, the ego,
a corrupt, self-absorbed king, dies during the night.

Let him go. In the dawn
breathe cold new air, the nothing of roselight.

A NEW IDEA

Every dawn we rise out of the east
and shine like grains in the light.

We thrash about between wet and dry,
being neither one nor the other.

We hear what the brass objects want,
Turn us into gold.

To help with that we rise up into the stars.
We become pieces of amber on a necklace.
Our patched robes change to elegant apparel.
The world's poison turns to sweetness in us.

We move to the center of the fighting,
this circle of bewildered lovers.
We give the sign.
We knock at the placeless door,
riding a horse of green air.

Soul becomes pure in the body,
purer, we move inside love and stand next to Shams,
our shoulders touching in the infinite house.

THE SKY OF THE BRAIN

Morning: a polished knife blade
and the smell of white camphor burning.

The sky tears his blue Sufi robe deliberately in half.
Daylight Rumi drags his dark opposite out of sight.
A happy Turk comes in. A grieving Hindu leaves.

The King of the Ethiopians goes. Caesar arrives.
No one knows how what changes changes.
One half of the planet is grass. The other half, grazing.

A pearl goes up for auction.
No one has enough, so the pearl buys itself.

We stand beside Noah and David
and Rabia and Jesus and Muhammad.

Quietness again lifts and planes out,
the blood in our heads gliding in the sky of the brain.

ONLY BREATH

Ah true believers, what can I say?
I no longer know who I am.

Not Christian or Jew or Muslim,
not Hindu, Buddhist, Sufi, or Zen.
I am not from the East or the West,
not out of the ocean or up from the ground.
Not natural or ethereal,
not composed of elements at all.
I do not exist.

I am not from China or India,
not from the town of Bulghar on the Volga,
nor from remote Arabian Saqsin.
Not from either Iraq, the one between the rivers,
or the one in western Persia.

Not an entity in this world or the next.
I did not descend from Adam and Eve or any origin story.
My place is the placeless, a trace of the traceless,
neither body or soul. I belong to the beloved,
have seen the two worlds as one,
and that one call to and know,
first, last, outer, inner,
only that breath breathing human being.

Friends, when I taste love's wine,
the two worlds combine,
and I have no purpose but this play of presences.

If I spend one moment outside you, I repent,
and when I have a moment of closer rapport,
I dance to rubble the ruins of both.
Shams Tabriz, this friendship is all I say.

WHO SAYS WORDS WITH MY MOUTH?

All day I think about it, then at night I say it.
Where did I come from, and what am I supposed to be doing?
I do not know. My soul is from elsewhere.
I am sure of that, and I intend to end up there.

This drunkenness began in some other tavern.
When I get back around to that place,

I will be completely sober. Meanwhile,
I am like a bird from another continent,
sitting in this aviary. The day is coming when I fly off,
but who is it now in my ear who hears my voice?
Who says words with my mouth?
Who looks out with my eyes? What is the soul?

I cannot stop asking. If I could taste one sip of an answer,
I could break out of this prison for drunks.
I did not come here of my own accord,
and I cannot leave that way.
Whoever brought me here will have to take me home.

This poetry. I never know what I am going to say.
I don't plan it.
When I am outside the saying of it.
I get very quiet and rarely speak at all.

Shams Tabriz, if you would show your face to me again,
I could flee the imposition of this life.

SILVER COINS

Put your cheek against this cheek.
Forget anger and men planning war.
When I hold out silver coins, take them,
and give me a cup of gold light.
You can open the wide door of the sky.
Surely you will open me.
All I have is this emptiness.
Give it a nickname.
Breaker and healer, break and heal this head.
Do not press your seal to that pistachio nut.
Put it here. There is that in me
that has to be told fifty times a day,
Stop hunting. Step on this net.

DAYBREAK

As the ocean waves of the king take us in to shore,
we give ourselves to the motion.

At the banquet where we will be the main dish,
Isaac leans his head down for the blade.

Only love has power over lovers. Death has none.
The beloved is giving as he appears to take away.

Breath diminishes as spirit flows stronger,
a falcon released to the wild.

A lover dies like Hallaj from his own words,
but not spoken in anger.

I will stop now before I say what cannot be said.

Shams is climbing up over the horizon,
snuffing whole banks of star-candles.

NEARER THAN YOUR JUGULAR

Whose idea was this,
to have the lover visible
and the beloved invisible?

So many people have died of their desiring
because of this. The lover cannot kiss
the lips he wants, so he bites himself.

Satisfaction is always two bow-shots away,
and yet something in the soul
prefers this unreachable lover
to anyone attainable.

This being locked in
is better than having the keys
to any consolation-house.

The beloved's rejection is wanted
more than anyone else's acceptance.

World-happiness is nothing.
Look for what Bestami had,
what Sanai and Attar wrote of.

A beautiful meal looks delicious.
Then one night passes, and the food passes
through you, becoming repellent filth.

Eat love-food.
Suckle the toes of a lion,
as the baby Abraham did in the cave.

But you should put away
what you learned as a fetus in your cave,
that need for blood.

There is a tall tower that love builds.
Live there in silence.

The one who knows all secrets is here *now,*
nearer than your jugular vein.

QUALITIES AND A BLUE-GREEN SEA

There is a sun-star rising outside the reality of form.
I am lost in that other beauty.

It is sweet not to look at two worlds,
to melt in meaning as sugar melts in water.

No one tires of following the soul.
I do not recall now what happens on the manifest plane.

I stroll with those I have always wanted to know,
fresh and graceful as a waterlily or a rose.

The body is a boat,
and I am waves swaying against it.

Whenever it anchors somewhere,
I pull it loose, or smash it to pieces.

If I get lazy and cold,
flames come from my ocean and surround me.
I laugh inside them like gold purifying myself.

A certain song makes the snake
put his head down on a line in the dirt.
Here is my head, brother. What next?

Weary of form, I came into qualities.
Each quality says, I am a blue-green sea.
Dive into me.

I am Alexander at the outermost extension of empire,
turning all my armies inward,
toward the meaning of armies, and Shams.

SPACIOUSNESS

Soul flies in empty space,
a single candle in the huge palace.

Bird-shadows cross whatever they happen to cross.
Lovers pay attention only to the ecstasy of their love.

I jumped off a cliff to find out the true nature of soul.
Do not sit inside the sadness of powerful, self-absorbed people.
Become the ground under your own feet.

The soul's joy enters a guest house
where Shams Tabriz is host.
No one is there.

THE EXUBERANT CONFUSION

A tree of fragrance from a garden rose,
the friend is the taste of this elaborate, particulate universe
and of the spirit that informs and streams beyond it.

An ash sapling and the stars wonder about the sun
as fish explore the restlessness they live within.

You turn faces toward light,
Joseph coming after so many years,
Khidr offering springwater.

Why are you still hidden?
Say openly where and who we are,
you, grace and content of the seen and unseen,
you, this exuberant confusion.

What kind of love is this
where the heart's eloquence and the way it is heard
keep explaining again
how the whole ocean makes a single pearl?

A BOWL THROWN OUT

Stay. Do not make excuses to leave.
Serve us more wine from this friendship's vineyard.
Do not turn to the window or the porch.
Live here in this circle.

Wanting what is outside is a bait that will trap you.
Step out onto sky through the round threshold.
Be alone in your search for absolute aloneness.

Be a bowl thrown out on the ocean,
not a bowl held out for more going kitchen to kitchen.
Time is bright, then dark, warm and cold by turns.
Live at the springhead where the flowing begins.

Do not find fault, and do not compliment anyone.
Do not offer pastry or garlic.
What's the use?

You may as well tell torches not to burn.
Say to whatever burns, *Burn*.
Except for the ache of separation.
But that is not always true either.
Anything put into words is questionable.

THE ARRIVAL

What shall we call the presence that arrives?
Beloved, friend? Pride and joy, love-thief, gratitude, patience?
I have no patience anymore.

Go away, you names and mental formations.
A new shape has come that flies our flag upsidedown,
the form no door lets in.

Rather, the walls around us fall outward.
Floor and roof too drop away.

ZERO CIRCLE

Be helpless and dumbfounded,
unable to say yes or no.

Then a stretcher will come from grace
to gather us up.

We are too dull-eyed to see the beauty.
If we say *Yes we can*, we will be lying.

If we say *No, we don't see it*,
that no will behead us
and shut tight our window into spirit.

So let us be not sure of anything,
beside ourselves and only that,
so miraculous beings come running to help.

Crazed, lying in a zero circle, mute,
we will be saying finally,
with tremendous eloquence, *Lead us*.

When we have totally surrendered to that beauty,
we will become a mighty kindness.

PART II
Quatrains (*Rubai*)

Introduction to the Quatrains

The astronomer Abd al-Rahman ibn Umar al-Sufi, commonly known as al-Sufi (903–986), lived in Isfahan and is known for his translation from Greek into Arabic of Ptolemy's *Almagest*. His most famous work is *Kitab suwar al-kawakib* (*The Book of Fixed Stars*), in which he gives the Arabic names for Ptolemy's constellations and stars. The careful science of this book spurred further work on astronomy in the Arabic and Islamic worlds and was a huge influence on the development of science in Europe. These images, reproduced here, are taken from a copy in the Library of Congress, produced somewhere in central Asia around 1730 and said to be an exact copy of a manuscript, now lost, prepared for Tamerlane's grandson, Ulug Beg of Samarcand, in 1417.

SPRINGWATER: RUMI'S SHORT POEMS

The short poem has been compared to discrete things that keep their mystery: a seed, a flower, a constellation of stars. Hence the categories here: knots, birdsong, a slice of tangerine, candleflame, a joke, an irrational number, a caboose, a feather, a tease. Lightning bug, grasshopper, bird's nest, hummingbird, shoe left behind stuck in the mud, boat tied up for the night. The list could go on until the whole world is here in singular items: nail, breath, drop. Cloud, lightning, waterfall. What would the language of a seed be like? All potential, a miraculously condensed life-form.

Rumi keeps saying throughout his oceanically in motion masterwork, the *Masnavi*, "This has no end." But short poems definitely *do* have a beginning and a quick end. They float in the delicious silence that surrounds them. It is for that they are so restrained, to get back to the silence, their source. Short poems have meditative properties and possibilities. They have often recorded or led into states of awareness that come with meditation. You feel this in the Japanese haiku, in South Indian poetry, Kabir, Tagore. In this regard, I love Robert Bly's work with short poems in his first book, *Silence in the Snowy Fields*, and that book's brother, James Wright's *The Branch Will Not Break*.[1] Those two books, I feel, contain the best work in the short form in this country since Emily Dickinson. She is the inimitable model for the short poem in American English. But there are also William Stafford, W. S. Merwin, and many others. Best not to make pronouncements. Mary Oliver has recently begun to write very short poems. She will find new aspects in the form.

Rumi's poems are often invitations into a mystery, an awareness that lives beyond the mind. "Do you want my head? Friend, I make you a gift." He has many ways of speaking of it. He lures us into a joy that has no reason. "I want to see beyond this existence." In his poems love messages are coming through. Be still and listen. It is a state of nonexistence that Rumi's *rubai* (quatrains) call us into. Here we are, they say, in the midst of visible, palpable existence. Then a presence comes, or something like a presence is sensed, felt, sometimes suddenly, "Lightning, your presence / from ground to sky," or gradually, "Birdsong, wind, / the water's face. / I know you are closeby." Imagine the short poem as a doorway leading to somewhere that is beyond the range of language, into a *you* that is both intimate and vast. There is often a leap or a stepping aside, a spontaneous effort. "What I most want / is to spring out of this personality, / then to sit apart from that leaping."

Or say that a Rumi quatrain is a form of sublime relaxation. He warns against moods and emotions that block the shift to nonexistence. Some of them are ambition, lust, boredom, guilt, and shame. Drinking wine made from grapes is also not much help either, whereas grief and longing are welcomed. They are conditions inherent in the shift. Sometimes there is a pronominal elision that registers in the poems. The *me* becomes a *you*. "You ask why I turn around you? / Not around you, I turn around myself." A dome rises overhead, composed of both. "I am the Capella.." "Union comes of nonbeing." It requires that one become profoundly unconditioned. Lose all your feathers, if you want to fly in this new air. "My living is composed only / of this trying to be in your presence." Some of the poems end up inside non-existence, where anything is possible. "In this kitchen stocked with fresh food, / why sit content with a cup of warm water? / Begin as creation, become a creator." Now that we are inside this new region, let's cook something up. "We can sail this ship lying down." Outrageous claims, like choicelessness, are made. We feel they are true.

Here are some images from the quatrains about the internal crossover into what I am calling nonexistence, or enlightenment, or emptiness:

The transition of birds from nest to flight ("The way of love . . . ,").

Going from an emperor in his finery of self-sufficiency to a nameless supplant in full prostration at the door ("Let your throat-song . . . ,").

Moving from descriptions of love in a book to the actual conversation of two lovers living together ("I have phrases . . . ,").

A wave that moves in to shore and becomes a stillness of fog against the cliff ("I was happy enough . . . ,").

A high desert plain with someone walking there in a peace beyond understanding ("There is a desert . . . ,").

Genuine solitude ("Which is worth more . . . ,").

We become evidence that there is a way from wanting to longing ("Be fair. Admit that love . . . ,").

The transition is not a way; it is more like nakedness ("Come to this street . . . ,").

A shift that leaves the intellect in ruins ("Come to this street . . . ,").

A gentle, nourishing form of insanity ("The mystic dances . . . ,").

In this crossing-over, separateness and connectedness are felt at the same time ("Spring overall . . . ,").

Pieces of cloud disappearing in sunlight ("This is how I would die . . . ,").

Being in nonexistence is like the strangeness of a dove who is unafraid of the hawk floating above it ("Someone who does not run . . . ,").

A burning emptiness ("Flowers open every night . . . ,").

There is no conventional love fulfillment in this new place ("Do not think for a moment . . . ,").

No ending, no place to rest ("A road may end . . . ,").

Language that comes in the moving-across is less like words than it is like the wind or the nightingale's song ("A light wind coming . . . ,").

Identities blend: "My own lips open, and in whatever I say, I hear you" ("Your fragrance fills . . . ,").

A new conversation ("I realize that the dawn . . . ,").

No confining limits ("Are you jealous . . . ,").

There is a new way of breathing ("There is a way . . . ,").

Rumi often comes back to the mirror as an image of the lover, the enlightened consciousness. The mirror does not do anything.

It just is a witness to whatever happens in front of it. Lover and worker become one as polisher melts into reflection. ("We are the mirror . . . ,").

A music we are part of that we do not control ("All day and night . . . ,").

One of the gifts from the friend, the mysterious you that is met in this shift, is that we can become a school with a greater presence nearby ("These gifts from the friend . . . ,").

Power is no longer wanted, except as something to surrender to ("Here is a magnificent person . . . ,").

This transition is about being truly alive, as a small stream enters a great river, or like suddenly discovering another dimension, as, inexplicably, oxen plodding in a flat circle around a millstone begin to move spherically ("If you want to live . . . ,").

The new life is fluid, a spring, but separate drops too ("Life is ending. . . ,").

Ignorance seems to be a primary characteristic of this crossover region of consciousness. It is a very positive form of ignorance ("I thought I had self-control . . . ,").

Here is one of his most precise images for the longing that drives this shift of awareness:

There is a path from me to you
that I am constantly looking for,

so I try to keep clear and still
as water does with the moon.

But any assertion *about* the transition into nonexistence is bound to be too formulaic to be true, too stiff. Rumi's poetry is a living flow that comes out of his evolving consciousness. We must allow the poems to stay uninterpretable, as a whole human being is, in motion, ineffable. "Transition," "shift," "crossover"—the terms are misleading. The state from within which Rumi speaks is more wavering and less definable than those words imply. There is doubleness, and tripleness. Absence and presence and something else ("I am the soul . . . ,"), revealing that enlightenment is a union *and* a unique separateness (individuality). Whatever it is is beyond language ("You are inside meaning, not words . . . ,"), full of wonder, in a surprising ecstasy, beyond time, losing interest in the createdness, yet feeling *inside* the beauty of the creator ("How long shall we delight . . . ,"). The main truth of enlightenment seems to be that the ego has dissolved, gone, *poof*. There is no shred of that, that I can detect, in Rumi's poetry. If these translations have traces of ego, that is my doing. I hope to be forgiven.

These poems are shorter than the usual English lyrics, shorter than sonnets and a little longer than haiku. The poems are like musical phrases, a single dance step with a gesture at the end. One whirl, a long flute note, invitation and answer. You hardly know what happened. Did anything? Where are we? And the atmosphere seems to me to stay profoundly playful. This is key.

There is a story about the origin of the Persian quatrain. It was a country-fair day. A poet and his friends were watching some children play a game. A boy threw a walnut so that it started along a groove of the pavement, jumped out, then rolled back in to hit the aimed-at spot. He had put English on the nut, and he celebrated with a chant, "Rolling, rolling, off and back, then home to the bottom of the ditch." The poet (some say it was Rudaki in the tenth century) heard a new rhythm in the boy's elation, repeated it with variations three times, and the Persian quatrain was born. The knack of making the crossover into a surrendered world, which I hear as the subject of many of Rumi's short poems, is full of playfulness and spontaneity. That is why they seem so fresh, and continuously refreshing, like cold springwater.

ORGANIZATIONAL NOTE

For symmetry with the first part of the book, I have divided the quatrains into twenty-seven groupings. Each is associated with a constellation or other celestial body. This is purely arbitrary. I felt they needed to be divided in some way, to make them more tasty and less dismaying to the eye, as is the sheer expanse of Emily Dickinson's 1789 nameless short poems in the Harvard edition. For the creative play of it then, and to give them space, to put them in an emptiness teeming with interpenetrating beings—transformative, protective, and dangerous—I have thrown them out among the galaxies like sparks from a campfire into the nightsky, where the laws of gravity may not quite apply the way we thought. The new pictures coming in from the refurbished Hubble telescope are as ecstatic as any Sufi.

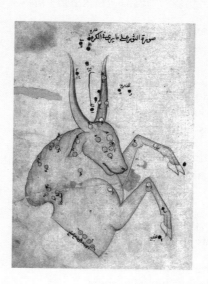

28.
Taurus: The Bull

Zeus transforms himself into a bull to abduct the princess Europa. He swims with her on his back to Crete. This constellation represents the front half of a bull, the part that would show above the waves of the Mediterranean as he swam.

———

Late, by myself, in the boat of myself,
no light and no land anywhere,
cloudcover thick.

I try to stay just above the surface,
yet I am already under
and living within the ocean.

———

I am crying, my tears tell me that much.
Last spring, they say, *the new-green, how weak you felt.*

Remember any night of all our nights,
but do not remember things I have said.

———

Friend, our closeness is this.
Anywhere you put your foot feel me
in the firmness under you.

How is it with this love,
I see your world and not you?

———

When I am with you, we stay up all night.
When you are not here, I can't go to sleep.

Praise God for these two insomnias,
and the difference between them.

———

When I die, lay out the corpse.
You may want to kiss my lips,
just beginning to decay.

Do not be frightened if I open my eyes.

———

This bleating eventually stops. The wolf appears.
We run off in all directions,
with always some thought of how lucky we are.

But nothing floats for long.
Death floods in at the mouth and the ear.
Every head goes under and away.

———

For years, copying other people, I tried to know myself.
From within, I could not decide what to do.
Unable to see, I heard my name being called.

Then I walked outside.

———

Today like every other day, we wake up empty
and frightened. Don't open the door to the study
and begin reading. Take down a musical instrument.

Let the beauty we love be what we do.
There are hundreds of ways to kneel and kiss the ground.

———

The breeze at dawn has secrets to tell you.
Don't go back to sleep.
You must ask for what you really want.
Don't go back to sleep.
People are going back and forth across the doorsill
where the two worlds touch.
The door is round and open.
Don't go back to sleep.

———

Take someone who does not keep score,
who is not looking to be richer, or afraid of losing,
who has not the slightest interest even
in his own personality. He is free.

———

Out beyond ideas of wrongdoing and rightdoing,
there is a field. I'll meet you there.

When the soul lies down in that grass,
the world is too full to talk about.
Ideas, language, even the phrase *each other*
doesn't make any sense.

———

I would love to kiss you.
The price of kissing is your life.

Now my life is running toward my life shouting,
What a bargain. Let's buy it.

———

We have this way of talking, and we have another.
Apart from what we wish and what we fear may happen,
we are alive with other life,
as clear stones take form in the mountain.

———

Someone who goes with half a loaf of bread
to a small place that fits like a nest around him,

someone who wants no more, who is not himself
longed for by anyone else.

He is a letter to everyone. You open it.
It says, *Live.*

———

Who sees inside from outside?
Who finds hundreds of mysteries
even where minds are deranged?

See through his eyes what he sees.
Who then is looking out from his eyes?

———

Looking for the ocean,
I find a piece of shell with a piece of foam on it.

I taste the ocean in the foam. I turn,
and the steep trail opens onto a high plain.

———

Your eyes are the mystery,
with thousands of lives living in the edges.

Your hair full of forgetfulness,
your face pure praise.

So clarity is decorated with mistakes.

29.
Ursa Major: The Great Bear, the Big Dipper

The Big Dipper is part of the Great Bear. It fits along his back like a saddle. You can find the North Star (Polaris) by sighting along the two stars that form the end of the cup. In one configuration the bear is on his haunches with his head in the air, sniffing. In another he is ambling along, being guided by the Herdsman.

———

The clear bead at the center changes everything.
There are no edges to my loving now.

You have heard it said that there is a window
that opens from one mind to another.

But if there is no wall, there is no need
for fitting the window, or the latch.

We take long trips.
We puzzle over the meaning of a painting or a book,
when what we are wanting to see and understand in this world,
we *are* that.

Does sunset sometimes look like the sun is coming up?
Do you know what a faithful love is like?
You are crying. You say you have burned yourself.

But can you think of anyone who is *not* hazy with smoke?

Daylight, full of small dancing particles,
and the one great turning,
our souls are dancing with you.
Without feet, they dance.

Can you see them when I whisper in your ear?

They try to say what you are, spiritual or sexual.
They wonder about Solomon and all his wives.

In the body of this world, they say,
there is a soul, and you are that.

But we have ways within each other
that will never be said by anyone.

This human shape is a ghost
made of distraction and pain.

Sometimes pure light, sometimes cruel,
trying wildly to open,
this image so tightly held within itself.

Stay in the company of lovers.
Those other kinds of people,
they each want to show you something.

A crow will lead you to an empty barn,
a parrot to sugar.

There is a light seed grain inside.
You fill it with yourself or it dies.

I am caught in this curling energy, your hair.
Whoever is calm and sensible is insane.

Do not think of good advice for me.
I have tasted the worst that can happen.
So they lock me somewhere, bound and gagged,
they cannot tie up this new love I have.

You don't have *bad* days and *good* days.
You don't feel sometimes brilliant and sometimes dumb.
There is no studying, no scholarly thinking
having to do with love,
but there is a great deal of plotting, and secret touching,
and nights you cannot remember at all.

The Sufi opens his hands to the universe
and gives away each instant, free.

Unlike someone on the street who begs for money to survive,
a dervish begs to give you his life.

There is a strange frenzy in my head,
of birds flying,
each particle circulating on its own.

Is the one I love everywhere?

Not until someone dissolves,
can he or she know what union is.
That descends only into emptiness.

A lie does not change to truth
with just talking about it.

Soul of this world,
no life, no world remain,
no beautiful men and women longing.

Only this ancient love
circling the holy black stone of nothing,
where the lover is the love,
the horizon and everything within it.

It may be sometimes noisy in the school of love,
but there is never any distinguishing past from present.

No judge decides a precedent here.
In matters of love, judges cannot speak.

30.
Corona Borealis:
The Northern Crown

The Greeks saw this circlet of stars as Ariadne's crown. Other Middle Eastern civilizations have seen it as a cracked dish. Australian aborigines call it the boomerang.

———

They say that paradise will be perfect
with lots of clear white wine and all the beautiful women.
We hold on to times like this then,
since this is how it is going to be.

———

Come to the orchard in spring.
There is light and wine and sweethearts
in the pomegranate flowers.

If you do not come, these do not matter.
If you do come, these do not matter.

———

Poles apart, I am the color of dying.
You are the color of being born.

Unless we breathe into each other,
there can be no garden.

So that is why plants grow and laugh at our eyes,
which focus on distance.

———

Think that you are gliding out
from the face of a cliff like an eagle.
Think you are walking like a tiger walks by himself in the forest.
You are most handsome when you are after food.

Spend less time with nightingales and peacocks.
One is just a voice, the other just a color.

———

For a while we lived with people,
but we found in them no sign of the faithfulness we wanted.

It is better to hide completely within,
as water hides in metal, as fire hides in a rock.

———

The mystery does not get clearer by repeating the question,
nor is it bought with going to amazing places.

Until you have kept your eyes
and your wanting still for fifty years,
you do not begin to cross over from confusion.

———

The minute I am disappointed, I feel encouraged.
When I am ruined, I am healed.

When I am quiet and solid as the ground,
then I talk the low tones of thunder for everyone.

———

I drink streamwater,
and the air becomes clearer, and everything I do.

I become a waterwheel,
turning and tasting you,
as long as water moves.

In pain I breathe easier.
The scared child is running from the house, screaming.
I hear the gentleness.

Under nine layers of illusion, whatever the light,
on the face of any object, in the ground itself,
I see your face.

Today I am out wandering,
turning my skull into a cup for others to drink wine from.

In this town somewhere there sits a calm, intelligent man,
who does not know what he is about to do.

I asked for one kiss. You gave me six.
Who was teacher is now student.
Things good and generous take form in me,
and the air is clear.

I am insane, but they keep calling to me.
No one here knows me, but no one chases me off.
My job is to stay awake like the nightwatchman.

When they are drunk enough, and it is late enough,
they recognize me. They say, *There's daylight.*

You who long for powerful positions,
keep worrying about that, and your land.

We burn inside union with one truth,

There is no reality but God.
There is only God.

A poet tries to say love's mystery,
why the reed flute grieves.

Listen and obey the hushed language.
Go naked.

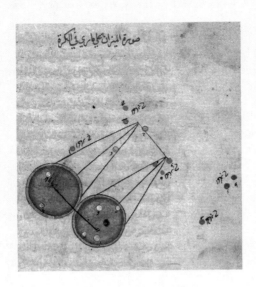

31.
Libra: The Scales

The Libra constellation is home to a star called Gliese 581, which has a planetary system of at least four planets. It was discovered in 2007 that three of these planets are Earth-like and of significance in establishing the likelihood of life outside of our own beloved sun's influence.

During the day I was singing with you.
At night we slept in the same bed.
I was not conscious day or night.

I thought I knew who I was,
but I was you.

Drinking wine with you, getting warmer and warmer,
I think why not trade in this overcoat made of leaves and dirt?

Then I look out the window.
For what? Both worlds are here.

———

Since we have seen each other, a game goes on.
Secretly I move, and you respond.
You are winning. You think it's funny.

But look up from the board now.
Look how I have brought furniture into this invisible place,
so we can live here.

———

The minute I heard my first love story
I started looking for you,
not knowing how blind that was.

Lovers don't finally meet somewhere.
They are in each other all along.

———

If you have any patience left, we know what to do.
If you love sleep, we will tear you away.
If you change into a mountain, we will melt you.
If you become an ocean, we will drain you.

———

You say you have no sexual longing anymore,
that you are one with the one you love.

This is dangerous.
Do not believe that I have a love like that.

If one day you see a picture of how you love,
you will hate yourself, openly.

———

I am not talking out loud.
I am talking to the ears of your spirit.
Remember what I have said.
Tomorrow I will say openly what I am saying tonight.

———

We have given up making a living.
It is all this crazy love poetry now.

It's everywhere.
Our eyes and our feelings focus together,
with our words.

———

We have a huge barrel of wine, but no cups.
That's fine with us.
Every morning we glow, and in the evening we glow again.

They say there is no future for us, and they are right.
Which is fine with us.

———

Do you think I know what I'm doing?
That for one breath or half-breath I belong to myself?

As much as a pen knows what it's writing,
or the ball can guess where it is going next.

———

Do not sit long with a sad friend.
When you go to a garden,
do you look at thorns or flowers?

Spend more time with roses and jasmine.

———

Inside the great mystery that is,
we do not really own anything.

What is this competition we feel then,
before we go, one at a time, through the same gate?

———

There is no light like yours.
No breeze quick enough to carry your fragrance.

When the intellect leaves its castle
and walks through your lane,
it does not know where or who it is.
It sits on the ground and babbles.

———

As salt dissolves in ocean,
I was swallowed up in you,
beyond doubt or being sure.

Suddenly here in my chest
a star came out so clear,
it drew all stars into it.

———

Show me yourself in the beauty of the world,
in the candle of Teraz.

No praying, no fasting.
When I am with you, everything is prayer.
Without you, there is no praising, and no grief.

32.
Gemini: The Twins, Castor and Pollux

Putting images and stories up in the nightsky is one of the most beautiful things people have done. Well, they used to. Now they assign numbers. The Ptolemaic system assumed that the sky was a spherical ceiling to decorate with images. Astrology reads those with astonishing subtlety as guides to the motions of individual, and collective, psyches. Dutch navigators and French astronomers came many centuries later and hung tools up, sextant, calipers, a microscope, as though the nightsky were a very eccentric suburban garage. Tools and fish.

———

We are the mirror, as well as the face in it.
We are tasting the taste this minute of eternity.

We are pain and what cures pain.
We are the sweet cold water and the jar that pours.

———

At night we fall into each other with such grace.
When it is light,
you throw me back like you do your hair.

Your eyes now drunk with God,
mine with looking at you.
One drunkard takes care of another.

———

We are walking through a garden.
I turn away for a minute.

You are doing it again.
You have my face here, but you look at flowers.

———

The one who floods the private sanctuary I have built,
who takes away sleep,
who drags and throws me under,

that presence is the joy I speak.

———

The center clears. Knowing comes.
My body is not singular like a corpse,
but singular like a salt grain
still in the side of the mountain.

———

The light you give off did not come from a pelvis.
Your features did not begin in semen.

Do not try to hide inside anger,
radiance that cannot be hidden.

———

All day and night, music,
a quiet, bright reedsong.

If it fades, we fade.

———

Sleep has no authority.
Night may as well stop looking for us,
when we are like this.

Invisible, except at dawn.

———

This night extends into eternity,
like a fire burning inside the friend.

Truly knowing this is what joy is.
Forgetting it is grief, and a lack of courage.

———

Days are sieves to filter spirit,
reveal impurities, and show the light of those
who throw their own shining into the universe.

———

Out of nowhere a horse brought us here,
where we taste love until we do not exist again.

This taste is the wine we always mention.

———

Earlier, to be ready,
I loosened the leg bindings.

Today, your scent.
Gratefulness rises on the air.

———

Yesterday was glory and joy.
Today, a blackened burn everywhere.

On the record of my life,
these days will be put down as *one*.

———

Love told me to reject mind, and also spirit.
Live with me.

For a while I did.
Then I left, came back, and left again.
Now I am back, here to stay.

———

You push me into the dance.
You pull me by the ears
like the ends of a bow being drawn back.

You crush me in your mouth
like a piece of bread.
You have made me into *this*.

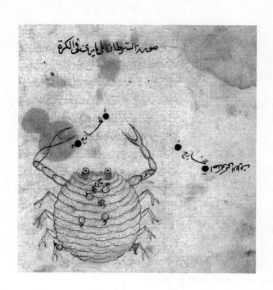

33.
Cancer: The Crab

The crab plays a small role in the myth of the twelve labors of Hercules. While Hercules is fighting the Hydra monster, the goddess Hera, who does not like Hercules, sends a crab to distract him. The crab bites Hercules' toe, but he barely notices and immediately crushes the crab with his other foot. Hera rewards the crab for its effort by giving it a place in the sky.

———

These gifts from the friend,
a robe of skin and veins, a teacher within,
wear them and become a school,
with a greater sheikh nearby.

———

There is no companion but love.
No starting or finishing, yet a road.

The friend calls from there,
Why do you hesitate when lives are in danger?

———

I pretended to leap
to see if I could live *there*.

Someday I must actually arrive *there*,
or nothing will be left to arrive.

———

Here is a magnificent person
holding a glass of wine, a vision of power,
over me, I hope, not *for* me.

———

Let the lover be disgraceful,
crazy, absentminded.

Someone sober will worry about events going badly.
Let the lover be.

———

The manner and appearance of a prophet,
our secret origins,
these are born of a woman who still lives inside us,
though she is hiding from what we have become.

———

If you have a spirit, lose it, loose it,
to return where with one word we came from.

Now, thousands of words,
and we refuse to leave.

———

If you want to live, leave your banks,
as a small stream enters the Oxus, miles wide,
or as cattle moving around a millstone,
suddenly circle to the top of the sphere.

———

Life is ending? God gives another.
Admit the finite. Praise the infinite.

Love is a spring. Submerge.
Every separate drop, a new life.

———

I thought I had self-control,
so I regretted times I did not.

With that considering over,
the one thing I know is,
I do not know who I am.

———

This piece of food cannot be eaten,
nor this bit of wisdom found by looking.

There is a secret core in everyone
not even Gabriel can know by trying to know.

———

You come to reading books late in life.
Don't worry if you see the young ones ahead of you.
Don't hurry. You are tired and ready to quit?
Let your hands play music.

———

I lay my forehead in the dust of your door,
very near the end.

Give me your mouth,
so that I can die out on your lips.

———

The early morning breeze tastes sweet like the friend.
Rise and take that in,
before it dissipates in wasted energy,
the many preparations that caravans make to leave.

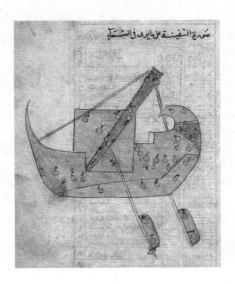

34.
Cassiopeia: The Queen

In the late autumn nightsky when Cassiopeia becomes visible, as a crooked *W*, the other players in the Andromeda myth become visible too: Perseus, the hero; Pegasus, his mighty steed; Cepheus, the king; and Cetus, the sea monster.

———

Some nights, stay up till dawn,
as the moon sometimes does for the sun.

Be a full bucket pulled up the dark way of a well,
then lifted out into light.

———

Tonight remove whatever remains.
Last night we lay listening to your one story,
of being in love.

We lay around you stunned like the dead.

386

No wine glasses here, but wine is handed around.
No smoke, but burning.

Listen to the unstruck sound,
and what sifts through that music.

———

We do not need wine to get drunk,
or instruments and singing to feel ecstatic.

No poets, no leaders, no song,
yet we jump around totally wild.

———

No better love than love with no object,
no more satisfying work than work with no purpose.

If you could give up tricks and cleverness,
that would be the cleverest trick.

———

I can break off from anyone,
except that presence within.

Anyone can bring gifts.
Give me someone who takes away.

———

Noah's ark is the symbol of our species,
a boat wandering the ocean.

A plant grows deep in the center of that water.
It has no form and no location.

———

What is this day with two suns in the sky?
Day unlike other days,
with a great voice giving it to the planet,
Here it is, enamored beings, your day.

———

Glass of wine in hand, I fall.
I get on my feet again, dizzy, deranged,
then sink down demolished,

not in this place any longer,
yet here, strong and sober, still standing.

———

The friend comes clapping,
at once obvious and obscure,
without fear or plans.

I am as I am,
because this one is like that.

———

The friend comes into my body
looking for the center, unable to find it,
draws a blade, strikes anywhere.

———

This night there are no limits to what may be given.
This is not a night but a marriage,
a couple whispering in bed in unison the same words.
Darkness simply lets down a curtain for that.

———

Last night, full of longing,
asking the wine woman for more,
and then more.

She teased me so lovingly
I fell into her and disappeared.
Then she was there alone.

———

The rider has passed,
but his dust hangs in the air.

Do not stare at these particles.
The rider's direction is *there*.

———

Listen for the stream that tells you:

Die on this bank.
Begin in me
the way of rivers with the sea.

———

If love is a battle
where swords are sharpened against our bodies,
let me drown in the uproar.

Tell my friends to save themselves.

———

Reason has no way to say its love.
Only love can open that secret.

If you want to be more alive,
love is your true health.

———

Love is beyond body, mind, heart, and soul.
A lover simply *is* love.

He or she has become *THAT,*
and if not, then not.

35.
Virgo: The Virgin

In Babylonian mythology this star grouping was thought of as an ear of
wheat. One star retains that association, Spica, which means in Latin
"ear of grain." The Greeks associated this constellation with the goddess
of wheat, Demeter, the virgin mother of Persephone. During the
Middle Ages in Christian countries she became the Virgin Mary.

Tonight is the essence of night,
the asking and what the asking wants,
generosity and the given,
something said back and forth with God.

A night full of talking that hurts,
my worst held-back secrets.
Everything has to do with loving and not loving.
This night will pass.
Then we have work to do.

———

I circle your nest tonight,
around and around until morning,
when a breath of air says *Now*,
and the friend holds up like a goblet
some anonymous skull.

———

I am filled with you,
skin, blood, bone, brain, and soul.

There is no room for trust or lack of trust,
nothing in this existence but that existence.

———

Do not forget the nut,
being so proud of the shell.

The body has its inward ways, the five senses.
They break open, and the friend is revealed.

Break open the friend,
you become the all-one, alone.

———

Keep walking, though there is no place to get to.
Do not try to see through the distances.
That is not for human beings.

Move within,
but do not move the way fear makes you move.

———

Walk to the well.
Turn as the earth and the moon turn,
circling what they love.
Whatever circles comes from the center.

———

The rose laughs at my long-looking,
my constantly wondering what a *rose* means,
and who *owns* the rose, whatever it means.

———

Two hands, two feet, two eyes, good,
as it should be, but no separation
between the friend and your loving.

Any dividing there makes other untrue distinctions
like *Christian* and *Jew* and *Muslim*.

———

Seeing you heals me.
Not seeing you, I feel the walls closing.
I would not wish for anyone else
such absence.

———

What keeps you alive without me?
How can you cry?
How can you know who you are?
How can you see?

———

Lost to one who seems not to care, I feel pain,
though even that is welcome from the Other,
who demands everything I am.

If I withhold it for now, as worthless,
the asking is precious.

———

Last night you left me and slept your own deep sleep.
Tonight you turn and turn.
I say, *You and I will be together until the universe dissolves.*

You mumble back
things you thought of when you were drunk.

———

There is no greater turbulence than unhappy love.
That is one we may never recover from.

It is not cured by hypocrisy, or courage.
A true love has nothing in it of power,
or of faithfulness.

———

The world is an open green in the middle of a garden.

Beings in various forms see their reflections and laugh,
love-messages flashing from every eye.

36.
Orion: The Hunter

Mythologies aside, look up and marvel *scientifically* at the stars in Orion's belt, Mintaka, Alnilam, and Alnitak. Each is a supergiant, twenty times the mass of our own sun. Alnilam's brightness is eighteen thousand times brighter than ours, and all three are about a thousand light-years away.

The Hunter is near his two companions, Big Dog and Little Dog. The game, the Hare, is at his feet.

———

My love hides on the path where the love-thief goes
and catches that one by the hair with my teeth.

Who are you? The love-thief asks,
but as I open my mouth to say,
he escapes into the desert.

———

I thought of you
and threw my glass of wine against the wall.

Now I am neither drunk nor sober,
jumping up and down, completely mad.

———

Our eyes do not see you,
but we have this excuse: Eyes see surface, not reality,
though we keep hoping, in this lovely place.

———

After being with me one whole night,
you ask how I live when you are not here.

Badly, frantically,
like a fish trying to breathe dry sand.
You weep and say, *But you choose that.*

———

There is a channel between voice and presence,
a way where information flows.

In disciplined silence the channel opens.
With wandering talk, it closes.

———

Day ferments. Eyes moisten with clouds.
Wind shakes trees, and they laugh,
just as the playful racket of children happens,
because mothers cry out, and fathers reach to touch.

———

You have said what you are.
I am what I am,
my head here in my hands
with something circling inside.

I have no name
for what circles,
so perfectly.

Why all this grief and turning pale?
Do not look at me.

Like any face reflecting other light,
the moon is a source of pain.

Someone who sees you and does not laugh out loud,
or fall silent, or explode into pieces,
is nothing more than the cement and stone
of his own prison.

Step barefooted on the ground and make it giddy,
pregnant with joking and buds.

A spring uproar rises into the stars.
The moon begins to wonder what's going on.

Those of you in the nightsky above the moon,
try walking damp ground.

Ecstatic singers in sacred taverns,
get up at dawn. Try not sleeping.

A secret turning in us
makes the universe turn.
Head unaware of feet,
and feet head. Neither cares.
They keep turning.

So delicate yesterday,
the night-singing birds by the creek.
Their words were:

You may make a jewelry flower
out of gold and rubies and emeralds,
but it will have no fragrance.

———

If you have times when you do not ache with love,
you should not be here with us.

Try to stay pointed like a thorn,
so at your side there will always be roses.

———

The one who is your being and your nonbeing,
the essence inside joy and sadness,

your eyes must not see that one,
else you would be completely that.

37.
Leo: The Lion

Leo is a crouching lion. The recognizable sickle-shape of six stars form the lion's jaw and neck. Pliny wrote that the Egyptians worshiped the stars of Leo, because the blessed annual inundation of the Nile (midsummer) coincided with the sun's entrance into those stars. Nile temples were typically decorated with lions' whisker bristles.

———

This moment this love comes to rest in me,
many beings in one being.
In one wheat grain a thousand sheaf stacks.
Inside the needle's eye, a turning night of stars.

———

Courage: a gazelle turns
to face a pack of lions.

A building that stands on bedrock stands.
Do you think my love will slump to the ground
when you leave?

———

Again, I am within my self.
I walked away, but here I come sailing back,
feet in the air, upsidedown,
as saint when he opens his eyes from prayer.
Now. The room, the tablecloth, familiar faces.

———

Listen, if you can stand to.
Union with the friend
means not being who you have been,
being instead silence, a place,
a view where language is inside seeing.

———

In the slaughterhouse of love, they kill only the best,
none of the weak or deformed.

Do not run away from this dying.
Whoever is not killed for love is dead meat.

———

Being is not what it seems,
nor nonbeing.

The world's existence
is not in the world.

———

When your love reaches the core,
earth-heavals and bright irruptions spew in the air.

The universe becomes one spirit thing,
that simple, love mixing with spirit.

———

Who ever saw such drunkards?
Barrels broken open, the ground and starry ceiling soaked.

And look. This full glass in my hand.

—

No intellect denies that you are,
but no one gives in completely to that.

This is not a place where you are not,
yet not a place either where you are seen.

—

One day you will take me completely out of myself.
I will do what the angels cannot do.

Your eyelash will write on my cheek
the poem that has not been thought of.

—

Inside water, a waterwheel turns.
A star circulates with the moon.

We live in this night ocean wondering,
What are these lights?

—

From the wet source
someone cuts a reed to make a flute.
The reed sips breath like wine,
sips more, practicing. Now drunk,
it starts the high clear notes.

—

I come to you, aching for you.
You say, *You are drunk. Go away.*

I say, *I am not drunk. Please open the door.*
You say, *You are. You are . . .
Go away.*

—

We do not have to follow the pressure-flow of wanting.
We can be led by the guide.

Wishes may or may not come true
in this house of disappointment.

Let's push the door open together
and leave.

———

There is a path from me to you
that I am constantly looking for,

so I try to keep clear and still
as water does with the moon.

———

Your love kills Turk and Arab.
I am slave to a martyr.
Your love keeps saying, *No one escapes me.*
You are right, my heart replies.

———

You that trade the pearl of your essence for a loaf,
you that find your heart in a crust of barley bread,

Nimrod also made such a mistake,
rejecting friendship with Abraham.
Later he fell in love with a mosquito.

———

My essence is like the essence of a red wine.
My body is a cup that grieves because it is inside time.

Glass after glass of wine go into my head.
Finally, my head goes into the wine.

38.
The Milky Way: Our Home Address Seen from the Side

The disk-shaped spiral galaxy we live in is 100,000 light-years across and 10,000 light-years thick. It contains about 400 billion stars. Our solar system is in an outer edge of one of the spiraling arms. This galaxy was named by the Romans, who saw it as a Milky Road (*via*) across the sky. It is fitting that Chaucer's road from the Southwark tavern toward Canterbury was known to the common people as the Milky Way. We are all Canterbury pilgrims.

———

At first, I sang and recited poems,
keeping the neighbors awake.

Now more intense, quieter.
When fire flames up, smoke vanishes.

———

When you confine, I am free.
If you rebuke, I am honored.

Your dividing blade is love.
Your moaning, song.

———

Listen to the presences inside poems.
Let them take you where they will.

Follow those private hints,
and never leave the premises.

———

Drunks fear the police,
but the police are drunk too.

People in this town love them both
like different chess pieces.

———

Night goes back to where it was.
Everyone returns home sometime.

Night, when you get there,
tell them how I love you.

———

Night comes so people can sleep like fish
in black water. Then day.

Some people pick up their tools.
Others become the making itself.

———

A voice inside both of us sings out,
a few lines from Khusraw, a stanza from Shirin.

At times a calm voice excites us.
Other times excited words make us quiet.

———

The morning wind spreads its fresh smell.
We must get up to take that in,

that wind that lets us live.
Breathe, before it's gone.

———

I am so small I can barely be seen.
How can this great love be inside me?

Look at your eyes. They are small,
but they see enormous things.

———

Where is a foot worthy to walk a garden
or an eye that deserves to look at trees?

Show me a man
willing to be thrown in the fire.

———

You speak and I start laughing.
Corpses come to life.
I am trying not to talk gibberish today,
though totally lost and wandering.

———

No one is ever depressed with you.
Those receiving light give out light.

Secrets cannot be kept
from a confidante.

———

I went to the doctor.
I feel lost, blind with love.
What should I do?

Give up owning things and being somebody.
Quit existing.

———

Longing is the core of the mystery.
Longing itself brings the cure.
The only rule is, *Suffer the pain.*

Your desire must be disciplined,
and what you want to happen in time, sacrificed.

———

Do not let your heart get rusty with grief,
and do not stay long with those
who are not in the presence.

———

A piece of dry bread and some watercress are enough.
Do not swagger yourself out in public
like the awn does, the spike tip at the top of a wheat stalk.

———

In the night when union comes,
a lover is lost inside what leaves no trace.

In that night the lover sees the stars from the inside out,
as the lightpoints in his eyes, her eyes.

———

Dust mote in sunlight,
fear giving in to peaceful breathing,
that is how I am with you,
flying without wings,
drawn like straw to amber.

———

Colorless words come from red lips,
coral being covered with playful life,
bright places in the flame of a torch.

We cannot talk as he talked.

———

Who cares what we call this thing that is hurting us,
this grief on the ground like a walnut?

Empty, we crush it. We are the heart.

———

I have tested my friend.
No spring-melt flood can make that river
other than it is, clear, majestic.

Only one day, I saw him frown.
I love him when he is alive. I love him dead.

―――――

Moses had a strange shepherd's staff.
When he threw it down, it separated out from the flock
those who live by aggression and those who hope for wealth.

The remnant went on with him through the wilderness.
Very few will understand this.

―――――

Have you heard the old advice?
For the two or three days before you die,
try hard for those days, to die.

It is probably good counsel,
the world being like an old woman
who has survived so many husbands,
more than you could ever imagine.

Do not waste your last days
talking to her.

39.
Bijou: The Black Hole

The black hole at the center of our galaxy has no name. I propose we call it Bijou, French for "jewel." We have a dark jewel turning majestically at the center of our home.

The theory now is that every galaxy has a nucleus, a black hole, and that the astonishing gravitational pull of the condensed energy of the one in the Milky Way gives our galaxy its spiral shape. The most powerful black hole discovered so far is called QSU B0827.9+5255. It contains more energy than a quadrillion (1,000,000,000,000,000) of our suns and 63,000 of our galaxies. I love to hear scientists talk about black holes, the event horizon, and possible wormholes into other universes. A black hole is the most physically extreme object in the universe, a maelstrom of unbelievable density. Black-hole research is one of those edges over which science and mysticism gaze with the same awe.

Who says the eternal being does not exist?
Who says the sun has gone out?

Someone who climbs up on the roof,
and closes his eyes tight,
and says, *I don't see anything*.

When you feel your lips becoming infinite and sweet,
like the moon in a sky,
when you feel that spaciousness inside,
Shams of Tabriz will be there too.

A ruby with a sweet taste,
absorbing wine-light.

I could tell you the name of this grape, but why?
I serve one who keeps secrets.

Already tightly bound,
we are wrapped with yet another chain.

We have lost everything,
but here is another disaster.

Held in the curls of your hair,
we feel a rope around our neck.

Those on the way are almost invisible to those who are not.
A man or a woman recognizes God and starts out.
The others say he, or she, is losing faith.

I want a poet who cannot leave the friend.
If he could, and still be always in love,
he would be a master, or he couldn't.

Give us poets like that.

———

The sun is love.
The lover, a speck circling the sun.

A spring wind moves to dance
any branch that is not dead.

———

Do not let your throat tighten with fear.
Take sips of breath all day and night,
before death closes your mouth.

———

If I gave up sanity,
I could fill a hundred versions of you.

There is no liquid
like a tear from a lover's eye.

———

I honor those
who try to rid themselves of any lying,
who empty the self
and have only clear being there.

———

God only knows, I don't,
what keeps me laughing.

The stem of a flower moves
when the air moves.

———

I reach for a piece of wood. It turns into a lute.
I do some meanness. It turns out helpful.
They say one must not travel during the holy month.
Then I start out, and wonderful things happen.

———

You are the pump of my pulse,
so the good or bad I do is due to you.

Now my eyesight is going,
which is also your fault,
since you are the lightpoints in my eyes.

Each moment you call me to you and ask how I am,
even though you know.

The love I answer you with
stirs like wind through cypress.

Your love fills my chest, then empties,
then comes back to put its baggage down.

Now it has gone again.
Please, I call out. *Stay still for a day or two.*

So you sit down here with me,
and evidently have forgotten how to move.

As you start out on the way,
the way appears.

As you cease to be,
true life begins.

As you grow smaller,
the world cannot contain you.

You will be shown a being
that has no *you* inside it.

Dear mind, such a traveler, always moving,
like a fish looking for the sea,
while the great heart's ocean waits,
all around *and inside it.*

How can you live outside this love?

You have not noticed the tears of the poor.
You are ecstatic, and the smoke of that clouds your sight.
There are those around you in great pain.
Still you talk about the subtle beauty.

Real love moves through humiliation.
Love has nothing to do with being admired.

The friend lives in the lover's eyes,
as the divine mystery does
in a plant or a fish.

What human beings are thirsty for
is flowing now from my eyes.

———

Every day your wind is blowing in my head.
I am restless and wildly alive with it.

This is nothing like being drunk,
with its joy of wine-rush,
then the sad hangover.

This is continuous,
blowing steadily throughout waking and sleeping,
your love, this wind,
moving the air so strongly and the same,
day after day, after night,
after day.

40.
Columba: Noah's Dove

The Dutch astronomer Petrus Plancius named the constellation Columba in 1592. It is a very small, faint constellation from our vantage point, as no doubt are we from its. The name refers to the dove sent out by Noah that came back with a piece of greenery, bringing the good news that the Flood was receding. *Columba* means "dove" in Latin.

Never too many fish in a swift creek,
never too much water for fish to live in.

No place is too small for lovers,
nor can lovers see too much of the world.

An ecstatic seed planted anywhere on earth
comes up with this crop we plant.

The music of a reed flute heard anywhere
floats in the air as proof of our loving.

———

I say, *Bring the simple wine that makes me free.*
You say, *There is a hurricane coming!*
I say, *Let's have some wine then,
and sit here like old statues and watch.*

———

The prophets were all commanded
to stay in the company of lovers.

We take warmth from fire,
but fire goes out in the presence of ashes.

———

I planted roses, but without you, they were thorns.
I hatched peacock eggs. Snakes were inside.
Played the harp, sour music.
I went to the eighth heaven. It was the lowest hell.

———

I say what I think I should do.
You say, *Die.*
I say my lamp's oil has turned to water.
You say, *Die.*
I say I burn like a moth in the candle of your face.
You say, *Die.*

———

Eyes. You say, *Keep them open.*
Liver. You say, *Keep it working.*
I mention the heart-center.
You ask, *What is there?*
Much love for you.
Keep it for yourself.

———

Secrets try to enter our ears.
Do not prevent them.
Do not hide your face.
Do not let us be without music and wine.
Do not let us breathe once
without being where you are.

We are confused as lovers always are.
You walk in and out among the confusions, unaffected,
but anyone trying to follow you will be confused.

Every day, this pain. Either you are numb,
or you do not understand love.
I write out my love story.
You see the writing, but you do not read it.

The sun coming up brings clear wine-air.
Being sober is not living.
Listen to the longing of a stringless harp.
Stand watch over this burning.

You come closer, though you never left.
Water flows, and the stream stays full.
You are a bag of musk. We are the fragrance.
Is musk ever separated from its scent?

When you are with everyone but me,
you are with no one.

When you are with no one but me,
you are with everyone.

Instead of being so bound up *with* everyone,
be everyone. When you become that many,
you are nothing. Empty.

If your guide is your ego,
do not rely on luck for help.

You sleep through the day,
and the nights are short.

By the time you wake up,
your life may be over.

———

Stay here today and tomorrow, my friend.
Wait with me.

Generous and selfish actions,
both come with every day.

Lovers take direct and also wandering ways,
with no treachery in either.

———

The great ocean of the heart plays and spends
its coral and its pearls, giving everything away,
holding nothing back.

The body, a seashell, opens its mouth.
Ah, says the ocean-heart,
if the soul could not find a way in,
how am I to fit?

———

There is a soul within your soul,
a jewel inside the mountain.

Solitary Sufi dervish going by,
you have the mystery of your journey's end
traveling with you.

41.
Draco: The Dragon

Draco was one of the original forty-eight constellations listed by the first-century astronomer Ptolemy, and it remains one of the eighty-eight modern ones. The ancient Egyptians associated it with a fierce protective goddess whose body was a composite of crocodile, lioness, human woman, and hippopotamus.

Whispering at dawn:
Do not keep from me what you know.

Answer: *Some things are to understand
but not to say. Be quiet.*

I saw you last night in the gathering,
but could not take you openly in my arms,

so I put my lips next to your cheek,
pretending to talk privately.

———

I want to hold you close like a lute,
so we can cry out with loving.

You would rather throw stones at a mirror?
I am your mirror, and here are the stones.

———

Someone who does not bloom at the sight of you
is empty and numb like a drum stored away.

Someone who does not enjoy the names of God
and the words of the prophets
remains apart from those.

———

Something opens our wings.
Something makes boredom and hurt disappear.
Someone fills the cup in front of us.
We taste only sacredness.

———

Christ is the population of the world,
and every object as well.

There is no room for hypocrisy.
Why use bitter soup for healing
when sweet water is everywhere?

———

My ego is stubborn, often drunk, impolite.
My loving, finely sensitive, impatient, confused.
Please take messages from one to the other,
reply and counterreply.

———

I will never look for somewhere else to live,
no longer shy about how I love.

My eyes open. You are everywhere.
Collyrium: Eye medicine for clearing sight
and strengthening circulation.

———

Love comes sailing through and I scream.
Love sits beside me like a private supply of itself.
Love puts away the instruments
and takes off the silk robes. Our nakedness
together changes me completely.

———

Much commotion at your door,
all attention drawn that way.

Remember, even though I have done terrible things,
I can still see the whole world in your face.

———

The wine forbidden in this place
creates life for the inner being.
Fill with that and forget consequences.
There is no beginning or end.

———

I hear you, and I am everywhere, a spreading music.
You have done this many times.
You already own me, but once more
you buy me back into being.

———

No longer a stranger,
you listen all day to these crazy love-words.

Like a bee, you fill hundreds of homes with honey,
though yours is a long flight from here.

———

I am a mountain. You call. I echo.
This image that looks like me was painted by the friend.

You think I am speaking these words?
When a key turns in a lock,
the lock makes a little opening sound.

———

Your presence is a river that refreshes everyone,
a rose-garden fragrance.

Do not worry about making doorways
between individual lovers
when this flow is so all around.

———

The one who is keeping time in me,
you that turn my heart inside out,
keep changing this shape,
however you want.

———

Who is this that lifts and fills my heart?
The same that gave you life.
Who sometimes puts the falcon's hood over your eyes.

Be still.
Who other times takes that away,
loosens the leg binding, and hands you to the sky.
Now, hunt.

———

La Hawl, No Strength, calls out for grace.
It sometimes protects, but at other times
troubles begin when you say, *No strength.*

What is this *No Strength, La Hawl?*
No strength but yours?

42.

Capricorn: The Sea Goat

The fish-tailed seagoing goat Capricorn is associated with Pan, who turned himself partly into a fish to escape the monster Typhon.

———

Lightning, your presence
from ground to sky.

No one knows what becomes of me,
when you take me so quickly.

———

The wind is what you say.
The nightbird is drunk with the syllables of your name,
over and over, like the strokes of a portrait
being carefully painted in the tall space inside of me.

———

Birdsong, wind,
the water's face.

Each flower, remembering the fragrance,
I know you are closeby.

———

I love this giving my life to you,
or to anyone who knows someone who knows you,
caught as I am in your curling hair,
inside your Kashmiri-witch eyes.

———

Held like this to draw in milk,
no will, tasting clouds of milk,
never so content.

———

Since I have been away from you,
I only know how to weep.

Like a candle, melting is who I am.
Like a harp, any sound I make is music.

———

What I most want
is to spring out of this personality,
then to sit apart from that leaping.

I have lived too long where I can be reached.

———

Happy, not from anything that happens.
Warm, not from fire or a hot bath.
Light, I register zero on a scale.

———

Burning with longing-fire,
wanting to sleep with my head on your doorsill,
my living is composed only
of this trying to be in your presence.

———

Begin as creation, become a creator.
Never wait at a barrier.

In this kitchen stocked with fresh food,
why sit content with a cup of warm water?

———

I stand up, and this one of me
turns into a hundred of me.
They say I circle around you.
Nonsense. I circle around me.

———

I cannot tell my secrets.
I have no key to that door.
Something keeps me joyful,
but I cannot say what.

———

A drunk comes in off the road with a flask.
The cup going round and round,
hand to hand, suddenly slips, shatters.

Cups do not last long among drunks.

———

They say I tell the truth. Then they ask me
to do a puppet show of myself in the bazaar.

I am not something to sell.
I have already been bought.

———

Some souls flow like clear water.
They pour into our veins and feel like wine.

I give in to that. I fall flat.
We can sail this ship lying down.

———

Love is a wine that ferments and draws us to meet in the tavern
where we sit to enjoy the company of lovers
who recognize in *us*
the fragrance that brought *them* here.

Light wind of early morning,
have you seen that heart that I know,
the sun that melts granite?

The moon rose but could not find us here, circling,
so it praised another *sema*.

Dawn comes deep red, ashamed
how pale and passionless we look.

We have not walked in your rose garden for a long time.
Your eyes, those rare flowers,
have been kept out of our sight
as royalty stay aloof from the people.

We need to see your face.

In the beginning touch was my music.
Then the fierce cooking started.
I began to see the kindness of that.
When I became you, you left.

43.
Hercules: The Hero

Hercules is given twelve labors by Hera, queen of the gods, as revenge for Zeus' infidelity with a mortal, Alcmene, his mother. His last labor is to descend into Hades and bring back Cerberus, the fierce three-headed dog that guards the gates and prevents the dead from returning to life.

———

When longing is sharp,
and the ruby color deep,
we welcome your grief,
but do not bring ambition or wanting,
or sleepy boredom.

———

Full moon. Quietly awake,
you look down from a corner of a roof,

reminding us that it is not time
to sleep, or to drink wine.

————

Tonight we are getting love messages.
For their sake we must not go to sleep.
The fragrance of your hair spreading through the streets
makes the perfumers wonder at such competition.

————

Grapes under feet that crush them
turn whichever way they are turned.

You ask why I turn around you?
Not around you, I turn around myself.

————

Gone, inner and outer,
no moon or ground or sky.
Do not hand me another glass of wine.
Pour it in my mouth.
I have lost the way to my mouth.

————

Hunted down, yet hunter.
Without a job, yet constantly working.

Do you want my head?
Friend, I make you a gift.

————

What is real is you and my love for you.
High in the air, unnoticed,
this reality rises into a dome.
I am the Capella.

————

I came and sat in front of you
as I would at an altar.
Every promise I made before
I broke when I saw you.

————

Do not come to us without bringing music.
We celebrate with drum and flute,

with wine not made from grapes,
in a place you cannot imagine.

———

Joyful for no reason,
I want to see beyond this existence.

You open your lips, laughing.
I think of a design for that opening.

———

I was a tiny bug. Now a mountain.
I was left behind. Now honored at the head.

You healed my wounded hunger and anger
and made me a poet that sings about joy.

———

Humble living does not diminish. It fills.
Going back to a simpler self gives wisdom.

When a man makes up a story for his child,
he becomes a father and a child together, listening.

———

You do not win here with loud publicity.
Union comes of nonbeing.

These birds do not learn to fly,
until they lose all their feathers.

———

Earlier, I promised myself
I would stay on the path.

Now, looking to the right and the left,
I see nothing but you.
Whatever I decide to do is inside you.

———

Step out on this road that has no end.
Seeing things at a distance is not the human experience.

A *strong heart* with many kinds of love
is what you most need for this setting out.
A *strong body?* Good for the animals.

———

The core of this wisdom is something like madness.
Love and insanity are often mistaken for one another.

As suffering deepens in your heart,
you become a stranger to yourself a thousand times.

———

Love comes and fills my skin,
veins and bones, every particle.

Only the letters of my name are left.
You are the rest.

———

Destiny does not obey our desiring.
Existence is meant to flow into absence.

All this is a shadow play
put on by our old nanny, a very skillful show,
but we are not actually here.

———

Inside the friend, where rose and thorn blend
to one opening point, the Qur'an,
the New Testament and the Old,
flow together to become one text.

But put nothing next to the beloved, no likenesses there,
where the lame donkey and the swift stallion are one mount.

———

Love's drum has no question and no answer.
The mystery is its emptiness.

Lovers obey no rule.
Love is not a matter of existence,
but rather of absence.

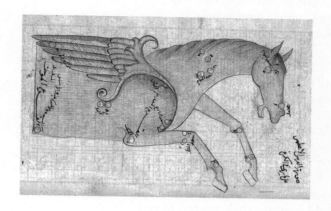

44.
Pegasus: The Winged Horse

One version of the birth of the stallion Pegasus is that he sprang from Medusa's neck as Perseus was beheading her. Wherever the horse's hoof touched the ground, an inspiring spring of water flowed forth, the most famous being the Hippocrene ("horse spring") on Mt. Helicon, the Muses' Mount. Pegasus was mortal. On the last day of his life, when Zeus transformed him into a constellation, a single feather fell to earth.

———

As long as I can remember, I have wanted you.
I have made a monument of this loving.

I had a dream last night, but it is gone now.
All I know is I woke up like this again.

———

Drawn by your soul's growing,
we gather like disheveled hair.
Even spirits come to bow.
We were dead. Now we are back.

———

My turban, my robe, my head,
those three for less than a penny.

My self, my name, not to be mentioned,
less than nothing.

———

At night you come here secretly,
and I want the darkness not to end.

But Night says, *Look, you are holding the Sun.*
So you are in charge of daylight.

———

The secret you told, tell again.
If you refuse, I will start crying.
Then you will say, *Shhhhh,*
now listen. I will say it over.

———

You were alone, I got you to sing.
You were quiet, I made you tell long stories.
No one knew who you were,
but they do now.

———

I have lived on the lip of insanity,
wanting to know reasons,
knocking on a door. It opens.
I have been knocking from the inside.

———

There is no love in me without your being,
no breath without that.

I once thought that I could give up this longing.
Then I thought again,
But I could not continue being human.

———

We are the night ocean filled with glints of light.
We are the space between the fish and the moon,
while we sit here together.

———

Sometimes afraid of reunion,
sometimes of separation.

You and I, so fond of the notion
of a *you* and an *I*, should live as though
we had never heard of those pronouns.

———

Two strong impulses.
One, to drink long and deep.
The other, not to sober up too soon.

———

The wine we really drink is our own blood.
Our bodies ferment in these barrels.
We give everything for a glass of this.
We give our minds for a sip.

———

Love enters, and the brilliant scholars get goofy.
The full moon becomes a simple dirt road.

Walk there with degenerates and saints,
with children and old people.

Be a slow pawn,
as well as the wide-ranging queen.
Then you will be king.

———

They end so quickly,
the noises we make.

A wolf tears open
the silly sheep's throat.

Look at the people going there
with their heads prancing along.
One downstroke and they are dead.

———

They say it is night,
but I cannot tell day from night
in your presence.

Day could learn a lot
about light from your face.

———

Your love spreads into the sky and beyond it.
Your strong hand touches here where I hurt.

Wherever your feet have walked on this planet,
I go there secretly to lay my cheek.

———

A nightbird in his rapture for the dark
makes a clear wind sound.
Music has never been so beautiful.

I stare into a stream or sit beside flowers.
Inside this friendship.

———

In the beginning you pampered me with gifts.
Then you burned me with grief and difficulties.

You were rolling me like numbered dice.
When I died and became you,
you threw me, the numbering, and the dice
out completely beyond any space for games.

———

A human being is made of clay and sky.
Spirit beings wish they could move as we do.
They want our agility and purity.

And sometimes Lucifer marvels
at our cruelty, the coldness of our turning away.

Wherever I touch my head to the ground,
you are the one I point this full prostration toward.

You are praised in each of the six directions,
north, east, south, west, up, and down,
and beyond all that.

Rose garden, nightingale, every beauty of existence
is a no-form of you, the livingness you are.

———

Shams is wine, but not the kind
that muddles and brings regret.

Shams is music and light and fire.
He brings the majesty that lives
in the deep center of everyone.

45.
Lepus: The Hare

In Egyptian mythology the hare is associated with collecting and protecting the sacred eggs of life. In many mythologies there is a link between hares and eggs and the moon. Our children continue to recognize this fertile, creative connection every Easter.

———

Wine to intensify love, fire to consume.
We bring these, not like images from a dream reality,
but as an actual night to live through until dawn.

———

In complete control, pretending control,
with dignified authority, we are charlatans.
Or maybe just a goat's-hair brush in a painter's hand.
We have no idea what we are.

———

We donate a cloak to the man who does the washing.
We feel proud of our generosity.
We stare at the infinite, suffering ocean.
We fall in.

———

You are cold, but you expect kindness.
What you do comes back in the same form.
God is compassionate, but if you plant barley,
do not expect to harvest wheat.

———

Wandering the high empty plain,
for some evidence you have been here,
I find an abandoned body, a detached head.

———

Wine and stout,
one very old, the other new.
We will never have had enough.

Not being here, and being completely here,
the mixture is not bitter.
It is the taste we are.

———

Lying back in this presence,
unable to eat or drink,
I float freely
like a corpse in the ocean.

———

Do not give me back to my old companions.
No friend but you.
Inside you, I rest from wanting.
Do not let me be that selfishness again.

———

You reach out wanting the moon with your eyes, and Venus.
Build a place to live with those dimensions.

A shelter that can be knocked down with one kick,
it is best to go ahead and knock it down.

Sometimes visible, sometimes not,
sometimes devout Christians,
sometimes staunchly Jewish.

Until our inner love fits into everyone,
all we can do is take daily these different shapes.

My work is to carry this love
as comfort for those who long for you,
to go everywhere you have walked
and gaze at the pressed-down earth.

Birdsong brings relief to my longing.
I am just as ecstatic as they are,
but with nothing to say.

Please, universal soul, practice some song,
or something, through me.

When a storm sets love's ocean wildly in motion,
not everyone can praise that mystery.

Only those who never break with the deep infinite
that sings underneath the changing surface.

You whisper into me,
and the way I love changes.
The way I think no longer exists.

What is it that you say
that is like a seed sown
and growing inside stone?

My king has gone,
my healing moon.

If he comes back,
and I am not here,
say, He had to leave,
just as you had to leave.

46.
Canis Major:
The Great Dog

Sirius is the brightest star in the Great Dog. It is the nearest sun to us, only eight and a half light-years away.

———

Tonight, a singing competition.
Jupiter, the moon, and myself,
the friends I have been looking for.

———

Tonight with wine being poured,
and instruments singing among themselves,
one thing is forbidden,
one thing: Sleep.

———

The way of love
is not a subtle argument.

The door there
is devastation.

Birds make great sky-circles
of their freedom.

How do they learn that?
They fall, and falling,
they are given wings.

———

Let your throat-song be clear
and strong enough to make an emperor
fall full-length, suppliant, at the door.

———

I have phrases and whole pages memorized,
but nothing can be told of love.

You must wait until you and I
are living together.

In the conversation we will have then . . .
Be patient . . . Then . . .

———

Sometimes I call you wine, or cup,
or sunlight ricocheting off those,
or faintly immersed in silver.

I call you trap and bait,
and the game I am after,
all so as not to say your name.

———

I was happy enough to stay still
inside the pearl inside the shell,

but the hurricane of experience
lashed me out of hiding
and made me a wave moving into shore,

saying loudly the ocean's secret as I went.
Then, spent there, I slept like fog
against the cliff, another stillness.

———

I used to have fiery intensity
and a flowing sweetness.

The waters were illusion.
The flames, made of snow.

Was I dreaming then?
Am I awake now?

———

I run around looking for the friend.
My life is almost over, but I am still asleep.

When it happens, if it happens,
that I meet the friend,
will I get the lost years back?

———

We search the world for the great untying
of what was wed to us at birth
and gets undone at dying.

We sleep beside a stream, thirsty.
Cursed and unlucky his whole life,
an old man finishes up in a niche
of a ruin, inches from the treasure.

———

There is a desert I long to be walking,
a wide emptiness, peace,
beyond any understanding of it.

———

When the soul first put on the body's shirt,
the ocean lifted up all its gifts.

When love first tasted the lips of being human,
it started singing.

———

Slave, be aware
that the Lord of all the East is here.

A flickering stormcloud
shows his lightnings to you.

Your words are guesswork.
He speaks from experience.
There is a huge difference.

———

Which is worth more, a crowd of thousands,
or your own genuine solitude?

A little while alone in your room
will prove more valuable than anything else
that could ever be given you.

———

Whoever drinks your love
takes in new life and new again.

Death used to follow me everywhere, threatening.
Then it caught your fragrance and left.

———

Pleasures end,
unless they fill with love.

Every rhythm must have love in it,
or it does not flow.

Rain pours down over the ocean.
Pearls form from one love-drop.

47.
Boötes: The Herdsman

The Herdsman is sitting down smoking his pipe, contemplating the stars he is made of, and the others he is not. In another version, he is herding the Great Bear. Arcturus, the chief star in this constellation, means the "bear herder."

———

I saw grief drinking a cup of sorrow,
and I called out,
                    It tastes sweet, does it not?
You have caught me,
                    grief answered,
and you have ruined my business.
How can I sell sorrow
                    when you know it is a blessing?

———

Love lit a fire in my chest,
and anything that was not love left:
intellectual subtlety, philosophy
books, school.

All I want now
to do or hear
is poetry.

———

Love is that that never sleeps,
nor even rests, nor stays
for long with those that do.

Love is language
that cannot be said,
or heard.

———

With your lips not here
I kiss rubies to remember.

When I cannot sip from you,
I put my lip on the cup's lip.

Instead of reaching into your sky,
I kneel and take handfuls of earth.

———

Be fair. Admit that love has in it
all the righteousness we need.

Confess that you are willing to forget
and be numb enough to call
some low desire a holy name.

Live as evidence
that there is a way
from wanting to longing.

———

You are from a country beyond this universe,
yet your best guess is
you are made of earth and ashes.

You engrave this physical image everywhere
as a sign that you have forgotten
where you are from.

———

Essence is emptiness.
Everything else, accidental.

Emptiness brings peace to your longing.
Everything else, dis-ease.

In this world of trickery
emptiness is what your soul wants.

———

We are not afraid of God's blade,
or of being chained up,
or of having our heads severed.

We are burning up quickly,
tasting a little hellfire as we go.

You cannot imagine
how little it matters to us
what people say.

———

Come to this street
with only your sweet fragrance.

Do not walk into this river
wearing a robe.

Paths go from here to there,
but do not arrive from somewhere.
There are no ways.
It is time now to live naked.

———

Soul serves as a cup for the juice
that leaves the intellect in ruins.

That candle came and consumed me,
about whose flame
the universe flutters in total confusion.

The mystic dances in the sun,
hearing music others do not.

Insanity, they say, those others.
If so, it is a very gentle, nourishing sort.

This love is beyond the range of language,
but you come in asking, *How is your heart?*
holding your robe up slightly.

I answer, *Hold it higher.*
This slaughterhouse floor is running with blood.

Leave, mind.
No one is *mindful* here.

Even if you shrink to one hair,
still there is no room.

Look at this morning light.
How could a candle ever improve this?

Hallaj the whirlwind said, *Anal-Haqq,*
and swept the dust from where he walked.

He dove in the ocean of emptiness
and found this pearl for both of us,
I am the truth.

You are gone from sight,
not from inside my love.
You are always there.

I travel about the world,
hoping at the end that you will show me
my wandering way home.

48.
Aries: The Ram

In Greek mythology Aries represents the golden ram that rescued Phrixos, taking him to the land of Colchis, where Phrixos sacrificed him to the gods and hung the skin in a sacred grove, where it became known as the Golden Fleece.

———

I want to be where
your bare foot walks,

because maybe before you step,
you will look at the ground.
I want that blessing.

———

Would you like to have revealed to you
the truth of the friend?

Leave the rind,
and descend into the pith.

Fold within fold,
the beloved drowns in his own being.
This world is drenched with that drowning.

———

Love perfected and whole, you arrive.
Words throng my soul, but none come out.

A traveler meets his joy
and his despair at once.

Dying of thirst, I stand here
with springwater flowing around my feet.

———

Spring overall.
But inside us there is another unity.

Behind each eye here,
one glowing weather.

Every forest branch moves differently in the breeze,
but as they sway, they connect at the roots.

———

A drunk sees me coming and claps his hands,
Look here. Our pilgrim has come back.
Against all his repentance vows.

It is true, but he does not know much
about glassmaking, the painstaking work.

Remember. The more effort goes in,
the easier we are to break.

———

Rain falls on one man,
he runs into his house.

But the swan spreads its wings and says,
Pour more on me of that power
I was fashioned from.

———

Around and around all night
in the house of the friend.

This is how it must be,
because the beloved needs
the cup empty, again empty.

———

What's the lover to do,
but humiliate himself
and wander your rooms?

If he kisses your hair,
do not wonder why.

Sometimes in the madhouse
they gnaw on their chains.

———

Last night the friend came to visit.
I asked night to keep the secret.

But look, said night,
behind you the sun is rising.
How could I show anyone anything?

———

My spirit saw how down and dull I was
and came and sat laughing on my bed.

Holding my brow. *Sweetheart,*
I cannot bear to see you like this.

———

This is how I would die
into the love I have for you.

As pieces of cloud
dissolve in sunlight.

———

Someone who does not run
toward the allure of love
walks a road where nothing lives.

But this dove here
senses the love-hawk floating above,
and waits, and will not be driven
or scared to safety.

———

Looking at form delights you,
but move beyond this circle of seeing.

There is no end to wisdom,
no boundaries for awareness,
no sky, no place to rest.

———

Leap up and dance when the song of the soul begins,
drum and flute notes moving together.

Your old grief jumps in the fire of that telling.
It is time to weep.

———

Only if you deny yourself,
will you die enough to know the mystery of union.

Not God filling you,
but you being emptied of self.
Anything else is arrogant and false.

49.
Delphinus: The Dolphin

Delphinus is a leaping dolphin, perhaps the one that saved the poet
and musician Arion. Dolphins are fabulously helpful. The four stars in
the dolphin's head are known as Job's Coffin.

———

Flowers open every night across the sky
as the peace of keeping a vigil
kindles the emptiness.

———

Do not think for a moment
that you have found the goal of your love.

Do not stand still in the ranks.
You have no place with uniforms at rest.

You might as well consent to be a corsage,
or a rose in some beautiful woman's hair.

———

A road may end at a single house,
but it is not love's road.

Love is a river.
Drink from it.

———

One who does what the friend wants done
will never need a friend.

There is bankruptcy that is pure gain.
The moon stays bright
when it does not avoid the night.

A rose's rarest essence
lives in the thorn.

———

A light wind coming downhill,
the nightbird's song.

The strange writing I read
on my lover's door

says the same message
now being called out over the rooftops.

———

My memory of your face
prevents my seeing you.

Lightning veils your brow.
Recalling our kissing,
I cannot kiss you know.

So strange, such sweetness
could keep us apart.

———

Your fragrance fills the meadow.
Your mouth appears in a red anemone,
but when those reminders leave,

my own lips open,
and in whatever I say, I hear you.

How long are you going to beat me like a drum
and make me sigh for you like a violin?

You answer, *Come. I will hold you close
and stroke you like a lute.*

But I feel more like a flute
that you put in your mouth and then neglect to blow.

I realize that the dawn when we will meet again
will never break,
so I give it up, little by little, this love.

But something in me laughs when I say this,
someone shaking his head and chuckling softly,
Hardly, hardly.

A bird delegation comes to Solomon complaining,
Why is it you never criticize the nightingale?

Because my way, the nightingale explains,
*is different. Mid-March to mid-June
I sing. The other nine months
while you continue chirping, I am silent.*

You thought union was a way
that you could decide to go.

But the world of the soul
follows things rejected and almost forgotten.

Your true guide drinks
from an undammed stream.

This mud-body is clear epiphany.
Angels wish they could move as I move.

Purity? Cherubim babies
long for my innocence.

Courage? Armies of demons
flee my uplifted hand.

———

The deepest grain markings in me are longings.
In the center of desire is that which wants to disappear
in the wine taste that has something of you in it.

———

Love weeps its grief.
Night whispers, Your hair.

As a cypress opens its branches to the dark,
I live blessed like a tree.

———

Do not withhold the good news about yourself.
Look at your companions smiling. They know.

Your love-room is not a prison,
though it does say above the door,
You will never leave this place.

50.
Cetus: The Sea Monster,
or Kraken

Andromeda, chained to a rock in the surf as a sacrifice to Cetus, is
rescued by Perseus. The constellation Cetus is in a region of the sky
called the Water, along with Aquarius, Pisces, and the River, Eridanus.
It is well away from the galactic plane and the Milky Way's obscuring
dust. As a result, far distant galaxies are visible, the brightest being
Messier 77, a ninth-magnitude spiral galaxy.

———

Spring paints the countryside.
Cypress trees grow even more beautiful,
but we stay inside.

Lock the door.
Come to me naked.
No one is here.

———

How will you know the difficulties of being human,
if you are always flying off to blue perfection?

Where will you plant your grief seeds?
Workers need ground to scrape and hoe,
not the sky of unspecified desire.

———

Rise. Move around the center
as pilgrims wind the Kaaba.

Being still is how one clay clod
sticks to another in sleep.

Movement wakes us up
and unlocks new blessings.

———

You walk in like you are about to say,
Enough of this.

But it will take more than frowns and harsh talking
to make my love leave.

This is the undauntable bird
who has never been caged, or felt fear.

———

Imagining is like feeling around
in a dark lane, or washing
your eyes with blood.

You *are* the truth
from foot to brow. Now,
what else would you like to know?

———

You that come to birth and bring the mysteries,
your voice-thunder makes me very happy.

Roar, lion of the heart,
and tear me open.

Love swells and surges the ocean
and on your robe of stormcloud
sews rain designs.

Love is lightning,
and also the *ahhh*
we respond with.

Pale sunlight,
pale the wall.

Love moves away.
The light changes.

I need more grace
than I thought.

In your light I learn how to love.
In your beauty, how to make poems.

You dance inside my chest,
where no one sees you,

but sometimes I do,
and that sight becomes this art.

You are the spring.
We are grasses trailing in it.

You are the king coming by.
We are beggars along the road.

You are the voice we are echoes of.
You are calling for us now.
How could we not return?

Lovers in their brief delight
gamble both worlds away,
a century's worth of work
for one chance to surrender.

Many slow-growth stages
build to quick bursts of blossom.

A thousand half-loves must be forsaken
to take one whole heart home.

You that prefer, like crows do,
winter's chill and the empty limbs,
notice now this that fills with new leaves
and roses opening and the nightbird's song.

Let your love dissolve also
into this season's moment,
or when it is over,
you will buy lamp after lamp to find it.

I shoot a random arrow arcing up.
It falls and strikes a believer in the heart.
He angrily asks, *Is this some secret design of yours
that has caused this accident?*

*No. The arrow I shot was from God's desiring.
The accident came from there.*

Calm and rational, I used to laugh at lovers.
Now I have become one,
dancing carefree in my misery,
it feels like this is how I have always been.

Since we see individuals,
we must not be inside the ONE.

Multiple, we make judgments:
good, bad, and somewhere in between.

That is how the ecstatic heart grows heavy.

I hear nothing in my ear
but your voice.
Heart has plundered mind
of all its eloquence.

Love writes a transparent calligraphy,
so on the empty page
my soul can read and recollect.

———

Joy moves always to new locations,
the ease of its flowing never freezing.

A long winter's tale is over.
Now with each spring day a new story.

———

Any cup I hold fills with wine
that lovers drink.

Every word I say opens into mystery.
Any way I turn, I see brilliance.

———

When school and mosque and minaret
get torn down,
then dervishes can begin their community.

Not until faithfulness turns to betrayal
and betrayal into trust,
can any human being become part of the truth.

———

While you are still yourself,
you are blind to both worlds.
That ego-drunkenness will not let you see.

Only when you are cleansed of both,
will you cut the deep roots of fear and anger.

———

Your eyes, when they really see
a rose or an anemone,
flood the wheeling world with tears.

Wine that stands a thousand years in a jar
tastes less mad than love only one year old.

51.
Andromeda:
The Chained Queen

In the Andromeda constellation is M31, the Andromeda galaxy, which is the major galaxy nearest to us. It is moving toward us at 500,000 kilometers an hour. In about 3 billion years the two galaxies will begin colliding and go on merging for a billion more years in a very complex gravitational pavane. It may be that the black holes at the center of each galaxy will eventually become one.

———

Drumsound rises on the air,
its throb, my heart.

A voice inside the beat says,
I know you are tired, but come.
This is the way.

Stars burn clear all night till dawn.
Do that yourself,
and a spring will rise in the dark
with water your deepest thirst is for.

Do not sleep now.

Let the turning night wheel through this circle.
Your brow, the moon, this lantern we sit with.
Stay awake with these lights.

Do not sleep.

If you want what visible reality can give,
you are an employee.

If you want the unseen world,
you are not living your truth.

Both wishes are foolish,
but you will be forgiven for forgetting
that what you really want
is love's confusing joy.

Gamble everything for love,
if you are a true human being.
If not, leave this gathering.

Half-heartedness does not reach into majesty.
You set out to find God,
then you keep stopping for long periods
at mean-spirited roadhouses.

In a boat down a fast-running creek,
it feels like trees on the bank are rushing by.

What seems to be changing around us
is rather the speed of our craft
leaving this world.

What is this that gives pleasure in a form,
then when not, turns dull, opaque?

This thing that slips away into infinity,
then strikes down to take another shape?

I say,
I will lift from your hand like a pigeon.
You say,
It will be my love that opens your wings.
I say,
Totally humble, like a dog
I will lay down at your feet.

Such glory for you,
you say.

The soul must suffer secrets that cannot be said,
public humiliation, people pointing in contempt.

While you are a human being,
stay inside the scorn.

Work there patiently with the others.
When you are pure spirit, quickly, leave.

Love is the way messengers
from the mystery tell us things.

Love is the mother.
We are her children.

She shines inside us,
visible-invisible, as we trust
or lose trust, or feel it start to grow again.

Childhood, youth, maturity,
and now old age.

Every guest agrees to stay
three days, no more.

Master, you told me
to remind you. Time to go.

———

Are you jealous of the ocean's generosity?
Why would you refuse
to give this joy to anyone?

Fish do not hold the sacred liquid in cups.
They swim the huge, fluid freedom.

———

Cypress moving, still, completely awake,
autumn's wing does not brush against you,
nor does the cruel wanting of those eyes.

You are a joining point for sky and ground,
soul as witness, green compassion.

———

Your confidence does not matter in this place
where the minute you come in, you must place a bet,
and it is your move.

Either you will be checkmated,
or you will win, or you both will win.

———

Dawn. As light becomes morning,
night-beings leave.

Your eyes, which have been closed to protect themselves,
open, looking for deeper dissolving.

———

It is as dangerous to refuse to help those traveling through your
    life
as it is to deny that the unseen worlds exist.

You do not know such secrets as this;
therefore you assume there are none.

———

A lover haunts the desert places
where the friend once put up a tent.
A lover looks for traces left on the ground.

Another kind of devotion
stays busy with rosary and ritual prayer.
Then he or she goes for bread.

The thirsty lover runs to water. The other is hungry.
Study the difference between hunger and thirst.

———

This is how it is with love: You take a bite,
you chew, you digest, then you start singing.

Grapes come unripe to the vineyard,
then gradually grow ready to be crushed for wine.

There is an appropriate progress to the spring.
You hear cats yowling. Later, a nightingale begins.

———

When you are poured in my empty glass,
those who have been living here invisibly
appear before me, as companions.

But those from the mosque and the tavern,
the conventionally religious and the conventionally ecstatic,
keep their distance.

———

Someone who does not make flowers makes thorns.
If you are not building rooms
where wisdom can be openly spoken,
you are building a prison.

———

If I hold you with my emotions,
you will become a wished-for companion.

If I hold you with my eyes,
you will grow old and die.

So I hold you here
where we both mix with the infinite.

———

Midnight, but your forehead shines with dawn.
You dance as you come to me

and curl by curl undo the dark.
Let jealousy end.

———

I could not have known what love is
if I had never felt this longing.

Anything done to excess becomes boring,
except this overflow that moves toward you.

———

The soul fell into the soup of nature
and started mixing with all manner
of delicious, and not so tasty, ingredients.

Our actions take on a tinge
of those we are near.
God keep us from bitter company.

———

Be clear and smiling
for those who are glad to see you.

Someone who is not, let his way darken
like a pen leaving a faltering ink trail.

52.
Scorpio: The Scorpion

Scorpio, in myth, is often associated with Orion, the great hunter, who brags one day that he will kill all the wild animals on earth. Apollo, who is responsible for guarding the herds, asks Gaia, the protector, to send a giant scorpion with impenetrable armor to sting and kill Orion. In one variation of the story he succeeds. In another, Orion swims out to sea to escape, only to be shot by Artemis, who is also allied with the animals.

————

Lo, I am with you always,
you promised that,
and when I realized that it was true,
my soul flared up.

Any unhappiness comes from forgetting.
Remember, and be back close
with the friend.

———

There is a banquet where grains of wheat
sit and eat and shout for more,
and more is brought.

These banqueter seed grains
never quit eating, and for eternity
the table stays replete.

———

You have so distracted me,
your absence fans my love.
Do not ask how.

Then you come near.
Do not . . ., I say
and *Do not . . .*, you answer.

Do not ask why
this delights me.

———

Real value comes with madness,
matzoob below, scientist above.

Whoever finds love
beneath hurt and grief
disappears into emptiness
with a thousand new disguises.

———

A bough with blossoms bears fruit.
The hawk descends with purpose.

Your image comes and goes
here inside me. Will you stay?

———

Poem, song, and story, the stream sweeps by,
moving along what was never mine anyway.

What I have done through an act of will,
well-meaning or mean, these are brought in briefly
by moonlight, then carried obscurely off.

———

Roses shine in the clay
beside your tomb.

Be aware, earth,
who sleeps inside you.

———

Spring lightning, poems being sung.
The drum gets quiet, but voices continue.

Venus appears,
bringing her gift to the music.

———

This season with the friend so near,
the body dims.
Heart-light grows more intense.

Stormclouds finally weep,
because the lightning has started to laugh.

With heavy tears everywhere coming down,
the fields get uncontrollably tickled.

———

The angel of death arrives,
and I spring joyfully up.

No one knows what comes over me
when I and that messenger speak.

———

When you come back inside my chest,
no matter how far I have wandered off,
I look around and see the way.

At the end of my life, with just one breath left,
if you come then, I will sit up and sing.

———

I called through your door, The mystics
are gathering in the street. Come out.

Leave me alone. I am sick.

I don't care if you are dead.
Jesus is here,
and he wants to resurrect somebody.

———

I set my heart out on the road
where it can be troubled.
I untie my feet, so I can run after you.

Now today with your fragrance in the air,
I give my love to the wind.

———

As the fig seller loves to sell figs,
so my soul, and yours, love to die
into the resurrection that comes
with every taste of this friendship.

It is just who we are.

———

Whatever is cooking us
draws us every night
into the tavern of absence.

Being cut off from who we were,
we become friendship itself.

———

I, you, he, she, we.
In the garden of mystic lovers,
these are not true distinctions.

———

From cane reeds, sugar.
From a worm's cocoon, silk.

Be patient if you can,
and from sour grapes
will come something sweet.

———

Morning breeze, bring news of beauty,
but slowly, please.
Let the fresh fragrance stay.

———

O heart, brighten yourself.
Here is Joseph's shirt.
Hold it against your face.
Rub your eyes with it.
Let them see again.

Little fish, O heart,
you cannot live without water.
Throw yourself back into the river.

———

You are inside every prayer,
in the deep listening of any sema,
inside every impulse to fast, every hajj.

I am the one who plays today.

You are the beautiful one,
the candle lit in Teraz,
and the source of these gifts
that keep falling from the sky.

53.
Sagittarius: The Archer

Sagittarius is the archer, a centaur, half human, half horse. The arrow of
his bow points toward the star Antares, "in the heart of the scorpion."

———

All our lives we have looked
into each other's faces.
That was the case today too.

How do we keep our love-secret?
We speak from brow to brow
and hear with our eyes.

———

Last night things flowed between us
that cannot now be said or written.

Only as I am being carried out
and down the road, as the folds
of my shroud open in the wind,

will anyone be able to read,
as on the petal-pages of a turning bud,
what passed through us last night.

———

When I remember your love, I weep,
and when I hear people talking of you,

something in my chest,
where nothing much happens now,
shifts as in sleep.

———

As essence turns to ocean,
the particles glisten.

Watch how in this candleflame instant
blaze all the moments you have lived.

———

There is a way of breathing
that is a shame and a suffocation.

And there is another way of expiring,
a love-breath that lets you open infinitely.

———

Lovers gather and give each other shade,
relief from the direct sun.

Stay closeby that community.
Be shade with them,
until you yourself are full of light
like the moon, then like the sun.

———

The rose took from another presence
its crimson grace,
as a thief on the gallows takes the breeze.

So the nightingale begs all night,
to no avail, the morning air,
Warn of what you bring.

———

Whoever loves,
loves the same sweetheart I do.

Lightning, there and there,
comes from one turning jewel.

Before creation,
gold was stamped with a seal,
so now no matter where it hides in the ground,
it belongs to me.

———

You are in my eyes.
How else could I see light?

You are in my brain.
This wild joy.

If love did not live in matter,
how would any place
have any hold on anyone?

———

Do not analyze enthusiasm.

The wheel that lifts some up
and drags others down,
we are not riding it anymore.

We have jumped off
the good-and-bad of that.

———

If you want money more than anything,
you will be bought and sold.

If you have a greed for food,
you will be a loaf of bread.

This is a subtle truth:
Whatever you love, you are.

———

You are not a slave.
You are a king.

If you *want* something,
release the wish, and let it light
on its desire, completely free of the personal.

Then sit and sound the drum
of nothing, nothing.

———

We start out from absence
into a night illuminated
with the wine of union.

Permissible wine,
lips, stay wet with that.

———

The heart keeps an image of the friend.
As long as that remains clear,
we move inside a profound health.

Whatever that love finds,
a thorn say, is better
than bushels of ripe dates.

———

Anyone who walks with us
will see many naked souls
inside each of our bodies.

Taste this sherbet
and you will recognize daylight
in this night we walk together in.

———

Now I lay me down to stay awake.
Pray the Lord my soul to take
into your wakefulness,

so that I can get this one bit of wisdom clear.
Grace comes to forgive, and then forgive again.

———

I do not regret how much I have loved,
and I avoid those who repent their passion.

Hundreds of sweethearts,
I am the lover and the one lovers long for.
Blue and a cure for blues,
sky in a small cage.

Badly hurt, but flying.
Everybody's scandalous flaw is mine.

———

I am here again
with that which burns sin,
and repentance, guilt, and holding back.

This flame says, *Nothing here but God.*
Everything, everyone, every moment,
this fire says, *That.*

54.
Pisces: The Fish

Pisces consists of two fishing lines knotted together, each with a dangling fish held by a cord tied around its tail. One might be a mackerel; the other a flounder. They are also the disguises that Aphrodite and her son Eros assumed to escape the monster Typhon. To early Christians, this constellation was a reminder of the miracle when Jesus fed the multitude with five loaves and two fishes (Mark 6:3–44).

———

The first morning air brings the presence
that angels in amazement watch.

Tears and a breathing silence together.
Then the morning itself,
growing stronger, calls out,

Who is loving who,
of these two?

———

I claimed my eyes.

*I will join them to the river
in rainy season.*

My loving. *Bloodred.*

But at least my body is mine.

*Before just a few days go by,
people will point at it and sneer
and drive you out of town.*

———

I placed one foot on the wide plain of death,
and some grand immensity sounded on the emptiness.

I have felt nothing ever
like the wild wonder of that moment.

———

I used to be shy.
You made me sing.

I used to refuse things at table.
Now I shout for more wine.

In somber dignity,
I used to sit on my mat and pray.

Now children run through
and make faces at me.

———

People want you to be happy.
Do not keep serving them your pain.

If you could untie your wings
and free your soul of jealousy,

you and everyone around you
would fly up like doves.

———

Revelation came to Muhammad.
Stay in the company of lovers.

Your fire can warm the whole world,
but if it gets covered over
with ash, it will go out.

———

Why let daily things bother you?
Have you forgotten how it is *in time?*

Your father has never met your mother.
The elaborate orchard garden you live in
has not yet been planted.

———

The work is always inside you.
This knot does not get untied
by listening to the stories of other people.

The well inside your house
is better water
than the river that runs through town.

———

You are inside meaning, not words.
You are the heart itself,
not any language of the heart.

You are the essence within the universe,
not the universe.
You are neither absence nor existence.

———

I am blessed with faith and cursed with forgetfulness.
Clear, but streaked with mud.
Mature, growing older, and still a baby.

When I die, do not say, *He is dead.*
Say, *He was dead. Then he came back to life,*
and his friend took him back into friendship.

———

These words I say do not belong to me.
I say them but I am not fully *aware* of what I am saying.

There is energy in them and something that depletes energy.
I have no control over any of that.

I know they come from my heart, from my love,
but I still do not know whose words they are.

———

Be a falcon with how you go straight to the point.
Be a lion in how you walk.
Majestic, with the way you pick a spot to rest.

Enter the realm of the soul as the treasure of that.
Walk fast to the place where there is no fast and slow.
Ascend beyond any high or low.

———

I am the soul in a hundred thousand bodies.
What is the soul? What is a body?
I am both, and there is someone else I am as well.

In order to please that one,
I put on various personalities. I say my lines.

———

If you could be master of yourself for one moment,
the knowledge that the prophets have would be yours.

The beauty the whole world wants, the emptiness,
the beauty of absence, would appear
in the mirror of your seeing.

———

I am so close, I may look distant.
So completely mixed with you, I may look separate.

So out in the open, I appear hidden. So silent,
because I am constantly talking with you.

———

Today, you have been inside my eyes all day.
I am confused, upside down.
You are so near and so obvious, I feel apart from you.
I am so aware of you, I know nothing.

———

How long shall we delight in these shapes that move through
    time?
How long shall we stay interested in these fragrances?

I am growing tired of creatures. I want the beauty of the creator.
But when I look there, I see myself.
When I look at myself, I see that beauty.

———

A lover is not a Muslim or a Christian,
or part of any faith.

The love religion has no doctrine
to be faithful or unfaithful to.

———

As long as my soul is in this body,
I bow to the Qur'an,
dust on the road Muhammad walks.

Do not interpret my words as different from his.
Whoever does that, I break with
and reject what he says.

———

You are an ocean in a drop of dew,
all the universes in a thin sack of blood.

What are these pleasures then,
these joys, these worlds,

that you keep reaching for,
hoping they will make you more *alive?*

———

Come, come, whoever you are,
wanderer, fire worshiper, lover of leaving.
This is not a caravan of despair.
It does not matter that you have broken your vow
a thousand times, still come,
and yet again come.

Acknowledgments

We are so grateful to be able to reproduce Mohamed Zakariya's calligraphy in the Odes section of this book, with his kind permission. To read about his amazing life and to see more of his transformative work, Google "Zakariya Calligraphy."

The illustrations in the Quatrains section of the book are reproductions of ink drawings from al-Sufi's *Book of Fixed Stars* by arrangement with the Library of Congress. And thanks to Muhannad Salhi in the Near East Section of the Library of Congress for his gracious help with finding these images.

Galway Kinnell's poem, "Prayer," is from *A New Selected Poems*, Houghton Mifflin (New York: 2001). Reprinted by arrangement with Houghton Mifflin.

I would like to acknowledge the help with many things, the quatrain references in particular, of Sergey Sechiv of Southfield, Michigan. Sergey has translated *The Essential Rumi* into Russian.

Alan Godlas, Professor of Religion at the University of Georgia, has been a great resource for the Notes. His award-winning Web site is an important scholarly tool: Islam and Islamic Study Resources.com

Kenneth Honerkamp, Professor of Religion at the University of Georgia, translated the Arabic around the constellation images. http://hnrkmp.myweb.uga.edu

Nicholas O. Splendorr's superb computer skills and careful attention to detail have been a continuous support. http://simolinic.com

Some of these poems appeared first in the following Maypop books (Athens, GA): *We Are Three* (1987), *Delicious Laughter* (1989), *Like This* (1990), *Birdsong* (1993), and *Say I Am You* (1994). Reprinted by arrangement with Maypop.

Some of these poems appeared first in the following Threshold Books (and later with Shambhala) volumes: *Open Secret* (1984), *Unseen Rain* (1986), and *This Longing* (1988). Reprinted by arrangement with Threshold/Shambhala.

Some of these poems first appeared in *These Branching Moments*, Copper Beech, 1988. Reprinted by arrangement with Copper Beech.

Some of these poems first appeared in *The Glance*, Viking, 1999. Reprinted by arrangement with Viking.

I should also acknowledge that, as I put this collection together, I felt drawn to relineate and revise, slightly, almost every poem. So with any future reprintings of these translations, I would prefer that these refreshed, 2010 versions be used.

PHOTOGRAPH CREDITS:

Photograph of Bawa Muhaiyaddeen by permission of Bawa Muhaiyaddeen Fellowship, 5820 Overbrook Ave., Philadelphia, PA 19131. bawamuhaiyaddeenfellowship.com

Photograph of Osho copyright © Osho International Foundation, Switzerland. www.osho.com

Photograph of Ramana Maharshi is by G. G. Welling and courtesy of Sri Ramanasramam.

The geometric patterns above the headnotes on #16, #17, #19, #26, and #27 are taken from Keith Critchlow, *Islamic Patterns* (London: Thames and Hudson, 1976; U.S. edition: Rochester, VT: Inner Traditions, 1999) and reprinted by permission of Keith Critchlow.

Notes

INTRODUCTION

1. The mystic Bayazid Bestami (d. 877) wrote nothing, but many of his ecstatic sayings have been preserved, of which "How great is my glory" is the most famous. Several others:

> I am the wine drinker and the wine and the cupbearer.
> I came forth from Bayazid-ness as a snake from its skin.
> Then I looked and saw that lover and beloved are one.
> I was the smith of my own self.
> I am the throne and the footstool.
> Your obedience to me is greater than my obedience to You.
> I am the well-preserved tablet.
> I saw the Kaaba walking around me.

Bestami illustrates the state of *fana,* of being so dissolved in God that what is said is said by the divine presence. In meditation Bestami developed an extremely daring sense of the numinous. His mystical experiences transcended any distinctions between subject and object. His sayings have been preserved and treasured in Sufi circles for over a thousand years. In Rumi's work he is often mentioned in balance with Junnaiyd (d. 910), who advocated spiritual sobriety: "There is a sobriety that contains all drunkennesses, but there is no drunkenness that contains all sobriety." Bestami's teacher in this way of mystical union was Abu Ali al-Sindi, who knew no Arabic. Bestami had to teach his teacher enough Arabic to say the prayers from the Qur'an. In return, al-Sindi led Bestami on the path of deep meditation. In Bestami we find the blending of Islamic and Indian mystic strains into an unnameable stream that flows through the friendship of Rumi and Shams Tabriz, becoming even more inclusive.

2. Franklin D. Lewis, *Rumi: Past and Present, East and West: The Life, Teachings and Poetry of Jalal al-Din Rumi* (Boston and Oxford: Oneworld, 2000).

3. The teacher Bawa Muhaiyaddeen used to refer to everyone as a member of a larger "family." Grandson, uncle, grandmother, brother, sister, father, mother—every human being is in a familial relationship with every other. Once when a child asked what religion she should say she was at her school, Bawa answered, "You are a Christian because you believe in Jesus, and you are a Jew because you believe in all the prophets, including Moses. You are a Muslim because you believe in Muhammad as a prophet, and you are a Sufi because you believe in the universal teaching of God's love. You are really none of those, but you are all of those because you believe in God. And once you believe in God, there is no religion. Once you divide yourself off with religions, you are separated from your fellow man" (quoted in Michael Green, *The Illuminated Prayer* [New York: Random House, 2000], p. 14). Bawa also said to those he was with, "You are the lightpoints in my eyes." I feel there is a deep truth about love and the melding of identities in that sentence. I do not know that he ever elaborated on it.

4. A. J. Arberry, *Mystical Poems of Rumi* (Chicago: University of Chicago Press, 1968).

5. I should say more about the kind of translations, or versions, these are. I do not speak or read Persian. I am not a scholar. I taught modern American poetry and creative writing, mostly to upper-division undergraduates, for thirty years at the University of Georgia in Athens. My publishing was mostly of my own poetry (the latest, *Winter*

Sky: New and Selected Poems, 1968–2008 [Athens: University of Georgia Press, 2008]). For the Rumi work I rely on scholars who know Persian (Farsi) to give me literal translations to work with. I am totally indebted and very grateful to all of them, to John Moyne most especially. When Robert Bly originally handed me a copy of Arberry's translations, he said, "These poems need to be released from their cages." My task was, and is, to rephrase those into valid poems *in English.* I claim to be able to recognize, as a poet must, when language has energy, when it delights, when it conveys grief truly, when the longing it expresses comes from the core. I do not know Persian, so I cannot sense the flavor of the phrasing there. But I am told by those who know that Rumi's language has the taste of his refinement, his learned lineage, as well as an easy colloquial, conversational tone. That blend of delicacy and sudden directness is part of what I hope to reproduce in American English.

There is a conversation going on now, in the blogo-Twittersphere of the Internet about the value of various kinds of translations, and of Rumi in particular. There is the faithful-literal-dull of the scholars and there is the free-falling musical asylum of the *matzoobs* (crazy-alive ecstatics), and all the country stops in between. Surely Rumi is vast and oceanic enough to accommodate any number of translators. Let us live happily, and ridiculously, together. When I read Rumi's poetry with music, I do not try to pretend that we are back in the thirteenth century (with *ney, rebab,* and *kudum*—flute, strings, and drum), but rather to bring his words over into *now* with accompaniment by cello, frame drum, sitar, tablas, banjo, oud, harmonica, serangi, gypsy violin, soprano sax, and stand-up bass, in whatever combination is available. This is fusion cooking, fusion poetry, and, I hope, fusion soul growth. My feeling is that the friendship of Rumi and Shams was revolutionary in the thirteenth century, and that translated into *this* time it will again break cultural molds and cross religious and national boundaries, fusing them into a new way of being, something at once planetary and tribal, indigenous and universal. We have no name or form for it, but we feel its approaching.

6. Galway Kinnell (1927–) is one of the greatest living poets. *The Book of Nightmares* (Boston: Houghton Mifflin, 1971), *Imperfect Thirst* (1994), *A New Selected Poems* (2000), and *Strong Is Your Hold* (2006) are some of his titles.

7. Elmer O'Brien, *The Essential Plotinus* (New York: New American Library, 1964).

8. "The Silent Articulation of a Face."

9. "Wooden Walkingstick."

PART I: ODES

Names for the Mystery

1. There are many variations of the ninety-nine names for God. These eighteen names are from Bawa Muhaiyaddeen's *Asmul-Husma: The 99 Beautiful Names of Allah* (Philadelphia: Fellowship Press, 1984).

Chapter 1

Introductory Note: *Great Song,* a book of Joe Miller's talks, edited by Richard Power, is available from Maypop Books (800–682–8637).

"Entrance Door": Mahmoud was a king whose name means "Praise to the end!" For his servant and friend Ayaz, just the presence of the king is more important than any form. In the story referred to here, no matter what value the courtiers put on the pearl, Ayaz is willing to crush it to powder when the king asks him to.

"A Garden Is Questioning the Dawn": *Khidr*, literally, means "the green one." Khidr is known throughout the Islamic world. He exists on the edge between the seen and the unseen. When Moses vows to find the place "where the two seas meet," meaning where the spiritual and the this-worldly mix, he meets Khidr. Although not mentioned by name in the Qur'an, Khidr is associated with the person described as "one of our servants whom We [God] had given mercy from Us, and We had taught him knowledge proceeding from Us" (18:64, Arberry translation). In this passage Moses wants to follow Khidr and learn from him, but Khidr says, "If you follow me, you must not question anything I do. You must be patient and wait for my explanations." Moses agrees, but as Khidr performs apparent outrages (sinking a boat, killing a boy), Moses cannot restrain his alarm, and Khidr leaves him after explaining the hidden reasons for his actions.

Khidr represents the inner dimension, which transcends form. He is the personification of the revealing function of the metaphysical intellect, the "prophetic soul." He especially appears to solitaries, those who are cut off from normal channels of spiritual instruction. The Sufi mystic Ibrahim, who gave up his external kingdom for the kingdom within, said of Khidr: "I lived four years in the wilderness. Khidr the Green Ancient was my companion. He taught me the Great Name of God." Khidr is connected philologically with Elijah and with Utnapishtim of the Gilgamesh epic. He may be a partial source, along with Druidic lore, for the enigmatic Green Knight in the magnificent Middle English poem *Sir Gawain and the Green Knight*.

Chapter 2

"Strange Gathering": The figures in this poem, from both Christian and Islamic romantic and heroic traditions, are having a very free-form party. It is important that the poem ends with those two figures who are so completely and insistently free of form, Hallaj and Shams Tabriz.

Chapter 3

"Green from Inside": The Sufi mystic, writer, and teacher Al-Hallaj Mansour was martyred in Baghdad in 922 for saying *Anal Haqq*, or "I am the Truth. I am God."

"Saladin": See note on "Goldsmithing" below in chap. 12.

"To the Extent They Can Die": There was a Platonic academy in Iconium (Konya), so there was probably a strong tradition of studying Plato's *Dialogues* as well as Plotinus's *Enneads*, and certainly the Muslim philosophers Ibn Rushd, known as Averroës (1126–98), Ibn Tufayl (d. 1185), Suhrawardi (1154–91), and Ibn Arabi (1165–1240).

"What the Sun Says Rising": Zuleikha is the wife of Potiphar the Egyptian. She is so lost in her love for the handsome Joseph that she sees everything that happens as a message from him. For Rumi she is a type of the lover, like Majnun.

Chapter 4

"A Bowl": Shams means "the sun," and almost every reference to sunlight in Rumi's poetry is a remembrance of Shams Tabriz. Rumi's son Sultan Velad writes that Shams passed through all stages of the lovers of God and became *qotb-e hama ma shugan*, the "pole of the beloved."

"Unfold Your Own Myth": "Chase a deer and end up everywhere" is a reference to the life of Ibrahim (d. 783). A prince of Balkh, Ibrahim represents to the Sufis someone who in one visionary moment gives up his external kingdom for his inner majesty. There are striking similarities between his life and Gautama the Buddha's. Balkh seems to have been an area, along the Silk Road, where Buddhism, Islam, Christianity, and other faiths met and blended. Lotus motifs, indications of a line of meditation, are on the ruins there of the school of Rumi's father, Bahauddin Velad. Here is Rumi's account in *Discourse* #44 of Ibrahim's epiphany:

Ibrahim, when he was still king, went out hunting. As he galloped after a deer, he became separated from his retinue. His horse was tired and lathered, but still Ibrahim rode. Deep in the wilderness, the fleeing deer turned its head and spoke. "You were not created for this chase. This deer body did not take shape out of nothingness, so that you might hunt. Supposing that you catch me, will that be enough?" Ibrahim heard these words deeply and cried out. He reined in his horse and dismounted. There was a shepherd nearby. "Take this royal jacket sewn with jewels. Take my horse and my bow. Give me your shepherd's robe of coarse cloth, and tell no one what has happened." The exchange was made, and Ibrahim set out on his new life. He made such an extraordinary effort to catch the deer and ended up being caught by God. All plans are subject to revision. God lives between a human being and the object of his or her desire.

There are other implied stories in many of the sentences of "Unfold Your Own Myth." I recognize the Moses, Jacob, Joseph, and Omar stories, but not the one that refers to Jesus. Does anybody out there know the source of that?

Chapter 6

"Glory to Mutabilis": *Glory*, *Penelope*, and *Mutabilis* are names of current varieties of roses. *Mutabilis* is Latin for "changeable" or "in the midst of change." I added them to this poem.

Chapter 8

"Rumi's Deathbed Poem": Aflaki, a contemporary of Rumi's grandson, says that this seems to be Rumi's last poem, spoken to his son, Sultan Velad, comforting him, sending him off to get some rest, and ending with the lighthearted jibe at his son's intellectual pretensions.

"Sanai": Hakim Sanai (d. 1150) was the first poet to use the *masnavi* form, rhyming couplets expressing mystical and didactic themes. Rumi loved Sanai and borrowed many images, phrases, and stories from him, particularly from his *Hadiqat'ul-Haqiqat* (*The Walled Garden of Truth*). Sanai's earthy style impressed Rumi. His remark that off-color, bawdy stories can be instructional finds its way into Book V of the *Masnavi*, where a number of such jokes are told and explicated. Sanai is also the source of the famous story about the blind man and the elephant, which Rumi changed to a number of people in a pitchblack room trying to define an elephant by where they happen to touch it. Sanai got that story from Indian sources. The tricky pun *bargi bi bargi* ("the leaves of leaflessness") also comes from Sanai. Rumi uses the image of no-leaves coming out on a winter tree as a beautiful symbol for the state of awareness that has abandoned the world without leaving (pun intended) it.

A story has come down to us, from Sirajuddin Ali's *Memoirs of the Poets*, about the central event in Sanai's transformation from a conventional court poet to the absolutely original mystic who wrote *The Walled Garden of Truth*. The sultan of Ghazna, Bahramshah, is starting out on a military campaign to India. Sanai is along to record the battles in verse and generally to celebrate Bahramshah's eminence, as court poets were paid to do. Sanai has just completed such a poem when the expedition passes a walled garden (*firdaus* in Persian, hence our word "paradise"). They hear beautiful music and singing coming from within the enclosure. They investigate and discover that it is the notorious Sufi mystic, drunkard, and teacher Lai-Khur.

Lai-Khur nods to the sultan and proposes a toast, "To the blindness of Bahramshah." Some of the officers object, and Lai-Khur explains, "Bahramshah is going on this foolish expedition to India when he is needed at home, and besides, what he is looking for is in himself."

Bahramshah recognizes the truth of what the Sufi says, but not enough to turn his army around.

Lai-Khur then pours another glass and proposes another toast, "To Hakim Sanai, and his even greater blindness."

"What do you mean?" asks Sanai.

"You are unaware of the purpose of your life. You will come before the throne of God bringing these silly poems in praise of political stupidity."

Sanai looks into Lai-Khur's eyes and suddenly he knows his life's purpose. He resigns from his court poet's post, even though the sultan offers him half the wealth of the realm and his daughter in marriage. Bahramshah is desperate, having received the same teaching as Sanai and been unable to respond. Sanai is unshakeable in his new state. To absorb the illumination, he goes on a pilgrimage. During this time he meets his Sufi teacher, Yusuf Hamadani. When he arrives back in Ghazna, he has with him *The Walled Garden of Truth.* I recommend the translation by David Pendlebury, *The Walled Garden of Truth* (London: Octagon Press, 1974).

"Sanai": *Rum* refers to the Roman-influenced part of the Anatolian peninsula, roughly everything east of Iconium (Konya) and sometimes, more specifically, to Byzantium, that ultimate bridge city between East and West. In the early thirteenth century the region around Konya was established as the Sultanate of Rum by a branch of the Seljuks. Rum-i means someone from Konya. In dialectical Arabic the adjective *rumi* refers to something Western or nonindigenous.

Chapter 9

"The Wave of That Agreement": The agreement referred to here is the covenant of *Alast*, when God addressed as yet uncreated humanity and asked, *Alastu bi-rabbikum?* "Am I not your Lord?" The "Yes!" that came instantly keeps propelling humankind forward and into spirit.

"Out of the Image-Making Business": Azar was Abraham's father and a famous maker of images. In the Qur'an Abraham asks his father, "Do you take idols for gods?"

Chapter 11

"The Deepest Rest": *Qutb* means "axis" or "pole." It is the center, which also contains the periphery, like a spiral. The *Qutb* is a spiritual being, or function, that can reside in a human being, or several beings, or in a moment. It is the elusive mystery of how the divine gets delegated into the manifest world. Very little can be said of it. In this poem Rumi suggests that one can be more open to that divine-human interaction, the *Qutb*. One can allow oneself to be seen and allow the taste of one's *wanting-oneness* stew to live as energy, as the chickpea eventually becomes the cook.

Chapter 12

Introductory Note: Hamza Yusef, *The Purification* (Louisville, KY: Starlatch, 2004).

"Goldsmithing": Saladin Zarkub, the goldsmith. There are hagiographic miniatures that show Rumi leading Saladin out of his goldsmith's shop to begin the *sema*. Rumi heard a transcendent music in the goldsmiths' hammering. He began to turn in harmony with that, and with the galaxies and the molecules, in the ecstasy of his listening. Saladin had come to Konya in 1235, already a student, like Rumi, of Burhan Mahaqqiq. When Shams arrived in 1244, the two would sometimes meet in Saladin's shop or in his home. After Shams's disappearance, Saladin became the friend that Rumi loved as a reminder of the deep presence. In 1248 when Saladin died, Rumi led a mystical dance with flute and drum through the streets of Konya to celebrate Saladin's *urs*, the union of a great soul with the divine mystery. The friendship of Rumi and Saladin was further strengthened by the marriage of Rumi's oldest son, Sultan Velad, to Saladin's daughter, Fateme Khatun.

Chapter 13

Introductory Note: In the May 2, 1977, dream I am sleeping out in a sleeping bag on the bluff above the Tennessee River where I grew up—five miles north of Chattanooga on the Baylor School campus. I wake up inside the dream, though still asleep, in a lucid state. A ball of light rises off of Williams Island and comes over me. It clarifies from the inside out and reveals a man sitting cross-legged with a white shawl over his head, which is bowed. He raises his head and opens his eyes. "I love you," he says. "I love you too," I answer. The landscape then, the curve of the river as it holds the island, feels soaked with dew. I feel the *process* of the dew forming in the night, and it feels like, it feels identical with, how love is mixing in with the world's matter. That is the dream. It felt initiatory. It is certainly the only credential I have for working on the Rumi poetry. A year and a half later, when I met the man in the dream, Bawa Muhaiyaddeen, he told me to continue the work on Rumi: "It has to be done."

Chapter 14

Fundamentalist orthodoxies have often opposed, and even killed, innovators who break with the past: Hallaj, Jesus, Suhrawardi, Socrates, Sarmad, Shams Tabriz. And now this enlightened master has possibly been murdered, in our time, by *us* (with our complicity) for his worldview and his mystical freedom. To be more factual, as much as I can be, I say this because I have met and talked to his personal doctor, George Meredith (Amrito), and I believe him. He says that Osho's health changed radically after the interlude he spent alone in an Oklahoma jail in November 1985, while supposedly being transferred from Charlotte (where he was arrested without a warrant) to Seattle for deportation. A trip that should have taken six hours took twelve days. Dr. Meredith thinks that Osho was poisoned with thallium, a heavy metal untraceable after a year, while he was in the Oklahoma jail. The symptoms of thallium poisoning are clearly set forth in the medical literature. Osho developed most, if not all, of them, and he had exhibited none of them prior to November 1985.

I am no student of the evidence, but by putting this information here, my hope is that someone might be able to trace the matter back to that Oklahoma jail and find out who put the thallium in Osho's orange juice (just a guess) and who arranged it. There are lots of good reasons for a democratic government to have effective secrecy: secure missions in wartime, terrorist surveillance, drug stings, and so forth. But should the secrets be permanently kept from public scrutiny? In a democracy, I feel, we must eventually (it has been twenty-five years) be able to find out who did what, who gave the order, and why. Otherwise we have government run not by the people or their elected representatives, but by secret agencies and multinational corporations. I am not much for "conspiracy theories," and mostly those who espouse them give me the willies. I do not know. I admit that. Maybe Dr. Meredith was wrong in his diagnosis. I myself cannot do the considerable research required to get to the bottom of this, but I hope that someone, at some future time, will. I am too lazy. My mind is not focused enough. And I have too many luxurious poems to write about my grandchildren, not to mention Rumi's *Masnavi* to joyfully drown in. Let me hear how it goes.

Chapter 15

Introductory Note: H. W. L. Poonja, *Wake Up and Roar* (Kula Maui, HI: Pacific Center Publishing, 1992), pp. 59–63. See also H. W. L. Poonja, *Wake Up and Roar*, vol. 2 (1993); *The Truth Is* (York Beach, ME: Samuel Weiser, 2000); and Gangaji, *Freedom and Resolve: The Living Edge of Surrender* (Ashland, OR: Gangaji Foundation, 1999).

Chapter 16

Introductory Note: The Carl Jung quotation is from a conversation cited in Miguel Serrano, *C. G. Jung and Hermann Hesse: A Record of Two Friendships*, trans. Frank MacShane (New York: Schocken, 1968), p. 56. The Heraclitus quotation is from Brooks Haxton, trans., *Fragments: The Collected Wisdom of Heraclitus* (New York: Viking, 2001), p. 45. The Bawa Muhaiyaddeen quotation is from *Questions of Life, Answers of Wisdom*, vol. 1 (Philadelphia: Fellowship Press, 1987), pp. 31–32.

"Drawn by Soup": There is a legend that when the Mongol armies led by General Bugra Khan got close to Konya, Rumi went out alone to meet them. The general was so impressed that he spared the city: "There may be more beings like this here. We must not harm them."

Chapter 17

"Hometown Streets": A *matzoob* is someone so ecstatic with just being conscious and here and in a body that he or she may appear insane to some. To others, *matzoobs* are the purest sanity.

"Border Stations": Majnun and Layla are types of the star-crossed lovers, like Romeo and Juliet. There are thousands of incidents in their story. Rumi likes to tell of the time when Majnun got dizzy and confused just with meeting Layla's dog on the street.

Chapter 20

"Who Is the Friend?": Mutanabbi (915–965) wrote in Arabic. In his youth he was imprisoned for leading an insurrection in al-Samawa, in which he set himself up as a prophet with a new Qur'an. "Mutanabbi" means "the man who pretended to be a prophet." I have not been able to locate the riddle that Rumi gives the answer to here. Perhaps it was "Who is the Friend?" or "Who pours this wine?"

Chapter 21

"Ramadan Silence": Ramadan is a time to experiment not only with how fasting deepens the connection to presence, but also with restraining language, not talking and not e-mailing so much, not reading. I once spent some silent days at the Meher Baba Center in Myrtle Beach. I recommend it. Huston Smith has beautifully described the difficulties of his decision to have silent days with his wife at his home in Berkeley.

Chapter 23

"Even Better," "Music Is My Zikr": [note on *Rehavi, Neva, Irak, Ispahan, Zingule*, etc.] The Persian musician and artist Reza DeRakshani tells me these are modes and ways of playing music in different parts of the country.

"Music Is My Zikr": *Zikr* means "remembrance." In a practical sense it refers to the internal or external repetition of the phrase *La'illaha il'Allahu*. ("There is no reality but God; there is only God.") The *zikr* (or *dhikr*) is said to have at least three parts. The first part, *La'illaha*, is the denial, the abandonment of everything, the depths. The second, *il'Allah*, is the actual intrusion, the explosion into the individual, of divine presence. *Hu*, the third part, is the out-breathing of that divine presence. Bawa Muhaiyaddeen advised his students to repeat and reflect upon the *zikr* with every breath. A student asked how that was possible. Bawa responded, "It is like driving a car. At first you think it is difficult, and it is, but you get used to it. It becomes natural. After a while, you can even drive and talk at the same time."

"Not a Food Sack, a Reed Flute": Averroës, as he is known in the West, is Ibn Rushd, born in Cordova, Spain, in 1126. He is best known for his commentaries on Aristotle and for his combining of medicine and theology into a philosophy of spiritual health. He had a profound influence on Christian thinkers in the Middle Ages, especially Thomas Aquinas.

Chapter 26

"Hallaj": See note on "Green from Inside" (chap. 3) above.

"*Mashallah*": *Ma sha Allah*, "What God wills," implying something ongoing, not completed. *Inshallah* refers to something that has not happened yet. *Alhamdulillah* gives praise for what God has already done.

"YHU": *Hu* is the out-breathing of the divine presence in the *zikr* (see chap. 23 note above). I have had a dream in which that was combining with the pronoun *You*, in big glowing letters, to make this elision of human and divine.

Chapter 27

Introductory Note: Bawa Muhaiyaddeen, *Questions of Life, Answers of Wisdom*, vol. 1 (Philadelphia: Fellowhip Press, 1991).

"Pearl": Nizami (1141–1209) is a Persian poet best known for his long narrative poems, especially for his version of the Layla and Majnun love story.

"Zero Circle": This poem is actually not from *The Shams*. It is a small segment of the *Masnavi*, Book IV, ll. 3748–3754, but it feels like a ghazal.

PART II: QUATRAINS

Introduction to the Quatrains

1. Robert Bly, *Silence in the Snowy Fields* (Middletown, CT: Wesleyan University Press, 1962); James Wright, *The Branch Will Not Break* (Middletown, CT: Wesleyan University Press, 1963).

Chapter 38

"A voice inside both of us sings out . . . ": This probably means, "A line from one lover, then a line from another. "

Chapter 54

"As long as my soul is in this body . . .": I do not hear this quatrain as a claim that Islam has an *exclusive* truth. Rumi is honoring the presence of Muhammad and the truth of the Qur'an. Others have heard this poem as proof that Rumi should be considered an Islamic poet, and that only. I would claim that there are many other passages that show how he and Shams honor the living, gnostic, experiential truth of every unique life, and that core of longing that is beyond doctrine and religion. I hear him as a planetary poet, and would point to the following passages: See "Inside the Friend . . . ," "I Am Not," "Almost in Sight," "A Question," "A Holiday Without Limits," "The Self We Share," "There You Are," "Waking Up, Dawn-Music," "Two Hands," and "Say I Am You."

I would align myself with Dag Hammarskjöld (1905–1961), U.N. Secretary-General and Nobel Prize winner, who quoted Rumi in *Markings* ("The lovers of God have no religion but God alone." [Dag Hammarskjöld, *Markings*. New York: Random House, 1964]) as representing the world-embracing tolerance we need, and with the many others over the last one hundred years, who hear in Rumi a universalist way beyond churches and religions, including Gurdjieff, Joseph Campbell, Erich Fromm, Meher Baba, Hasan Shushud, Sam Lewis, Pir Vilayat Khan, Reshad Feild, Idries Shah, Hamid Karzai, and wonderfully, Barack Obama.

I should explain the Obama reference. In the fall of 2009 Richard Holbrooke, Special Envoy to Pakistan and Afghanistan, asked his assistant in the State Department, Frank Archibald, who knows a friend of mine, Angela Elam, to contact me and ask if I would sign a book for President Obama. *A Year With Rumi* was the one requested. The request from Holbrooke as it moved along to me was accompanied by the sentence, "Rumi is Obama's favorite poet." I signed the book, "For President Obama. Barack, your presence is fresh air for this country to breathe. Much love to you and your beautiful family, Coleman Barks." I found out his birthday, Michelle's, and the two girls, Malia's and Sasha's, and put birthday messages on the appropriate pages of *A Year With Rumi*.

I am not at all sure that I am saying these things with proper respect, awe, for the grandeur of Rumi's surrender, and for that of Shams Tabriz. There is a story that Shams tells in his *Maqalat*.

One day the companions of the Prophet came to see him. There is a man here who is neither with the deniers, nor the Muslims. We see him pray, and we do not see him occupied in gaming or other such things. We do not see the attributes of the mad in him, nor the seeking of livelihood of the sensible. A feeling of compassion arose within the Master. He said, "Now go, and when you see him, convey my greeting to him, and say, 'Our Master wants very much to see you.' Do not command him to come here; do your best not to injure his feelings!" They came near the man, and at first, they were not able to greet him. After some time passed, the opportunity opened and they conveyed the greeting of the Prophet to him, and his love and his strong wish to see him. All the while, he kept silent. They obeyed the command of the Prophet about not creating trouble for him and did not speak further. After a while, they saw that the man had come to visit Muhammad. For some time, he sat silently in the gathering. The Prophet sat silently, and he was silent too. At last, Muhammad stood up from his place. Both when the man arrived and when he was leaving, the Prophet behaved with great humility towards him. He said, "Abundant light has poured upon you—Great grace has poured down upon you. Our medrasah is this—these four walls made of flesh. The instructor is very great. I cannot say who He is. And His tutor is the heart; just as some people of God have said, 'My heart has informed me about my Lord.'" (*Rumi's Sun: The Teachings of Shams of Tabriz*, trans. by Reflik Algan and Camille Adams Helminski [Sandpoint, ID: Morning Light Press, 2008] p. 387).

I love the feeling of Muhammad's presence in this story, and the silence that seems to be the gist of his conversation with the visitor. I once visited Omani Chisti in Herat, Afghanistan. He has studied and taught the *Masnavi* for eighty years. We were sitting side by side. I leaned against him and asked, "Who is Shams?" He answered quickly. *Shams is the doctor who comes when you hurt enough. In the thirteenth century the intensity of longing was strong enough so that he came. Now it is not so strong.* May our longing increase to what is needed to bring such a doctor again. I am told that some Sufis have a custom of meeting secretly with mystics from various traditions. The designated meeting place is the one with a single rose above the door. These meetings need no longer be secret.

"Come, come, whoever you are . . .": This is one of the most frequently quoted quatrains. It has long been associated with the Mevlevi Order in Konya. A Turkish version with English translation is in a glass case in the Rumi Museum in Konya with a copy of the quatrains, but it may well not have been written by Rumi. A similar quatrain is attributed to Abil Khayr (d. 1049). The invitation itself remains open.

Note on These Translations

Since New Year's Day 1977 until the mid-1990s, the Persian scholar John Moyne sent me literal translations of Rumi's poems from *The Shams*. These have been used to produce many of these versions, as have A. J. Arberry's scholarly translations: *Mystical Poems of Rumi* (Chicago: The University of Chicago Press, 1968), *Mystical Poems of Rumi*, vol. 2 (Boulder, CO: Westview Press, 1972), and *The Rubaiyat of Jalal al-din Rumi, Select Translations into English Verse* (London: Emery Walker, 1949). Reynold Nicholson's *Divani Shamsi Tabriz* (Bethesda, MD: Ibex Publishers, 2001) and Nevit Ergin's twenty-two-volume translation of *The Shams* (San Mateo, CA: Echo Publications and the Turkish Ministry of Culture, 1995–2003) have also been used.

Index of Familiar First Lines